RUNNING INTO THE SKY

ADVENTURES IN POWERED PARAGLIDING

Chris Wolf

with Michael Maikowski

Published by Jefferson Technology Press
Federal Way, Washington

Printed in the United States of America

ISBN 0-9678917-0-1

*This book is dedicated to
Hugh Murphy,
who taught me to fly a powered paraglider,
and who wisely nodded agreement
when I finally screwed up my nerve and said
"Let's get this sumbitch in the air!"*

Thank you for giving me wings.

Acknowledgement

A good editor is worth his weight in gold. He deflates the puffery, redlines the junk, rewrites the awkward sentences, and gets rid of all those damned commas. And so I hereby acknowledge George Hawkins, fellow powered paraglider pilot, for his tireless efforts in editing this book. Without George this book would still exist, but it wouldn't be half as good.

And thanks to Doug Tews, who designed the cover, and to Hugh Murphy, who took the pictures.

Contents

Why You Should Buy This Book...

The purpose of this book is to explain what it's like to learn to fly a powered paraglider. Not *how* to fly a powered paraglider (although there's plenty of that), but what it's *like* to fly a PPG. In other words, this book is primarily for anyone who wants to know what it's really like to get into the sport, acquire the equipment, get trained, and fly a PPG before he shells out good money for equipment and training. There's nothing worse than investing a lot of time and money in a sport, only to find out that you really don't like it. And the truth is, there are a lot of discouraged dropouts in the sport of powered paragliding. Without proper training, it can be a difficult sport to master. I want to tell you about the good and the bad of powered paragliding, so that you can make an informed decision.

What is a PPG? It's the world's smallest and simplest powered aircraft. It's been described as a "bedsheet with a weedeater," and that's not too far from the truth. It's an aircraft that you can literally put in the trunk of your car (provided you take the propeller off). If you imagine a modern-day skydiver, flying along under his ram-air parachute, but with a gasoline-powered engine and propeller on his back, you'll pretty much have it. The engine permits the pilot to go up, as well as down. The engine also permits the pilot to foot launch from virtually any flat field, with no need for a hill in order to get into the air. In other words, you can simply lay out the PPG wing on the ground, strap the PPG engine to your back, start it up, run forward a few steps to inflate the wing, and launch yourself into the sky, just like a bird.

And that's why people love to fly powered paragliders. It lets you fly just like a bird.

PPG manufacturers and dealers are in the business to make money. Thus, they'll tell you all the good stuff about the sport, but frequently fail to mention the problems and the drawbacks. And there *are* drawbacks.

When I decided to get into this sport, there was a real dearth of information.

It's somewhat better now, thanks to the Internet, but I had no idea what I was getting into. I ended up making a lot of mistakes due to simple ignorance. Some mistakes were expensive (buying the wrong equipment), and some were downright painful (a broken rib). I decided to write this book so that YOU can profit from my hard-won experience. Far too many people get into this sport, are poorly trained by fast-buck operators, and end up spending thousands of dollars on equipment that ends up gathering dust in their garages, or gets sold for ten cents on the dollar. I don't want that to happen to you.

I will take you, step by step, through my firsthand experience in learning to fly a powered paraglider. I will show you the good and the bad. Nothing will be left out. I will change some names and places to avoid embarrassing anyone (and to avoid lawsuits), but every incident will be told exactly as it actually happened. I have no product to promote, and no axe to grind. I simply want to tell it like it is. I want to make you aware of the options that are available, and hopefully keep you from repeating my errors. I also want to show you all the useful tips and tricks that I've learned and invented during my first year of flying that will make your flying experience much more comfortable, easy, and fun. Powered paragliding is a very new sport, and it's still under development. A lot of PPG pilots are still doing things the hard way. I'll show you some easier ways.

Then you can decide if you want to follow in my footsteps. I hope that you do, because powered paragliding is the most fantastic flying there is.

So why should you buy this book? Because if you've never flown a PPG, I'll show you what it's like to fly one. And if you're already flying a PPG, I can show you ways to make your flying easier and more fun. Even if you have no plans to fly a PPG, I think you'll greatly enjoy reading about my experiences (like the ping-pong balls that I dropped at a company picnic, and how the ostrich ate 'em).

But why should you buy a book written by a novice? After all, I've only been flying for about a year. I'm still pretty green myself.

You should buy this book because I *am* a novice. Unlike an experienced professional, I still remember what it's like the first time you sling that heavy motor on your back, clip that wing to your harness, and try to fly. I still remember the fear and the anxieties. I know what's going through your mind, because it's still going through mine! I remember what's important to a beginning pilot, and what isn't. I still remember how a tiny little training hill, less than fifty feet high, looked like Mount Everest (and twice as scary!). Most important of all, I still remember all the little things that are so important to a beginning pilot, but that have long since been forgotten by an experienced pilot.

An experienced pilot tends to rewrite history to conform to the way he would *like* the sport to be. I'm still new enough to the sport to tell you the way it really *is*.

Let's start by taking an actual flight in a powered paraglider. I'll take you along on a recent flight I made. The wing is laid out on the grass, the engine is strapped to my back, the propeller is spinning, and we're almost ready to take off.

If you'll just turn the page, we'll be on our way…

Chapter 1

Over the Waterfall

It's 6:00 p.m. I'm standing at the edge of a large grassy field, surrounded by tall pine forests. The temperature is a delightful 70 degrees, sunny, with only a couple of clouds in the sky. The thermal updrafts have pretty much died down for the day, leaving the air very smooth and unruffled. In my opinion this is the very best time of the day to fly a powered paraglider (PPG).

My paragliding wing is laid out on the ground, ready for inflation. I'm standing immediately in front of my wing, wearing my PPG engine like an oversized backpack. The engine is warmed up, and idling at just under two thousand revolutions per minute. The three-bladed, carbon fiber propeller is spinning inside its protective aluminum cage. I'm ready to give the engine a full power run-up test before I take off.

I make certain that the prop wash is pointed away from the wing, then I slowly squeeze the pistol-grip throttle in my right hand. The engine starts to roar with increased power. I have to brace myself to keep from being pushed over by the increased thrust. At full throttle, I glance down at the tachometer on my vest. It reads just under seven thousand revolutions per minute. The propeller is now pushing on my body with over one hundred pounds of thrust. Everything is as it should be. I ease off the throttle, the thrust drops off, and the engine quickly returns to idle.

My flying field is part of a stretch of fertile farmland that borders the western slope of a long range of mountains. The whole area is very scenic. The closest mountain is just half a mile away and rises four thousand vertical feet into the air. It looks a lot like Half Dome, in Yosemite. Surrounding me is a vastness of forests, farms, mountains, rivers and waterfalls. In my opinion it's one of the most beautiful spots in the United States.

It's time to fly. I take a handful of wing lines in each hand, including the left and right steering lines. I reach over to my Cateye altimeter, strapped to my wrist, and hit the button to start the built-in stopwatch. The twin digital display will constantly give me my altitude and elapsed flight time. This little altimeter came all the way from South Africa to fly with me. We've become very good friends.

I glance across the field at my flying buddy, Mike. He's making a last check of the wind with the Skywatch digital wind meter. That electronic wind meter was the best seventy bucks I ever spent. Mike holds up two fingers to tell me that the wind is blowing at a speed of only two miles per hour. It's perfect for a forward launch.

A last check to make certain that everything is clear around me, and I start to run forward. I always feel incredibly slow and clumsy, running with nearly seventy pounds of engine on my back. It seems utterly impossible that I'm about to run into the sky. Suddenly the wing lines go taut in my hands and I feel the wing start to inflate and rise off the ground behind me. As the wing leaps into the air, I keep my hands in contact with the wing lines. This lets me know where the wing is, and what it's doing at any given moment. Maintaining constant control of the wing is critically important during takeoff. As my arms rise above my shoulders, I squeeze the throttle. The engine roars at full power and it suddenly becomes much easier to run; pushed forward by one hundred pounds of thrust.

As I start to gain speed, I glance up to make certain the wing has completely inflated, with no twists or snags in the lines. As usual, the wing looks fine. I keep my eyes on the wing as I run, ready to move to one side or the other in order to stay centered under the wing. I feel the weight of the engine disappear as the wing lifts it from my shoulders. Now the wing is trying to lift the engine *and* me. But I'm pretty heavy, so I keep on running as fast as I can. As the lift increases, my strides become longer and longer as my weight rapidly diminishes.

I've run about fifty feet, and now my feet are starting to lightly slap the earth as the wing struggles to lift me into the air. My feet are becoming more of a drag than a help, so I gently tug on both steering lines. This is like lowering the flaps on an airplane; it gives the wing a bit more lift. It works. Suddenly I feel nothing under my feet. The ground is dropping away. The only thing still on the ground is my shadow. I keep some pressure on the steering lines for a few seconds while I gain a little altitude, then I slowly ease off the pressure to permit the wing to reach maximum flying speed as I soar into the sky.

I am flying! Like a bird!

Why does every takeoff always feel like the first time? My heart is racing and my pulse is pounding. Will this ever become routine?

I certainly hope not!

Thirty seconds later I'm approaching the end of the field. My Cateye altimeter says I'm at 120 feet, just about level with the treetops. I keep the engine at maximum thrust and continue to gain altitude. I pass over the tops of the trees with about thirty feet to spare. Rather than fly out over the forest canopy, I execute a slow right turn, still climbing at full throttle, and fly back over the field.

I'm still hanging in the leg straps, and it's starting to get a bit uncomfortable. I reach down and release the footbar. The footbar is just a piece of aluminum tubing about eighteen inches long. It hangs from the bottom of my seat from a couple of short nylon cords. It looks like the rung of a ladder. I reach back with my right foot, catch the dangling footbar on the bottom of my boot, and push it forward. The seat, which has been stowed away between me and my motor frame during takeoff, is dragged down and forward. I slide into the padded seat just like a playground swing. Ah, much better! As I reach the other end of the field I note that I'm nearing three hundred feet of altitude. Time to start my trip.

I wave goodbye to Mike and head east, over the trees. Soon I'm flying over a nearby golf course. Since it's a warm, pleasant evening, the course has a fair number of people still on it. Most of them look up and wave. I hope the noise of my engine isn't annoying them.

Two hawks are diving and soaring just in front of me. As a kid I always wanted to fly with the birds. Well I finally got my wish.

And the flying is very easy. I have a steering line in each hand, and a throttle in my right hand. When I want to turn left, I simply pull on the left steering line. To turn right, I pull on the right steering line. When I want to go up, I squeeze the throttle. To go down, I ease off the throttle. Most of the time I don't do anything at all. The wing flies itself; all I have to do is steer. That's all there is to it. It truly is the world's simplest aircraft.

My speed isn't much; barely more than twenty miles per hour, but I'm not flying for the speed. I'm up here for the view and the fun. I don't have to worry about stalling because the wing automatically flies itself at a constant airspeed. Even if the engine quits, the only thing that will happen is that the wing will slowly start to descend. The wing is such a good glider that I always turn off the engine just before landing.

I pass over the golf course and over a large hay field. There's the river, just ahead. This is as far as I've ever flown in this direction. Not only is this going to be a cross-country flight, but it's also going to be a flight over new territory.

It's my intent to follow the river to the edge of the plateau where the river plunges three hundred feet over a magnificent waterfall. The falls are about eight miles downstream, so I should be there in less than half an hour.

Right away I can see that I need more altitude. I'm rapidly leaving the flat hay fields behind, and passing over rugged, unbroken forest. Many of these Douglas Fir trees are over one hundred feet tall. Not a good place for a tree landing. When you fly a craft that's basically a bed sheet and a weedeater, it's always a good idea to keep an emergency landing field within gliding distance, just in case the engine suddenly decides to quit. So I squeeze the throttle and start to climb. About four minutes later I'm at one thousand feet. Just ahead I can see one of the plants of the local paper company. They've thoughtfully logged off a big chunk of the forest, and even took out the tree stumps. Their property would make a fine emergency landing field. Across the river is a small town. The high school soccer field would be another good place to land if the engine quits.

God, but the view up here is fantastic! The rivers, the forests, the mountains, the farms. I can see *everything!* And there is nothing, absolutely nothing, between me and rest of the world. It's like sitting in a playground swing a thousand feet above the earth. It's so different from flying in a plane, where you're inside a machine that's moving through the air. Flying my paraglider, *I'm* the one who's moving through the air. I've strapped on my wing, run into the sky, and now I'm flying. Just like a bird.

My view is unobstructed in almost every direction. If I look down, the only thing I see between me and the planet Earth are my dangling feet. If I look to either side, I can see a short nylon strap connecting my shoulders to the wing. Even a helicopter does not afford such an unobstructed view. If I look over either shoulder, I can see the edge of my propeller cage. Inside the cage, my propeller is whirling at more than sixty revolutions per second. The propeller is blasting out a column of air at nearly ninety miles per hour, sufficient to push me forward and to permit my wing to climb against the force of gravity.

I can certainly feel the power and vibration of the engine, just a few inches behind my back, but it's a reassuring type of presence. With my helmet and earplugs, the noise of the engine doesn't bother me at all.

Down at the high school the kids are playing soccer. One of them spots me. The game stops for a moment while everyone looks up and waves. They're probably shouting something, but I can't hear them over the noise of the engine. I wave back and fly on.

Soon I've left the town behind me and I can see the spray of the falls, just ahead. It's the height of the tourist season and there are lots of people on the observation platform overlooking the falls. I'll give them something extra to look at today.

I fly over the edge of the plateau and circle just above the falls like some gigantic bird. The view is outstanding. The falls are a tall, Yosemite-type plunge, more than twice as high as Niagara Falls. Since this is August, the dry season, there's not that much water going over the edge, but it's still breathtaking. I must fly here again, in the Spring, when the snow is melting in the mountains, flooding the river and giving the falls about twenty times their present volume. That should be quite a sight!

I'd love to fly lower, over the falls, but the closest emergency landing field is another golf course at a new housing development further along the lip of the plateau. It's a fair distance away. In fact, if my engine quit right now, I'm not certain that I could reach the golf course. I immediately increase power to climb a bit. In less than a minute I've gained enough altitude to permit me to glide to safety if I have to.

Immediately below me is a gigantic abandoned railroad trestle climbing up from the valley to the edge of the plateau. From my seat in the sky I can see exactly where the old railroad used to cut through the forest. I decide to fly over the new housing development on the plateau. I've been reading about this development for the past year, but I've never actually seen it before. It is huge! Some of the homes are still under construction. The houses are very big, luxurious, and expensive. In the middle of it all is the golf course that is my emergency landing field. I decide to drop down for a closer inspection.

Even though it's early evening, there are still a fair number of pickup trucks and other vehicles driving around the development. Several of the drivers stop, get out, and stare up at me. I'm tempted to land on one of the fairways, then take off again. Nah, better not. This place is still closed to the public. Fortunately they can't lock up the sky.

I glance at the stopwatch on my Cateye altimeter. I've been flying for half an hour. I use my wrist mirror to check the fuel in the tank behind my back. Plenty of fuel remaining, but in less than an hour it will be gone. I think I'll start heading back. I'd hate to have to walk home.

I head southeast for about a mile until I cross the Interstate highway. There are lots of farms to the south of the Interstate, with plenty of good emergency landing fields. I cruise over the farms, waving to the people below. Lots of cows and horses and dogs and kids. The dogs always bark, and the kids always wave.

Until this moment, the air has been smooth as silk. Suddenly my wing hits a bit of stray turbulence and starts to shake and buffet. I look up. The wing is rocking back and forth a bit, but there's no sign of trouble. My Pro Design Compact wing is handling the turbulence nicely. Good wing!

But I'm puzzled. Where did this sudden turbulence come from? I glance up, past the wing, to see a big twin-engine aircraft passing high overhead, about half a mile away. I would estimate he's about eight hundred feet higher than I am. I'm in just the right position to have flown through the turbulance coming off his wing. Good thing he wasn't a heavy jet, or my ride might have been much rougher. Once again I'm reminded that I'm not the only flying machine in the air. I need to keep my eyes open for other air traffic. Given my small size, and low profile, I'm probably not the easiest thing to spot in the air.

About twenty minutes later I'm approaching my landing field. I must have picked up a little tailwind on the way back. I happen to look down in one of the hay fields, and spot a herd of elk. There must be a dozen of them. They've just come out of the forest to graze. I decide to drop down for a closer look. The elk stare up at me for a few seconds, probably trying to figure out if I'm dangerous or not, then they scatter back into the forest. I laugh and head for my landing field.

I check my fuel again, and estimate that I have at least another twenty minutes of flight time remaining. I decide to fly toward the local mountain; the one that resembles Half Dome at Yosemite. The base of the mountain is heavily forested, but quickly becomes too steep for the trees. I fly along the tree line for a couple of minutes. What a monolith! What a view! Good mountain to respect. Someday I'll fly over the summit, but for now I decide to land before my fuel runs out. I turn back toward my landing field.

I ease off the throttle and let the engine idle. As the engine thrust lessens, I start to descend. I slowly drift down over the trees at the end of the field. As soon as I see that I'm clear of the irrigation system at the end of the field, I kill the engine and slide out of my seat for the landing. Once again I'm hanging in my leg straps and ready to run.

After the constant roar of the engine, the silence is equally deafening. I can hear the wind whispering around my head, and singing in the wing lines. The grassy field is coming up pretty fast. I know that I'm only flying about twenty miles per hour, but it always seems like sixty. There's my flying buddy, Mike, out in the middle of the field with his video camera. This landing is gonna look great on television!

At about three feet of altitude, I smoothly pull the steering lines down just below my shoulders. The wing immediately levels out, and I shoot across the grassy surface. I'm trading airspeed for extra lift. About two seconds later, as my remaining airspeed bleeds off, I pull the steering lines all the way down to my waist. The wing promptly stalls and comes to almost a complete stop. I settle softly to the ground for a perfect, no-wind landing. I run about three steps to absorb the last tiny remnant of my forward velocity, and then come to a complete stop.

The wing is still flying above me, but it's ready to collapse. If I do nothing, the wing will fall on top of me, and my hot muffler might melt the suspension lines. I spin around one hundred and eighty degrees and take a few steps backward, keeping the suspension lines taut. The wing moves backward, away from me, and slowly collapses to the ground. In a moment it's just a little pile of cloth and string. I unstrap the engine and set it down on the ground. I pull off my helmet and gloves and remove my ear plugs. Then I just stand there, looking around. There's a puffy cloud hanging over the summit of the mountain, and the whole mountain is glowing orange in the soft light of the setting sun. How beautiful!

I'm flooded with a wonderful feeling of accomplishment. I've strapped on a wing, launched myself into the sky, flown miles over scenic countryside, and then returned to earth for a feather-soft landing. This is what I live for. This is why I stay alive. For moments like this.

What a great flight! What a fantastic flying machine! Who would have ever thought that with a little gasoline engine, a dollar's worth of gas, and some cloth and string, that I could fly like a bird.

Life is very good.

If you've enjoyed this story, then please keep reading. I will tell you some more of my flying stories. Some are funny, some are exhilarating, and some are downright scary. I will also tell you exactly how I reached this point. Almost anyone can do it. You too, can fly like a bird.

Chapter 2

The Odyssey Begins

I've always wanted to fly.

Don't ask me why. I don't know myself. Maybe it was from watching all those Superman TV shows starring George Reeves, when I was a kid. Maybe it was from watching Commando Cody as he got into his rocket-powered flying suit, twisted the two knobs on his chest marked UP and FAST, and leaped into the air. Maybe it was from watching those wonderful 1950s television series, "Whirlybirds" and "Ripcord," about helicopters and skydiving.

If you have any idea what I'm talking about, you're probably over the age of forty. If you have no idea what I'm talking about, don't worry. It's not important.

As a kid growing up, I was very easy to get along with. All I ever asked for was my own way. I remember my first plane ride, at the age of nine. It was a seaplane ride in Wisconsin and I absolutely loved it! I was amazed to discover how small everything looked from my perch so high in the sky, and how slowly the earth seemed to move beneath the plane. I had a small box camera and I shot an entire roll of totally unmemorable pictures in beautiful black and white film. When I got the pictures back I discovered that one cow looks very much like another from half a mile up.

I remember my first helicopter ride at the age of twelve. It was a tourist ride over Mt. Rushmore in South Dakota. I worked very hard to get on that helicopter. Not to get the money to buy a ticket, but to get my folks' permission. My folks hated airplanes with a passion. Even today they hate to ride in a jet to Hawaii. And the only reason they ride in a jet to Hawaii is because they can't find a ship sailing there from Indiana. And the only thing they hate more than jets, are helicopters.

Fortunately for my aviation career, my folks finally decided that dying in a fiery helicopter crash was preferable to listening to my constant, nonstop pleading and whining from the back seat of the car to *please, please, please, please, please* let me go on the helicopter. I wanted to ride that helicopter more than anything else in the world. I'll never forget that moment, sitting next to the pilot, the rotor whirling overhead, when the helicopter slowly rose from the ground and soared away over the pine forests surrounding the monument. I was absolutely thrilled with the ride, but my folks were scared to death that it was going to crash. (As an interesting aside, that very same helicopter ride over Mt. Rushmore DID crash about a year later, killing all aboard. Rather ironic.)

When I was growing up I always wanted to learn to fly, but I never had the money for flight training. My folks wouldn't waste good money on "such nonsense." Fortunately I met guys in college who were pilots, and they were glad to share the cost of the plane, just to get flying time. So I spent all of my spare cash helping them to rent Cessnas.

Then when I was a senior in college, in 1972, I discovered skydiving. Jumping out of airplanes looked like even more fun than riding in them. It's a credit to my courage and naiveté that I actually asked my parents to give me permission to jump. I might as well have asked for permission to cut my throat. My parents hadn't yet accepted the fact that I was flying around in little airplanes. Jumping out of the plane, wearing only a parachute, was their idea of suicide AND insanity.

So I decided to wait another year, until I turned 21. Then I could jump without their permission. And so on January 13, 1973, I climbed out onto the strut of a Cessna 182 and stepped off into 2800 feet of empty space. Naturally I was totally terrified. When the jump door opened next to me, I wanted to climb over the pilot and hide under his seat. But I went ahead and did it. For a few seconds after leaving the plane I was convinced that I was falling to my death, but then my static line pulled the parachute open and I made a slow, fantastic descent to earth. It was one of the high points of my life. Now this was FLYING!

Over the next four years I made over one hundred parachute jumps. I made freefalls lasting as long as one minute from an altitude of twelve thousand feet. I linked up in the air with other freefalling skydivers. I graduated from plain old military surplus parachutes to fancy Para-Commander skydiving parachutes, and finally to a ram-air parachute that wasn't even a parachute, but was actually a flying wing.

I loved that ram-air wing. It was faster than any parachute I had ever owned, and I could actually fly it around, just like an airplane. Because it was a wing, and not a parachute, I had to make an approach before landing, and then flare the wing at the moment of touchdown. If I flared too high, I stalled the wing and fell to the ground. This happened a couple of times before I got the hang of it. Fortunately I wasn't too high when I stalled, so I didn't fall very far, or get hurt. Not much anyway.

Flying the ram-air wing soon replaced my love of freefall. I loved to get out of the plane at seven thousand feet, fall for a few seconds, then open the wing and fly it around; especially above the clouds. That way I could get a ride of several minutes before finally being forced to land. I could go in any direction, but up.

After college, I was forced to hang up my canopy. The ram-air wing was wearing out and I didn't have the money to replace it. Also I'd pretty much had my fill of skydiving. Even with the ram-air wing, skydiving had become routine. It required a lot of time, money, and preparation for just a few minutes of flying under the ram-air canopy. So I contented myself with riding around in a Cessna.

But the flying dream dies hard. Twenty years later, the memories of skydiving were still vivid. I remembered how much fun it had been, flying that ram-air canopy. I started to look at hang gliders. They could stay up a lot longer than a ram-air canopy. They could even soar on thermals. But then, in 1996, I happened to open the yellow pages of the phone book to the "parachute" listings, and a whole new world suddenly opened up.

I didn't know it at the time, but I was looking at an ad for a powered parachute (PPC). It had a big ram-air wing that was connected to a three-wheeled cart made of aluminum tubing. It looked like a big gyroscope on wheels. The cart had a seat for the pilot, and directly behind the seat was a small gasoline engine and a propeller. This thing could fly! Like an airplane! It looked like the world's simplest aircraft. The pilot started the engine and taxied forward until the ram-air canopy was inflated and pulled into the air overhead. Then he increased the power, and flew. He steered the craft with his feet by pushing on a hinged bar on either side of the cart. Each bar pulled on a line that was attached to the trailing edge of the wing. To go up, he increased power. To come down, he reduced power. It not only looked like the world's simplest aircraft, but also the safest. If the engine quit, the pilot simply glided down to a gentle landing. Best of all, no license was required to fly the beast.

I didn't pursue the ad, but I did keep it in mind. It sure looked like a fun way to fly. And it also looked like a fairly inexpensive way to take to the air. Then about a year later I saw another ad for a school that taught people how to fly a powered parachute. I decided to give them a call.

The owner of the school was very helpful. He explained that he did not deal in powered parachutes, but rather taught powered and unpowered paragliding. He patiently explained the differences to me.

Paragliders were high-performance ram-air wings that were foot launched from hills or mountains. Instead of a wheeled cart, the pilot merely dangled from the wing in a parachute-type harness. Since paragliders had no engines, paraglider pilots depended on thermals, or other types of rising air, to gain altitude and stay airborne, just like a regular glider or sailplane.

Powered paragliders (PPGs) consisted of a paraglider wing and a gasoline-powered engine that was small and light enough for the pilot to wear on his back (at least in theory). Like an unpowered paraglider wing, the PPG had no wheels, and was footlaunched by the pilot. Unlike the unpowered paraglider wing, the powered paraglider could be launched from a flat field. It wasn't necessary to find a mountain.

I think I was instantly hooked by the idea of the PPG. The idea of slipping on a backpack engine and literally running into the sky was more addictive than heroin. I decided to get on the Internet and gather as much information as I could. I was especially interested in how much these powered wings cost. Given their simplicity, I figured they couldn't possibly cost more than three or four thousand dollars. Needless to say, I went into sticker shock when I learned that a brand-new powered parachute cost around ten thousand dollars! Okay, how about a brand-new powered paraglider? Here was one called the "Pagojet." Argh! They wanted twelve thousand dollars for it!

Okay, how about used equipment? There was plenty of it, and some of it was available for only a few thousand dollars. But was the used equipment any good? Or was it simply an example of that old maxim about making sure to sell your horse before he dies?

Obviously I needed more information. Did the library have any books on the subject? Nope. Not a thing. But the PPC and PPG dealers offered videos for sale, so I ordered copies of all of them. And I learned there was a magazine called

Ultraflight that covered the PPC and PPG scene, so I immediately subscribed to it.

Which one to buy? Powered parachute or powered paraglider? Both types of craft had their advantages and disadvantages. The PPC wheeled cart obviously made for easy takeoffs and landings, but it also weighed several hundred pounds and had to be hauled around on a trailer. The PPG engine had to be carried on the pilot's back during takeoff, but it weighed less than a hundred pounds and could be hauled in the trunk of a car (which I thought was pretty cool for a flying machine). Both craft cost about the same when new; around ten thousand dollars. Not cheap, but pretty inexpensive for an aircraft.

(The PPG has come down a bit in price in the last couple of years. New PPGs can now be had for $7,000 to $8,000. New PPCs can range in price from $8,000 to $16,000.)

I decided that I could not make an informed decision without actually going for a training flight in both types of craft. I made an appointment with a nearby PPC dealer to go for a demo ride. He told me to show up on his doorstep at 6:00 a.m. That meant I would have to get up at 3:30 a.m.

Ladies and Gentlemen, I wanted to fly very badly, but I would not willingly get up at 3:30 in the morning, even for a ride in the Space Shuttle.

When I inquired as to the reason for the dawn departure, I was told that PPCs flew best in the smooth, unturbulent air at dawn. Flying later in the day, when the thermal updrafts were active, could be rough and bumpy, and passengers frequently became airsick. I suggested flying in the evening, near sunset, after the mid-day turbulence had died down. The dealer said that would be fine.

My demo flight was set for the civilized hour of 6:00 p.m. I drove out to the dealer's house and met him. He was a nice friendly guy, named Steve Rambo, who worked a regular day job and sold PPCs on the side. He answered my questions and never resorted to the hard sell. I helped him load the PPC onto his trailer. After watching all those PPC videos, it was interesting to finally see one in the flesh (or at least in the aluminum). The craft appeared sturdy and well-made, with two seats (sort of). It also weighed about 350 pounds.

We drove out to a nearby pasture and unloaded the PPC from the trailer. The dealer quickly spread the big ram-air wing out behind the cart. Then he fired up the fifty horsepower engine and let it warm up for a few minutes. Finally he handed me a helmet and showed me where to sit. I climbed aboard and fastened my seatbelt.

The dealer's PPC was a two-place machine, meaning that it was barely possible to pack two bodies onto its aluminum frame. I sat immediately above and behind the dealer. My legs were on either side of his body, and rested on little pegs. There was very little wriggle room. The dealer had a control stick for steering the front nosewheel while on the ground, and there was a hinged footbar on either side of the nose of the machine that controlled the steering lines for the ram-air wing.

When everything was ready, the dealer advanced the throttle and the engine roared. The cart began to roll forward and the ram-air wing began to inflate and rise into the air. The wing rose to about a forty-five degree angle, and stayed there as we rolled down the field. The ride was a bit scary. The cart was only going about twenty-five miles per hour, but it seemed like sixty. I started to wonder just what it would take to make this three-wheeled cart roll over. Then I started to wonder if we were going to get airborne before we hit the fence at the end of the field, which was coming up rather quickly. The ram-air wing was still stuck at a forty-five degree angle, behind us, and we weren't lifting off.

Suddenly the dealer reduced power momentarily, then immediately increased it again. This seemed to "goose" the wing, and it quickly moved directly overhead. A moment later, we lifted off.

The climb out was rapid and smooth, and the view was fantastic. With no cabin walls around us, it was almost as good as hanging in a parachute harness. The sun was just setting as we cruised along at an altitude of five hundred feet. Steering the craft was very simple. When the dealer wanted to go right, he pushed on the right-hand steering bar with his right foot. When he wanted to go left, he pushed on the left-hand bar with his left foot. More throttle to go up; less throttle to come down. That was about it.

We didn't have radios or an intercom, so the dealer shouted his explanations of how everything worked, over his shoulder. Over the roar of the wind and the engine I could barely understand a word he was saying, so I just nodded and smiled a lot. Truthfully I would have been just as happy if he hadn't said a word during the entire flight. All I wanted to do was relax, sit back, and absorb the experience. I did notice that our speed was much higher when going downwind than when going upwind. Obviously this craft was not intended to be flown in much of a wind unless you were only planning to go downwind.

During the landing approach I noticed how rapidly the craft descended when the engine was idling. Obviously the ram-air wing did not have much of a glide ratio. I later learned that the wing would glide forward about 3.5 feet for every foot of vertical descent. Just before we reached the ground the dealer added power to level out, and then gently eased us down onto the ground for a very smooth landing.

After the flight, I helped the dealer load the PPC back onto the trailer. I thanked him for the training flight, took some literature, and said goodbye. I realized that every time the dealer wanted to fly, he had to do a lot of loading and unloading of a rather heavy machine. I decided that a PPC would be fine if I lived on a farm, but trucking the PPC back and forth between my suburban house and the flying field would get old pretty quick. Now I understood why many PPC owners kept their craft in hangars, at airports, just like regular airplanes.

At this point, even though I had not yet taken a training flight in a powered paraglider, the PPG was starting to look better than the PPC. I realized that a PPG, in the trunk of my car, would be a lot less hassle and effort to haul around than a PPC on a trailer. Also, if I wanted to travel, a PPG could be packed up as airline luggage and travel with me, while a PPC could not. And a PPG required less distance for landings and takeoffs. That meant a PPG would have more flying fields open to it.

On the other hand, the PPG required the pilot to carry the engine on his back, and run with it for takeoffs and landings. Obviously takeoffs and landings would be easier in a wheeled PPC. But were they worth the extra trouble and expense of hauling the PPC around on a trailer? To me, there was something almost magical about an aircraft that you could wear on your back and carry in the trunk of your car. It rather appealed to the romantic swashbuckler in me. Rocket Man lives!

None of these things disqualified the PPC. Obviously the PPC was a fine little flying machine, with many advantages. It was really just a question of personal preference. Which craft would give *me* the most enjoyment?

Obviously it was time to go for a training flight in a PPG. I discovered a PPG dealer just a few miles from my house, checked out his web site, ordered his video, and finally called him up for a chat. Yes, he did give training flights in a PPG. Even better, he had a storefront where I could actually look at some PPGs. I decided to pay him a visit. I took a friend along who was also interested in learning to fly a PPG.

The storefront was in one of those little strip malls. It was stocked with flight suits, helmets, boots, and other sundry equipment. There were several PPG engines sitting on the floor. The place was also infested with high-pressure salesmen.

As soon as I walked in and said that I was interested in a PPG, the jerk behind the desk immediately went to work on me. He tried to sell me a variometer for eight hundred dollars. Knowing that a beginning PPG pilot has very little need for a variometer, I was immediately unimpressed with the jerk's character and honesty.

When we were introduced to the store owner, and dealer, I was even less impressed. I'm over six feet tall and weigh about 220 pounds. The first thing the dealer asked me was, "Do you think you can run with an eighty pound PPG engine on your back?" Of course, having never tried to do such a thing, I had no idea. It struck me as an odd way to make a sale. It was as if the dealer was trying to discourage me from buying.

I had many questions about PPGs that I wanted to ask the dealer, but he was constantly being interrupted by phone calls, all of which he took. Obviously making a sale was not as important as answering the telephone. I ended up getting most of my questions answered by one of the sales clerks. Unfortunately the clerk was not very knowledgeable, and could not answer all of my questions.

I was rapidly become disenchanted with the quality and professionalism of this establishment, but I still wanted to go for a training flight in a PPG. The dealer said he could arrange it, and named a date a couple of weeks away. Each flight would cost $80, so the total cost for me and my friend would be $160. The price was okay, but the dealer wanted the entire payment *now*. This made me very suspicious. Why not pay at the time of the actual flights?

When I told the dealer that we preferred to pay at the time of the flight, he seemed to lose all interest in us, even though he agreed to our request. I started getting suspicious. Was it possible that this entire operation was about to go out of business? Did the dealer simply see an easy way to make an extra $160, knowing that he wouldn't be around to deliver the goods?

On the way home, I told my friend that I doubted we would ever get to make those training flights. It was just a hunch I had, based on my bad feeling in the store. However it turned out that I was right. Several weeks later, only an hour before we were scheduled to make our flights, the PPG dealer called up and said he was forced to cancel the flights. He said he would call back later, and reschedule them. He never did. I decided to take my PPG business elsewhere.

Why the dealer failed to deliver on the training flights, simply because we refused to pay for them, weeks in advance, is still a mystery to me. What's even more unexplainable is why he was so willing to blow the sale of two PPG units, collectively worth about twenty thousand dollars. A very strange way to do business.

Even though my experience with the PPC dealer had been quite pleasant, and my experience with the PPG dealer had been really lousy, I finally decided to go with the PPG. The deciding factors were greater portability for the PPG, and a larger choice of flying fields.

As I learned later, after getting deeper into the PPG business, these reasons were mostly true, but not totally true. More on this later.

There were a few other reasons that contributed to my decision to go with the PPG. The PPG was simpler and less complicated than the PPC. Instead of a wheeled cart weighing several hundred pounds, you had a parachute harness and an engine weighing less than one hundred pounds. There were fewer lines and cables to mess with on the PPG, and fewer things to go wrong. The PPG engine was simpler and less complicated than the PPC engine. In fact, the two-cycle, air-cooled PPG engine was about as simple as an engine can get. It was basically a fancy lawnmower engine.

The PPG also takes up far less storage space than a PPC. The PPG can sit in a closet, or occupy one corner of your garage, and still leave room for the car. The PPC fills the garage, and the car has to live outside.

It's true that the PPG pilot must carry his engine during the takeoff, but it's also true that he only carries the engine for a minute or two until he's in the air. Once airborne, the wing carries the weight of the engine, not the pilot. The truth is, both PPCs and PPGs are very comfortable craft to fly when properly sized and adjusted.

Of course the PPC offered some benefits that the PPG did not. The PPC had wheels, which meant easier takeoffs. The PPC also put wheels and a metal frame between the pilot and the ground, which offered some protection in case of a hard landing. The PPG put *nothing* between the pilot and the ground, except the pilot's own legs.

I decided that 350 pounds of aluminum frame and wheels, that had to be trailered, was too high a price to pay for something that was only used for a few seconds during landings and takeoffs.

Another benefit of the PPC, which I was not aware of at the time, was the fact that the PPC requires much less training to learn to fly. You can easily learn to fly a PPC in a day. To learn to properly fly a PPG takes at least a week. Anyone can learn to fly a PPC, but learning to fly a PPG is an athletic skill that takes some time to master. Also you need to be in reasonably good shape to be able to run with sixty to eighty pounds of engine on your back. Landing and taking off, while wearing an engine on your back, takes a certain amount of coordination and quick response. There were times during my PPG training when I felt that I had made a mistake in choosing the PPG. Sort of like a new recruit who has just joined the Army, on his first twenty mile hike with full pack, and is bitterly regretting it every step of the way.

However there was one other very important reason for choosing the PPG that I think I sort of knew, intuitively, at the time. Flying a PPC is like flying a stripped-down airplane. You're quite aware that you're sitting in a metal frame with wheels and levers and lines all around you. Flying a PPG is flying like a bird. You don't just sit in a PPG; you *wear* it. You strap it on, and literally run into the sky. It's very different than flying a PPC. It's like flying through the air while sitting in a playground swing. There is literally *nothing* between you and the ground. When you look down, all you see is your feet.

Rocket Man lives!

In Hindsight, What Would I have Done Differently?

Not much. I did a very thorough job of researching both PPCs and PPGs. I collected all the information possible at the time, but it wasn't enough. I wish I could have gotten a training flight in a PPG, but after the local PPG dealer bailed out on me, there was no one else in my area offering the flights. However I don't think a flight in a PPG would have affected my decision to go with a PPG. It would only have reinforced it.

Nevertheless, I think training flights are the very best way to get a true picture of how a particular craft operates. Videos are great, but it's just not the same as an actual flight. In the videos they're always very careful not to show the warts. And there are *always* warts!

How I wish I could have read this book! Then I would have known about the warts. (paid advertisement)

Chapter 3

Build Your Own PPG!

Wow! What a deal!

That's what the web site said. Build your own PPG for only $900! It seemed that an outfit in Oregon, called Easy Up, was offering a set of plans for building your own PPG. The cost of the plans was $100. They also offered a book for twenty dollars called *Going Up In A Parachute*. I decided to order both. I was still barely over the ten thousand dollar sticker shock for a brand new PPG. The Easy Up deal sounded great!

The book and the plans arrived a few days later. The book was a little paperback, about 100 pages long, that gave a really excellent overview of powered parachuting. The fundamentals of both PPG and PPC were covered. The diagrams were simple and easy to understand, and there were several pictures. I consider this book an excellent introduction to the sport of powered paragliding, and would recommend it to anyone just getting started.

The plans looked pretty good too. There were about a dozen pages. Each page was three feet long and two feet wide. All the necessary materials were listed, and there was a separate book that showed how to fabricate the more challenging parts, like the bent aluminum tubing for the prop cage. There were also tips on locating used engines and used wings, and suggested sources for parts and materials. All in all, a rather complete package that seemed well worth the money.

The book included a picture of the homemade PPG unit, called a Parapropter. It looked like a decent unit. Building it seemed to be mostly a matter of bending aluminum tubing and hacksawing various aluminum shapes out of sheet metal. I decided to show the plans to a friend of mine who used to make wing spars for Boeing 747s. He looked the plans over and pronounced them good. He even offered to help me fabricate the parts if I decided to build the machine.

According to the Easy Up people, their Paraprotper had been built for a total cost of three thousand dollars. They bought the best used engine and best used wing they could find. This gave them a savings of seven thousand dollars over a new unit. The Easy Up people also claimed that with a great deal of bargain hunting, it would be possible to build the unit for only $900.

I thought long and hard about building my own machine. I certainly wouldn't mind saving seven thousand dollars. However, in the end, I decided to pass on the homebuilt option for two reasons. One, this wasn't a go-cart or an end table. It was an aircraft, and my life would depend on its being airworthy. With a backpack engine I would be unleashing a great deal of power just inches from my body. Knowing almost nothing about the nuts and bolts of PPGs, with their spinning propellers and tanks of explosive gasoline, I was concerned that I might overlook some fundamental detail that might cause me grief later on. If I were an experienced PPG pilot I might take a crack at building my own rig, but at this point I didn't feel comfortable attempting to do so.

The other problem with building your own PPG is that there is very little of it that you can actually build yourself. You still have to buy a wing, a harness, and an engine. And if you end up buying a new engine, you might as well buy a new unit. You're not going to save very much money by building your own rig, particularly if you consider the value of the many hours you will spend in the process.

You see, a PPG is mostly just a few pieces of bent aluminum tubing, welded together to make a frame on which to mount the engine, plus some more aluminum tubing welded together to make a protective cage for the propeller. The frame and the cage are the parts that you get to make yourself, but that's only a very small part of the total aircraft. Everything else; the engine, harness, and wing, must be purchased. If you buy all of that equipment new, you're going to have almost as much invested as if you had simply bought a brand new rig. Also, you're not going to have some of the nicer features that can be found on the commercial rigs, like electric start, an anti-torque system, or an anti-gyroprecessional system, unless you spend even more money.

If you're going to make your own rig, the only way to make it work, financially, is to buy good *used* equipment; used engine, used wing, etc. That way you can save a bundle of money. The drawback, of course, is that you may very well spend a great deal of time locating these used items. Also you need to know that what you're buying is of good quality. Unfortunately, if you're a beginner you probably don't have the necessary experience to do so.

If you want to save money by building your own rig, and are willing to spend the time finding the used items, there's certainly nothing wrong with the idea. Me, I decided I'd rather be flying. Also, at the time I was considering making my own rig, I didn't know enough about engines, wings, and harnesses to guarantee that I wouldn't end up buying worthless junk.

So having decided to buy a new PPG, it was time to get some firm prices. And to settle on a PPG dealer. But first I needed to decide which PPG I wanted to buy.

Far fewer brands of PPGs are offered for sale in the United States than in Europe. Powered paragliding hasn't caught on here, the way it has in Europe and Japan. I suspect this is due to the ready availability of PPC craft in the United States (which are easier to learn to fly than PPGs). In Europe, PPCs aren't readily available, due to high regulatory costs, so the choice is between General Aviation, which is VERY expensive in Europe, and relatively inexpensive PPGs. This makes the PPG very popular in Europe. It's the poor man's airplane. On the other hand, only a few brands of PPGs are sold in the U.S. I looked at the DK Whisper, the La Mouette, the Paramotor, the Pagojet, and the Adventure. (And if I were looking today, I'd add the South African Xplorer and German Fresh Breeze to the list. Along with the Italian Miniplane.)

The DK Whisper was made in Japan, so it was likely to be extremely well-engineered. But it only had a 1.7 gallon fuel tank, which, coupled with its high rate of fuel consumption, provided enough fuel for about one hour of flying. Would that be long enough? And the DK only had a reported thrust of 115 pounds. Would that be strong enough to fly me? I'm over six feet tall, and weigh 220 pounds. On the plus side, the DK engine only weighed a little over fifty pounds. Easier to carry than some of the heavier models. It also had an electric start. Just press the button on the hand throttle, and the engine starts. Nice! Put the engine on, stand up, *then* start it. Shut the engine off in flight, glide for a while, then restart it and fly some more. Very nice!

The Adventure unit came in several sizes, but the large model weighed around eighty pounds. That was pretty heavy. The smaller sizes weighed less, but they also used the Solo 210 motor, and I'd heard that the Solo could be a difficult engine to start. (Of course I'd also heard that it was a very easy engine to start. Take your pick.)

The Paramotor sounded okay until I got a closer look at one. The picture showed the fuel tank above the motor. That looked dangerous to me. What would happen if the fuel tank started to leak, and dripped gasoline on the hot motor? Barbecued pilot? I decided to pass on that one.

The French La Mouette looked like a solid engine. The thrust was an impressive 155 pounds, but it was also one of the heaviest engines on the market; weighing more than 80 pounds. After adding fuel and a reserve parachute, the pilot could easily end up carrying 100 pounds! That's a lot of weight to carry on your back, especially on a hot day.

The Pagojet had what many agree is the best engine; the three-cylinder, German-made Koenig. The Pagojet also had the biggest price tag; a whopping $12,500. It was also a little short in the features department. No electric start. Not even a very good pull-starter. The video showed the pilot wrapping a rope around the hub of the propeller and giving it a tug. The engine started right up, but the propeller blades barely missed the pilot's fingers. It looked like an accident waiting to happen. Also, you couldn't put the engine on, and then start it, unless you had a friend to pull on the rope for you. For twelve grand, I expected a little more. On the other hand, the Pagojet had a five gallon fuel tank; enough for 3-5 hours of flying. (Assuming you could handle the weight of that much fuel.)

Both the La Mouette and the DK Whisper had the advantage of having local dealers. In fact there were several DK Whisper dealers in my state. I decided that it would be nice to have a local dealer, for after sale support. It would also be nice to get my flight training locally.

I talked to two local DK dealers at length. Both of them seemed very happy to answer my questions, and both appeared to be very knowledgeable and safety-conscious. Both agreed that the DK Whisper was the best unit on the market (not too surprising, since they sold it).

I finally decided to go with the DK Whisper. It had all the features I was looking for, including electric start. It didn't weigh too much, and I was assured that it had enough thrust to get me off the ground. As I discovered later, this was mostly true, but not entirely true. The 1.7 gallon fuel tank did concern me, but the dealer assured me that one hour of flying, in a PPG, was plenty long enough. (As I discovered later, it wasn't.)

It was a tough decision to decide between the DK dealers, but I finally made my decision based on physical location. I picked the dealer who was closer to me. Less distance to drive for lessons, and cheaper phone calls. We'll call this dealer "Ralph."

I considered asking for references from Ralph, but in the end I decided not to. Not only did Ralph sound very experienced and professional, but he had also written some articles for the ultralight flying magazines, and his name was frequently mentioned in the ranks of a national ultralight organization. I figured this made him a Guaranteed Good Guy. Which was a Very Dumb Assumption on my part.

The DK Whisper Plus engine cost seven thousand dollars. I had a friend named Mike who was interested in sharing the cost of the rig with me. Yay! But there was just one problem. I weighed 220 pounds, while Mike only weighed 160 pounds. Could we fly the same wing? Most dealers said no. They said the weight difference was just too great. We could share the engine, but we each needed our own wing. (This is another area where PPCs have a definite advantage. With a PPC, the pilot's weight is a much smaller fraction of the total payload, so differences in individual pilot weight can be largely ignored when it comes to wing size.)

Contrary to the other dealers, Ralph said there was a wing that Mike and I could both fly. It was called the A5 Sport, from Flight Design. Ralph said it was a top-of-the-line wing. I hoped so, because Ralph wanted $3600 for the A5 wing, and that was about a thousand dollars more than the other PPG dealers around the country were quoting for their wings. Of course it was still cheaper than buying two separate wings.

I asked some of the other PPG dealers how they felt about the A5 wing. Most of them seemed to think that the A5 was too demanding for a beginner, but that it would make a good second wing after I'd gotten some flight experience. Most of the dealers who felt this way also recommended the Pro Design Compact wing as a good beginner wing. The Compact was also cheaper, costing around $2500.

In the end, Mike and I decided to go with Ralph's recommendation. The cost of the entire package, wing and engine, was $10,600, but that included my training to learn to fly it. Ralph said that he would be willing to train Mike to fly the unit for an additional $800. Or if Mike also bought an engine, then the training would be included in the engine price.

Unfortunately we couldn't buy the engine, or the wing, right away. Both Mike and I had our money tied up in an old house that we had bought a few months earlier, and were fixing up to sell. We had bought the house in May, and I was hoping to have it finished and sold by September or October. Talk about naïve!

By mid-December we were still working on the house, with no end in sight. Ralph let us know that DK was planning to raise the price of their engine, in January, by one thousand dollars. Wouldn't we like to buy our engine right now, and save a thousand bucks? Ralph explained that when DK originally introduced their engines to the United States, they sold them at a big loss to get market share, and now they needed to raise the price to stay profitable.

Being prime suckers, Mike and I took the bait. Even though it would be a financial hardship, we decided to go ahead and buy the engine at the end of December to avoid paying an extra thousand bucks later. We decided to buy the engine now, and then buy the wing after the house was sold.

Ralph's terms were very simple. We would pay him the entire seven thousand dollars up front, and then he would order the engine from Japan.

I wasn't very comfortable with those terms, and neither was Mike. I had no particular reason not to trust Ralph, but this was sport aviation, and it was shot through with stories of customers who paid for the entire plane, up front, and then never got it. Or else they signed up to buy a kit, but only got some of the pieces. This business was filled with fly-by-night operators, just plain crooked dealers, and well-meaning individuals who go bankrupt and are Very Sorry To Have Spent All Your Money, But There's Nothing More I Can Do For You.

Ralph tried to reassure us that nothing bad would happen if we would only do exactly what he wanted us to do. It reminded me of the line I used to give my girlfriends. Ralph explained that he would have a contractual obligation to us, and if he failed to deliver the engine his reputation would be ruined. Big deal! We'd still be out our seven grand, with no way to get it back. It happens all the time in this business. A friend of mine had just finished losing $75,000 in a precious metals scam, despite having been a personal friend of the President of the company for ten years. I vowed that was not going to happen to us. Seven thousand dollars was more money than we could afford to lose. If we paid the money, and didn't get the engine, we couldn't afford to buy another one.

We told Ralph that we wanted to pay for the engine at the time of delivery. Ralph said that wasn't possible. He said that he couldn't afford to tie up so much money in inventory. We debated taking our business elsewhere, but Ralph was local, and that was a great advantage. He might not be the world's greatest businessman, but he did sound like the world's greatest instructor. Also I liked the guy personally (and still do). Wasn't there some way to make this deal fly?

Ralph happened to mention that other dealers normally required a one thousand dollar deposit in lieu of the entire amount up front. Hey! I liked that idea, and so did Mike. Losing a thousand bucks would hurt, but it wouldn't be the catastrophic loss that seven thousand dollars would be. We offered to put down a one thousand dollar, non-refundable cash deposit, with the balance to be paid on delivery of the engine. Ralph agreed, and confirmed the agreement via e-mail. We sent Ralph the deposit and he ordered the engine. It was just a few days before Christmas.

In the first week of January, Ralph called to say that the engine had arrived. Yay! Then he dropped a bombshell. He said that he wanted the six thousand dollar balance due on the engine. No problem, I told him. Haul the engine down to my house and we'll trade the money for the engine. Just as we had earlier agreed to do. Or I'd be happy to bring the money to Ralph's house and trade it for the engine.

Ralph said that he couldn't do that. He claimed the deal was that he would get the rest of the money when the engine arrived in the United States; not when it was delivered to me personally. That didn't sound at all like our original agreement. I dug out Ralph's old e-mail. It read, "If what you are saying is that as soon as I have it in my hands, and can change actual physical ownership to you, then I will be paid the balance for the machine, then great, let's do it!"

It sounded to me like Ralph had forgotten the terms of our original deal. To my way of thinking, I didn't care if the engine was sitting in a factory in Japan, or sitting on a dock somewhere in the United States. If the engine was not in my physical possession, then my money was still at risk. We had paid the one thousand dollar deposit, precisely to avoid this sort of problem.

Ralph claimed that he had the actual engine in his physical possession. I asked Ralph why we couldn't simply trade the money for the engine. He explained that he couldn't turn the engine over to us because we hadn't been trained to use it, and we might get hurt with it. He said he couldn't afford to take the legal risk.

I didn't agree. To my way of thinking, a PPG engine was no different, fundamentally, than a lawn mower. Both have gasoline engines and blades that spin.

Ralph never told us that we would be required to have training before we could take physical possession of the engine. I began to suspect a scam. This looked like a last-ditch effort by Ralph to get the entire seven thousand dollars, up front, without delivering any merchandise. That was precisely the situation I was determined to avoid. Thank God we had only risked a thousand dollars!

But I didn't want to lose a thousand bucks. I just wanted to get my engine! I proposed several solutions to solve this latest problem. I suggested that Ralph give me whatever training he felt was necessary to relieve him of liability. Then he could turn the engine over to me, and I could pay him the balance due.

Or we could trade the money for the engine, and I could give Ralph my personal guarantee that the engine would sit in my garage, chained to the floor, where no one would touch it until Ralph was satisfied that I had received enough training to be trusted with it..

Or we could trade the money for the engine, and I could sign a waiver releasing Ralph from all liability.

Unfortunately, none of these solutions was satisfactory to Ralph. So I finally suggested that he deliver the engine to me, minus the propeller. End of liability problem. Then I could pay him. Ralph reluctantly agreed.

On January 14, Ralph delivered the DK Whisper Plus engine to me. What a beauty! Instead of removing the propeller, Ralph had merely removed the spark plugs from the twin cylinders, making the engine impossible to start. Ralph sternly warned me that any attempt to install new spark plugs, and run the engine, would destroy the engine. I knew that wasn't true, but I really didn't care. I had my engine! I assured Ralph that the engine would sit, chained to the floor of my garage, until I could afford to buy the wing and start taking lessons.

After Ralph left, I spent several hours drooling over my gorgeous new engine. The usual Japanese attention to detail was everywhere. The rig looked extremely "finished" and polished. The aluminum weld joints were very well done. Everything fitted together perfectly. There was a simple aluminum frame that held the engine securely in place. A padded, parachute-style harness was attached to the frame. Attached to each side of the harness, at shoulder level, was a big metal carabiner that would connect the wing to the harness. A shiny, jet-black, 3-bladed, carbon-fiber propeller was mounted on the engine. The propeller looked huge and menacing, but it was shielded from the pilot by a cage of aluminum tubing. The propeller cage attached to the engine frame with velcro straps, and the cage itself could be broken down into four pieces for easy transport. A 1.7

gallon fuel tank was mounted below the engine. Just behind the fuel tank was a large muffler.

The engine included a small electric starter. On top of the engine was a simple carburetor with an air foam filter and a sliding choke. Directly in front of the carburetor was a nicad battery pack that powered the starter. The battery was about as big as four hot dogs taped together. There was a very nice hand throttle, made of molded plastic, to control the engine speed. There were two buttons on the hand throttle; one to start the engine and one to kill the engine. The hand throttle also included a cruise control to lock the throttle in any given position. This made it unnecessary to maintain constant finger pressure on the throttle during the flight. Nice!

The engine was a two-cylinder, two-cycle, air-cooled powerplant with simultaneously-firing, opposed cylinders. It said so in the literature. (What I knew about engines, at that point in my life, you could write on the head of a pin.) At the moment, each cylinder was missing the vital spark plug. I didn't care, as I had no interest in starting the engine until I'd received proper training.

The engine came with an instruction manual that was obviously written by an author for whom English was a second language, but it was good enough.

I sat down on the floor and strapped the engine to my body. There were two leg straps and a chest strap. There was also a large, zippered vest that covered most of the chest area, and was an integral part of the harness. The whole thing fitted very snugly, but seemed comfortable enough. There was a stiff, padded seat between the leg straps to sit on, in flight. It would be like sitting in a playground swing.

I managed to get to my feet while wearing the engine. It wasn't an easy thing to do with 50 plus pounds on my back. About like getting up with a heavy backpack. Was I really going to be able to run fast enough with this heavy load on my back, to get airborne? With the leg straps secured, and the rigid seat positioned under my butt, I couldn't stand up straight. I was bent over like a hunchback. Obviously the harness would need to be properly adjusted for my height.

I walked around with the engine on my back. The sight of it scared the cats. I managed to only knock over one lamp with the prop cage. Obviously I was going to have to learn to maneuver carefully with this big rig on my back; especially when the engine was running.

But the important thing was that the engine was here, and it was MINE! ALL MINE! This was the engine that was going to let me fly through the air. I felt like I'd reached a very significant milestone in my life.

I had a hard time getting to sleep that night. Sleep had difficulty competing with visions of soaring through the air in my own personal flying machine. Fortunately I had no idea of the trials and tribulations that lay ahead of me.

Now that I had the engine, Ralph said that I could start my lessons anytime, using one of his wings. I was very eager to get started, but I wasn't sure just how long it was going to take to finish remodeling that damn house, get it sold, and get the money I needed to buy my own wing. Ralph said that I would not want to wait too long after finishing my lessons before starting to fly on my own, and for that I would need my own wing. I decided that it would be better to wait until I actually had my own wing before starting my lessons. Sob! I also decided that I would prefer to learn to fly on the same wing that I would be flying after I finished my lessons.

Ralph admitted that he already had my wing in his possession. He had ordered it from the wing dealer at the same time that he had ordered the engine; hoping that I might be able to come up with the money to buy the wing, too. Oh how I wanted to say yes! I had the cash, but I knew that it might be needed to finish the house. Reluctantly I told Ralph to send the wing back to the dealer.

The months dragged by as I continued to work on the house. At the start of each month I was convinced that I was just a couple of weeks away from finishing the house. But new problems kept popping up, pushing the completion date farther and farther into the future. Every few days I wandered out into the garage and gazed longingly at my beautiful new engine, sitting chained to the floor. It was like watching a beautiful captive bird. Sometimes I gave the propeller a half-turn, just to hear the pistons moving inside the cylinders.

As the months passed, Ralph inquired regularly as to my progress on the house. He told me that he couldn't hold onto the wing much longer. The wing dealer either wanted his money, or the wing. In May, five long months after taking possession of the engine, I got an idea. The house WAS nearing completion, and cash was not quite so tight, but I still couldn't fork over $3600 for the wing. However I could make smaller monthly payments on the wing until the house finally sold, and then I could pay off the balance on the wing. That way I could start my training immediately, and the dealer could start getting his money now, rather than later. Ralph proposed the idea to the wing dealer, and the dealer accepted. We settled on monthly payments of $500. Finally I could start flying!

Well no, not quite. As soon as the local Weather God received word that I was getting ready to fly, it began to rain. And rain. And rain. Enough rain to keep me grounded for the rest of May. And through the month of June. And half of July! More rain than this area had seen in the last fifty years! But finally the clouds ran dry, and the sun reappeared. Finally I could start flying!

Well no, not quite. Suddenly I got word from my parents that they were coming for a visit during the last week of July. They wanted to see the house that I'd just finished remodeling. So the start of my flying career got pushed back a little further. But the good news was that the house sold almost instantly, and for top dollar. Yay!

Finally, at the beginning of August, *seven freaking months* after taking possession of my engine, I notified Ralph that I could finish paying for my wing and start my training. Hallelujah!

I had no idea that I was about to walk into Hell.

In Hindsight, What Would I have Done Differently?

Get the dealer agreement in writing!
Get the dealer agreement in writing!
Get the dealer agreement in writing!

Oral contracts aren't worth the paper they're not written on. Even the e-mail I received from Ralph might not have stood up in court if matters had come to that. A simple written agreement, signed by me and Ralph, spelling out how the deal would be conducted, would have prevented a lot of hassle and grief after the engine arrived in the U.S.

Get it in writing!

Also, get at least three references from the dealer, call them up, and ask them if they are satisfied with the product, the service, and the training. This is critically important! There are lots of dishonest, incompetent dealers out there. Don't end up as one of their victims! Many people buy PPGs, get one or two flights during their inadequate training period, then go home and are too scared to fly again. They realize that they haven't been properly trained, and they frequently end up selling their engines for a fraction of what they paid for them.

If you need a good dealer recommendation for learning to fly a powered paraglider, contact me at cwolf41@attbi.com.

One thing I did right was to not pay the entire amount for my gear, up front. Ideally you would pay for the gear on delivery, but few dealers can afford to get stuck for the total cost of a gear package if the customer should change his mind. So if the dealer seems to be trustworthy (you did check his references, right?) then it's okay to give him a small down payment with the balance due on delivery. The down payment should be non-refundable if you fail to take delivery of the gear, or to pay the balance due. Fair is fair.

Never pay the entire amount up front unless you're paying by credit card. There are simply too many dishonest dealers in this business. The sport aviation market swarms with stories of people who paid up front, and never got their flying machine.

If you had it to do over, would you have made your own PPG from the Easy Up plans?

No. And I'm glad I didn't try to build my own. I really don't think it's a job for an amateur (like me). On the other hand, if I was an experienced machinist, or had plenty of experience in working with engines and frames, I might very well go the homebuilt route. As many homebuilt pilots can tell you, there are few things more satisfying than flying a machine that you've built with your own hands. But keep in mind that you will be building something on which your life will literally be hanging. You can't afford to make mistakes.

Having flown a PPG for a year, I can say that the Easy Up plans still look good to me. The Parapropter looks like it would get the job done. The problem is that until you've actually flown a PPG for awhile, you may not know what you really want. The Easy Up plans would produce a machine that would satisfy some pilots, but not others.

Would you still get an engine with electric start?

The answer to that question is a definite "maybe." Personally I like an electric starter. I love being able to start up my engine just by pressing a button on my hand throttle. I love being able to start the engine and warm it up, then turn it off, put it on, get ready to take off, restart the engine with the press of a button, and take off. Of course my flying buddy, Mike, could always start the engine for me, after I put it on, but I'd rather have him off in the distance, getting ready to video my flight.

If you're flying alone, without electric start, then you have no choice but to start up the engine, warm it up, then put it on and get to your feet. However it's much easier and safer to put on the engine, get to your feet, and *then* start it up.

When my engine suddenly quit during one of my flights, my electric starter enabled me to restart the engine. Some engine makers claim that their engines can be restarted, in flight, by hand. I have no experience in this area, and so am unable to comment on this, but other pilots appear to confirm the claim. If so, that would be very nice.

If I was planning on doing an aerial restart, by hand, I would insist on testing this feature while wearing the running engine, while hanging from a couple of ropes from a tree limb. While suspended in the air, I would stop the engine and then try to restart it by hand. As we all know, sometimes the practice doesn't quite live up to the theory.

Of course it must be remembered that an electric starter adds weight and complexity to the engine. It's something else to go wrong. Being electric, there's always the possibility of an in-flight electrical fire, which is why frequent inspections of the wiring are so important. PPG engines are great places to practice the KISS principle. (Keep It Simple, Stupid!)

If you have an electric starter, the battery is also a pain to keep charged unless you have one of the expensive Pulse Chargers that permit a nicad battery to be recharged, at any level of discharge, without suffering from the nicad's infamous "memory" effect. Most nicad battery chargers cannot properly recharge the battery unless the battery has first been completely drained. This frequently results in a dead battery, in the field, just as you're getting ready to take off.

But even with all that, I still love my electric starter. However I will probably omit it on my next engine, simply to save the weight.

If you had it to do over again, would you consider buying used equipment?

Yes. Used equipment can be an excellent bargain. But if you're a first-time buyer, find a trustworthy dealer who can make certain that you're getting good equipment. An honest dealer will be happy to inspect and evaluate your used equipment, for a fee, even if you don't buy your equipment from him.

What's the most important thing to do when buying a PPG engine?

Try it on! Try it on! Try it on! Never buy a PPG engine until you've actually tried it on, and sat in it while hanging suspended from a couple of ropes, just as you would hang from the wing. Fit is critically important, and some PPGs are much more comfortable than others. Remember, you're going to be sitting in this thing for a couple of hours at a stretch. It must fit your body comfortably, or you won't want to fly it. I had one PPG pilot tell me that the Pagojet was the most comfortable PPG he had ever flown. Another pilot told me that the Pagojet was the most *un*comfortable PPG he had ever flown. Everybody is different. If the dealer won't let you try the engine on, and sit in it while hanging from the ropes, find another dealer. Would you buy a car from a dealer who wouldn't even let you sit in it?

I was dumb enough to buy my engine without ever actually trying one on. If I had tried a DK Whisper on, before buying, and hung it from the ropes, I would have immediately known that it was too small for me. I love my DK Whisper, but I had to go through a lot of hassle to make it fit my oversized body. Remember, no motor is perfect for everyone.

At the same time, it's important to remember that while comfort is very important when flying through the air, it doesn't mean diddly-squat while walking around on the ground, carrying your engine. All PPG engines are heavy, and none of them are designed to be comfortable while being carried around on your back, on the ground. However you only have to carry the motor for a minute or two, when launching, so comfort on the ground is not that important. (Later on I will show you some tricks to improve comfort on the ground.) As long as the engine feels good when you're sitting in it while suspended from the ropes, it doesn't matter too much how it feels when riding around on your back. As long as you can physically lift the damn thing, and run a few steps with it on your back, you'll be okay. Of course, the lighter the better. Don't put up with the extra hassle of an eighty pound motor if a fifty pound motor will fill your needs.

Did you end up saving a thousand bucks by buying your engine early?

Go away and quit bothering me!

Okay, the truth is, DK never raised the price of their engines. Instead they *lowered* the price of their engines by one thousand dollars, just a few months later. What happened to all of this inside information about a price increase? Apparently something got lost in the translation from Japanese to English. Another fine lesson from the School Of Hard Knocks.

Chapter 4

First Flight

It was Saturday, and the first week in August, and it was pretty hot. I'd been given directions to a farm where my flight training was to take place. I hadn't been told to bring anything except myself, so I didn't.

When I got to the farm there was only the farmhouse and one other car parked alongside the road, next to an empty pasture. I parked behind the other car, got out, and introduced myself to the driver. Yes, this was the right place and we were just waiting for the rest of the group to arrive.

The training field was a long pasture with a line of trees at the far end. As we stood in the hot sun, I found myself wishing that I had brought a hat and some water to drink. I was also wondering where they kept the restroom.

In a few minutes the rest of the group arrived. There was Ralph, his assistant Jake, and half a dozen other students; mostly men. They all seemed to know each other. As the new kid in the class, I felt a little awkward and out of place.

We all piled into two pickup trucks and were driven to the far end of the field, next to the trees. I watched as Ralph and Jake set up the scooter tow. Several paraglider wings were unpacked and laid out in the sun. I just stood around, waiting for somebody to tell me what to do. The other students seemed to know what was going on, and what they needed to do. Nobody told me anything, and I was feeling a bit disconnected. I hadn't been given a course syllabus, a description of what was to happen, or any idea of what the training would encompass. I'd been given a paragliding instruction manual to read, and I had read it, but there was a lot of material to absorb. It was difficult to know which points were important to a beginner, and which were not. The whole training operation seemed a bit on the rough side. As someone who values orderly procedures, I found it a trifle disconcerting. In fact, after all the time I'd spent eagerly waiting to start my glorious flight training, the whole thing seemed a bit of an anticlimax. I felt a little bit disappointed. But of course, reality is almost always a bit of a letdown compared to the dream.

But one thing I did notice. This operation did not seem to be a *training* facility; it was more like a *processing* facility. There's a difference. Training is to achieve a goal. Processing is to fulfill an obligation.

As the morning wore on, two things were happening. Students were being towed aloft with the scooter, while other students were practicing forward inflations of their paragliding wings. I watched both operations, trying to learn as much as possible. I wondered when it would be my turn. Or was I going to spend my first day of training, just standing around?

The forward inflations were interesting. This was the first time I'd seen a paraglider wing up close. It looked very much like the ram-air skydiving canopies I'd flown twenty years earlier, but there had obviously been some significant changes. I felt a little like Rip Van Winkle, waking up to find that twenty years of progress had taken place while I slept.

Each wing had a top and bottom layer of zero-porosity fabric, sealed at the back and sides, and open at the front to permit air to rush in and inflate the wing. Across the front of the wing, about every eight inches or so, there was a vertical "rib" of fabric, cut in the shape of an airfoil. These ribs divided the wing into numerous "cells." When the wing was pulled forward, the open cells scooped up the air and forced it inside; inflating the wing into an airfoil shape that could generate lift, just as my old skydiving ram-air canopy had done.

There were some important differences, of course. Twenty years of improved technology had produced a much more sophisticated wing shape than my primitive skydiving canopy. Another big difference was in the thickness of the suspension lines. They were much thinner than the suspension lines on my skydiving canopy. The paraglider lines hardly seemed more than kite string. (Of course they were much stronger than kite string.) Obviously since these wings were not intended to be opened at a speed of one hundred miles per hour, they didn't need to be made nearly as strong as a skydiving wing.

Each fabric rib in the wing had several suspension lines attached to the bottom of the rib. The suspension lines were gathered together into groups, and the groups were finally gathered together into two sets of nylon straps called "risers." Each riser ended in a single nylon strap with a loop in the end that permitted it to be attached to the pilot's harness via a steel carabiner.

The wing had a steering line for each hand. The steering lines were attached to the trailing edge of the wing on either side of the pilot, and permitted the wing to be steered left or right. When the pilot pulled down on a steering line, it pulled down the trailing edge of the wing on that side, increasing drag and causing the wing to turn in that direction. There were no other flight controls. The pilot's suspended weight kept the wing at the right pitch, and also prevented the wing from rolling from side to side. This was called Pendulum Stability. Nor was it necessary to control the yaw. If the pilot kept his hands off the controls, the wing would automatically fly straight, and without stalling. The pilot's input was only necessary for steering. It was the world's simplest aircraft. Obviously it was very easy to fly. The trick would be in the landings and takeoffs.

The pilot's harness greatly resembled a skydiving harness. About the only difference was the presence of a rigid seat for the paraglider pilot to sit in, after launch.

Since the wind was very light, the students were doing forward inflations. Each student laid his wing out on the ground, on its back. Then he attached the wing risers to each side of his harness, put on the harness, and took the risers and steering lines in each hand. Then he ran forward as fast as he could. As the suspension lines went taut, the leading edge of the wing would be jerked off the ground, the cells would scoop up the air, and the wing would be inflated and pulled up into the sky. Once the wing was flying overhead, the student could keep it there by running forward as fast as he could, and by steering it with the steering lines.

At least that was the theory. That was the way it was supposed to happen. Most of the time it didn't. The wing would start to rise into the air, but then would fall off to one side or the other. Or else the wing would rise overhead, then shoot past the pilot and crash nose-first into the ground with a loud *whump!*

The problem was that none of the students seemed to know what they were doing. And the fact that it was hot and sunny, with almost no breeze, made the whole process pretty miserable and uncomfortable. Since I had nothing else to do, I helped to lay out the wings on the ground. The activity was making me very hot and thirsty. Some of the students had water bottles or drinking bladders, but there seemed to be no community water supply. Unfortunately I had also made the mistake of wearing long pants, instead of shorts. I was also starting to worry about sunburn, since I had brought no sunscreen for my arms, head, or neck.

Truthfully I was surprised to discover that my first lesson was to be held outside. I was under the impression that paragliding lessons always started with classroom instruction on the basic aerodynamics of the paragliding wing. Apparently that was not Ralph's method of teaching.

The real problem was that there were not enough instructors to go around. There were just two instructors, Ralph and Jake, and they were both needed to operate the scooter tow system. When the students weren't being towed, apparently they were supposed to get along as best they could on their own. The whole thing struck me as low-rent, and rather disorganized.

The scooter tow was an interesting mechanism. An ordinary motor scooter had been mounted on a stationary frame. The front wheel had been removed and replaced with a large spool of strong line, several thousand feet long. The line ran all the way down the field, passed through a pulley at the far end of the field, and then ran all the way back to the motor scooter where it was attached to the student's harness. This placed the student very close to the instructor who was operating the motor scooter (a good safety feature).

The student who was to be towed, laid out his wing, got into his harness, and clipped on a radio. One of the instructors attached the tow line to the front of the student's harness with a quick-release link. Then the tension was slowly taken up on the tow line. When the student felt the tow line begin to tug, he signaled to the instructor on the motor scooter (the towmaster) to begin towing. As the student ran forward, inflating his wing, the towmaster gunned the scooter's engine. If all went according to plan, the wing would quickly rise overhead, the tow line would provide the forward speed, and the wing would lift the student into the air. Under the pull of the tow line, the wing would climb until it had reached an altitude of several hundred feet. Then the student would release himself from the towline and glide back to Earth under the radioed guidance from the instructor on the ground.

Each tow session took about fifteen or twenty minutes from start to finish. Everybody got a tow but me. Since I had not yet been taught how to do forward inflations, I could not take a turn on the towline. While I waited patiently for my turn to come, I managed to borrow a Coke and some sunscreen, but I was still terribly thirsty.

After a couple of hours of towing, Ralph called a halt to give some instruction on forward inflations. Ralph also told me that he had brought my wing out to the farm with him, and that it was in his truck. I quickly located the large, black nylon bag. I opened it up and unpacked my brand-new wing.

What a beauty! It was an A5 Sport from Flight Design. The wing was bright orange in color, and it fairly gleamed in the sun. The material was so new that it still crinkled. And the wing was enormous! It appeared to measure about thirty feet from wingtip to wingtip, about ten feet from front to back, and was about one foot thick. I laid the wing out on the ground and drooled over it. This was the wing that would give me the freedom of the skies. This was my wing!

Finally it was time for me to get some instruction in forward inflations. I was given a hockey helmet to wear, and a pair of gloves to protect my hands from line burns. Then I was given a harness to put on, and was hooked up to the wing. I was given some perfunctory instructions, and shown how to hold the risers and steering lines.

I stood in front of the wing, risers and steering lines in my hands, and crouched like a Olympic sprinter. I counted down from three, and then ran forward as fast as I could. When I felt the lines go taut, I pulled forward with both arms, as I had been instructed. As the wing shot up into the air, the drag from the rising wing stopped me in my tracks. No matter how hard I pulled, I couldn't overcome the wing's tremendous drag. It was like pulling on a rope that was tied to a tree. However in only a moment or two the wing was flying overhead, and I was once again able to run forward. In fact, that's exactly what I should have done; run forward as fast as I could to keep the wing flying. A wing can only fly as long as it moves through the air. But not knowing any better, I just stood there, looking up at that big beautiful wing flying overhead. At that point, of course, the wing stopped flying and promptly fell on top of me, enfolding me in billowing folds of cloth and dangling lines.

As I untangled myself from the wing, I reflected on my first attempt at forward launching. Obviously this was going to take some practice. It suddenly occurred to me that not only did I need to learn to pull the wing into the air, and keep it there, but that I also had to be able to do it with sixty pounds of engine on my back. It sounded like an impossible task, and I hoped that I hadn't bitten off more than I could chew.

While I laid out the wing again, Ralph assisted some of the other students in doing forward launches. I waited patiently for him to return and supervise my second forward launch, but instead he went back to the tow line. I stood in front of the wing, in the hot sun, for nearly half an hour, waiting for an instructor to come and help me. When none came, I finally decided to try the forward launch again, by myself. This time the wing came only part way up and then fell off to one side, just as I had seen it happen with some of the other students. I wondered what I was doing wrong, but there was no one to whom I could ask my questions.

Finally I gave up, unhooked the wing, and wandered over to the tow line. I figured I might be able to pick up some tips by watching the towing process. Having bought ten thousand dollars worth of equipment from Ralph, I really didn't feel like I was getting my money's worth in the training department.

If the instructors were less than impressive, the paragliders most assuredly were not. Whereas my old skydiving wing had been rectangular in shape, and relatively flat, these wings were elliptical and took the shape of a gentle arch when they were flying. They were extraordinarily beautiful against the blue sky, and they flew like birds. As wings, they were obviously much higher performance than my old skydiving ram-air wing.

I later learned that the paragliding wings had a 7 to 1 glide ratio; meaning they flew forward seven feet for every vertical foot they descended. Their forward speed was generally between twenty and thirty miles per hour, and their landings were very gentle (if properly done). Normally the pilot simply pulled both steering lines down to his waist as he neared the ground. This caused the wing to flare, converting forward speed into vertical lift and slowing the rate of descent. Finally the wing stalled, which brought it to a virtual stop in the air. Then the pilot merely stepped down onto the ground. If done properly, it was like stepping off a curb. If the pilot still had some forward velocity, he simply ran a few steps before coming to a stop. All in all, it was a most impressive flying machine.

If the paragliders were beautiful in flight, the process of getting them into the sky, via the towline, could only be described as "scary." The launching itself wasn't too difficult. I soon learned that the pull of the tow line could correct for many student handling errors. Basically if the student simply ran forward, did not trip over his own feet, and managed to get the wing even a few feet into the air, he usually became airborne without too much trouble. Sometimes it was necessary to back up and start over before the student finally got airborne. Sometimes several tries were necessary.

However the real thrills began once the student was in the air. All the student had to do was steer, and keep the wing perpendicular to the tow line until it was time for release. If the wing was drifting to the right, a pull on the left steering line would bring the wing back into position. If the wing was drifting to the left, a pull on the right steering line was all that was needed.

Unfortunately some of the students just couldn't seem to master this skill. They would take off, start to climb, and immediately begin to drift to one side or the other. Ralph would start shouting into the radio, "Left steering!" or "Right steering!" Sometimes the student would respond properly and correct the problem. Sometimes, especially if it was the student's first time aloft, he pulled on the wrong steering line and kept pulling on it in spite of Ralph's shouted orders. Even when Ralph told the student that he was pulling on the wrong steering line, this sometimes only made the student pull even harder!

The result of this was to send the paraglider and student all over the sky; sometimes as much as forty-five degrees from the direction of the tow line. I began to wonder just how far to one side a paraglider could fly before it would start to slip sideways and fall out of the sky. I learned later that this was called "lockout," and was a very real possibility. I think some of the students came awfully close to disaster. In the case of a lockout, the only hope would be to cut the tow line and hope the wing recovered in time before striking the ground.

When the student reached an altitude of three or four hundred feet, it was time to release the tow line and fly the wing back to Earth. When the release command was given over the radio, the student was supposed to kick his legs to signal that he was ready. Since the student already had a steering line in each hand, it was necessary to let go of one of the steering lines in order to reach for the tow line release. Accordingly, the student was told to place both steering line handles in one hand, and then use his free hand to pull the tow line release. Then he was supposed to pull both steering handles down about six inches, to stop the forward surge of the wing when it was suddenly released from the tow line tension. Then the student was supposed to return the steering lines to the appropriate hands and steer according to his radioed instructions. I thought it was a lot of detail for a first-time flier to have to remember.

Since the tow line pulled the student far out ahead of the wing, the sudden release of tension on the tow line caused the student to fall backward. This caused the wing to surge forward, ahead of the student, and dive toward the ground before regaining its flying attitude. While this surge was not particularly dangerous, it could be frightening to the student, and it did cause some altitude to be lost, which shortened the subsequent flight.

The whole process struck me as a fairly complicated procedure for someone who had never done it before. Unfortunately the only training the student received, before making his towed flight, was a set of verbal instructions from Ralph, delivered just moments before launch. Naturally most of the students completely forget the detailed instructions once they were in the air. When the order came to pull the tow line release, usually the student just let go of the steering lines and reached for the release. Then after the wing surged forward, and altitude was lost, the student managed to re-acquire the steering lines and started piloting the wing. (Fortunately paragliders are very forgiving wings.)

One woman had a particularly memorable flight. After several aborted attempts, she managed to launch and get airborne. She then proceeded to trace giant arcs back and forth across the sky, like the swinging pendulum on a grandfather clock. Never once did she manage to stay lined up with the tow line for more than a few seconds. Finally, as she reached maximum altitude, Ralph gave her the order to release the tow line. She let go of the steering lines, reached for the tow line release, and pulled it. Then she put her hands back on the steering line handles and started flying the wing.

All well and good except for just one little problem:

The tow line had not released! The student was flying a wing that was still tethered to the ground!

The student made a perfect one hundred and eighty degree turn, and headed back toward the rest of us. The tow line dangled from her harness, reaching hundreds of feet down to the ground. In less than a minute she would have used up all the slack in the tow line, and the line would go taut, just like an anchor. What would happen then? I was pretty sure that the sudden drag would cause the wing to plunge forward and fall out of the sky. I reached for my pocket knife to cut the tow line, if necessary. (I learned later that Ralph kept a knife handy for just such an emergency.)

Fortunately it wasn't necessary to cut the tow line. Ralph radioed instructions to the student, telling her how to release the line. She finally managed to do it, and the rest of her flight was quite ordinary. She seemed quite unperturbed after landing. Personally I had been scared to death. Was I the only one aware of how close she had come to tragedy? Later, I privately questioned Ralph about the incident. He agreed that it had been quite dangerous, and pretty scary.

Paragliding was beginning to look like a rather dangerous sport. I wasn't too worried about myself, because I already knew how to fly a ram-air wing. All I had to do was learn how to get it into the air. I knew that I would have no problem steering as I was towed aloft, or as I flew back to Earth.

Nevertheless, this towing business struck me as rather dangerous for beginners who had never flown before. Eventually I realized that it wasn't the towing itself that was dangerous; *it was the complete lack of training before towing.*

Flying though the air while suspended under a big kite, is not a natural act. When a student is towed aloft for the first time, his brain typically goes into sensory overload. His instinctive fear of falling kicks in, and he hangs onto the harness for dear life. That's okay if he doesn't have to do anything, like on those parasail rides they give at beach resorts. But if the student has to steer the wing, or control it in any way, he needs to have been trained to do so. And it's not enough simply to have described the proper procedure to the student just before he takes off. The student needs to have been hung up in a harness from a tree branch or swing set, with a pair of steering lines in his hands and a hunk of tow line attached to his harness, held by the instructor.

The student needs to learn what it's like to hang in a harness, what the tow line looks like when the wing starts to drift to the right or left, and which steering line should be pulled to restore the wing to its proper orientation behind the tow line. The student needs to know which line to pull when the instructor says "right steering" or "left steering." The student also needs to be trained in how to release the steering line after the turn is finished. I've seen untrained students stop the turn by pulling down on the *opposite* steering line. They end up with both steering lines pulled down, and risking a stall. Even more important, the student needs to have been trained in the proper procedure when it's time to release the tow line.

In other words, the whole towing process needs to be physically rehearsed so that the student has some idea what's coming, and how he will need to respond. When the student is finally in the air, and his poor brain has just gone into sensory overload, the only thing he can fall back on is his training; his "muscle memory." If he hasn't had any training, then he has nothing to fall back on, and it will be sheer luck if he does the right thing. It will be sheer luck if the student pulls on the proper steering line when the instructor shouts "Right steering!" Unfortunately, the student is all too likely to pull the wrong steering line, *and to keep on pulling it* no matter what the instructor says. The student's brain simply issues the command to "Do Something! Anything!"

Unfortunately, such a lack of training is all too common in the paragliding business.

Around noon, Ralph announced that we were finished towing for the day and that it was time to head over to Mount Wilson for some tandem flying. He reminded everyone to be sure to bring warm clothes, as it would be much cooler on top of the mountain. No one had told me to bring warm clothes. Fortunately I had a windbreaker with me.

On the way to Mount Wilson I stopped in a nearby town for some food and drink. I don't think I've ever been so thirsty in my life. Then I drove over to the landing zone at the base of Mount Wilson. The LZ was a big grassy field surrounded by trees on three sides, and a busy highway and power lines on the fourth side. There was a parking lot, and it was already full of cars. There were several paragliders soaring high overhead. I watched them fly for several minutes. There are few things in the sky more beautiful than a paraglider in flight.

The access road to the top of Mount Wilson was gravel, and was best suited for pickup trucks and four-wheel drive vehicles. I left my car in the LZ parking lot and rode up to the top of the mountain in the back of a pickup truck. There were no seats or seatbelts. We simply piled in along with the gear. As we whizzed down the paved highway at sixty-five miles per hour, and then roared up the gravel access road to the top of the mountain, I realized that if this vehicle were to have an accident, or to be involved in a collision, we would very likely be severely injured or even killed, since we weren't wearing seat belts or shoulder harnesses. This whole operation struck me as unsafe. It just felt wrong.

But I wanted to fly in the worst way, so I hung on as the pickup truck lurched and swayed as it wound its way up the side of the mountain. The mountain was completely forested with tall timber, but occasionally the trees would part and give us a momentary glimpse of the surrounding area. The view was quite impressive.

After about forty minutes of travel time, we finally arrived at the top of the mountain. There was a small parking lot nearly filled with trucks and cars. I helped to unload the gear. We carried the gear a short distance through a stand of trees and out to the launching area.

What a view! The trees had been logged off on a little promontory on the shoulder of the mountain, just below the summit, creating a magnificent window onto the landscape below. We were standing on the summit of a heavily-wooded mountain, looking out across a valley full of farms, fields, and homes. We were almost two thousand feet above sea level and it was quite a bit cooler than it had been down on the flat lands.

I walked out to the edge of the launching area and looked down. Miles and miles of empty space stared back. It looked enormous. And terrifying. The grassy promontory quickly gave way to rocks and trees. Not a good place for a crash. Not really a good place for a beginner to fly.

A gentle breeze blew up the wooded flanks of the mountain. I watched several paragliders launch, and soar out over the valley. I could not quite see the landing zone, two thousand feet below. It was hidden by a small ridge. Just as I was starting to be thankful that I wasn't first in line, Ralph told me to get ready for my first tandem flight. Oh God, I *am* first in line! And I don't want to be! I'm about to run right out into empty space and fall off the edge of the world. And I'm the guy who's afraid of rollercoasters! Let somebody else go first!

But nobody stepped forward to take my place. So with my heart in my mouth, and beating at about twice its normal speed, I put on my windbreaker, harness, and helmet. Ralph quickly laid out an extra-large paraglider wing and hooked his harness to it. I was told to stand directly in front of Ralph, facing forward. There were two nylon straps attached to the front of Ralph's harness. Each strap curved around my body and attached to the twin carabiners on my own harness, just above my hips. These twin straps were the only things connecting me to Ralph, and to the wing. I knew that each strap was rated to carry a ten thousand pound load, so I wasn't too worried about either of them breaking. Still, it didn't seem like a whole lot of support for my 220 pound frame. Perhaps a logging chain would have seemed about right.

But I was more worried about being the first one to run off that cliff, just ahead of Ralph. If there was an accident, I would be first on the scene. Literally. Ever ride in the first car on a rollercoaster? You can't even pretend that if there's an accident, the people ahead of you will hit first. I knew that those nylon straps would hold me, but I also felt like I was about to run off that cliff with nothing at all to keep me from falling. Intellectually I knew I was safe. Emotionally I knew I was doomed.

I looked down on the homes of the people who lived down on the flat land. They were going about their safe, mundane lives. I could be one of them. Nobody was forcing me to come up here and run off a cliff with only a fancy bed sheet to hold me up.

As Ralph finished his takeoff preparations, he explained to me what I would need to do. "When I say run, you run forward as fast as you can. Don't worry if the straps hold you back for a few seconds. Just keep running until I tell you to stop. We should be airborne in just a few seconds, but even after we're in the air, *keep running.* We might settle back onto the ground for a couple of steps, and if you're not running, you'll fall down and abort the launch. *So keep running!*" I decided that I would do my very best imitation of Wiley E. Coyote chasing after that damned Roadrunner. Beep! Beep!

Ralph had the risers and steering lines in his hands, and he was waiting for just the right moment to launch. Out of force of habit from my skydiving days, I looked down at my harness to make certain that everything was properly fastened. I particularly wanted to check the twin nylon straps that connected me to Ralph's harness, since they were the only things that would keep me from falling to my death.

The left nylon strap was securely fastened to the left carabiner on my harness, but when I checked the right strap, my heart skipped a couple of beats. *The right strap was not fully attached to the carabiner!* When Ralph pushed the right strap against the hinged gate on the carabiner on my harness, he did not make certain that the strap had cleared the gate, which would have permitted the gate to snap closed behind the strap. Instead, the strap was hung up on the carabiner gate, and the gate itself was being held open by the strap. During the flight it would have been possible for the strap to slip out of the open carabiner and completely detach from my harness!

I instantly pointed out the problem to Ralph. He reached down and pushed the strap all the way inside the carabiner, and then snapped the gate closed behind the strap. "Glad you caught that," was all he said.

I felt sick to my stomach. For me, this operation was growing less impressive by the minute. Ralph had failed to perform the most elementary safety check on my harness. He had failed to make certain that the student was safely secured. This was a grievous violation of basic safety precautions. For a moment I seriously considered canceling the flight. After all, what other safety precautions might Ralph have overlooked?

But I didn't. My skydiving experience assured me that I was now safely strapped in. If Ralph could get this assembly into the air, there seemed every chance that we would fly. So I decided to proceed with the launch. I really, really, *really* wanted to fly!

What would have happened if I had not noticed the problem with the strap, and we had taken off? Probably nothing. The tension on the strap would have kept it tightly pressed against the top of the carabiner and would probably have prevented it from slipping off. And even if the strap had become detached during the flight, I would still have been solidly secured to Ralph's harness by the other strap. I could not have fallen.

But could we have flown safely? I don't know. If my right strap had become detached, I would have lost all support on my right side. My body would have pivoted around the remaining strap on my left side. In addition to giving me a few moments of stark terror, it would have instantly put all of my two hundred plus pounds on the left side of Ralph's harness. This would have resulted in a tremendous "weight-shift" under the wing, and would have caused the wing to start turning to the left. Could Ralph have countered the turn by pulling on the right steering line? I don't know. I do know that if we had been flying close the mountain at the moment of the detachment, there might not have been enough time to stop the turn, and we could have flown into the mountain and crashed.

In aviation, safety is a full-time job. Nothing less than 100% attention to detail will do.

But now it was time to fly. *"Run!"* Ralph yelled. I started running as hard as I could, right out into empty space. My adrenaline level shot off the scale and my thrill meter instantly pegged. I probably only got two steps before the drag of the wing, coming up fast behind us, brought us to a complete stop. But I continued to strain forward, and in only a second or two we were moving again as the wing climbed overhead and started to fly. I managed to run a few more steps, then I was suddenly picked up into the air. The grass was falling away, and I was now running on air. I continued to run, even though the ground was now twenty feet below me.

"You can stop running," Ralph said to me. "We're up. Slide back in your seat and enjoy the ride."

And that's exactly what I did. That ride, Ladies and Gentlemen, turned out to be one of the most fantastic flights of my life. It was like nothing I had ever experienced before, or had ever imagined. We were flying about twenty-five miles per hour, just a short distance above the giant trees that covered the side of the mountain. The view was absolutely stupendous. I was flying through the air and there was *nothing* between me and rest of the world. I was flying like a bird; the way I had always flown in my dreams, but never in real life. Until now.

It took me a few minutes to get used to just hanging there in space, with no obvious means of support, and to trust the harness to hold me up. My hands wanted to grasp and clutch something, *anything*, for dear life. Quite irrationally I clutched at the twin nylon straps that connected me to Ralph's harness.

Instead of flying out and away from the mountain, we turned and flew parallel to it. At some points we were only a few feet above the tops of the trees. I could have almost kicked them. A gentle wind was rushing up the side of the mountain, giving us free lift. We neither climbed nor descended. We just flew. Like a giant bird.

Skydiving had never been like this. In freefall I was always thousands of feet above the Earth. I was never near anything on the ground, except just before landing. Now I was never more than a hundred feet from the trees. I could see everything, and the detail was incredible!

We swept along the face of the mountain for about a quarter of a mile, then turned around and retraced our path. There were at least half a dozen other paragliders in the air with us. Occasionally one would pass close by. We waved, and the other pilot always waved back.

As we flew back and forth along the face of the mountain I became aware that we were slowly gaining altitude. Obviously the air, rushing up the side of the mountain, was rising faster than we were descending. This was called "soaring."

At one point Ralph let me take the steering lines and make a couple of turns. It was very easy to do; just like my old ram-air skydiving wing. Then Ralph took us out over the valley, away from the mountain, so that he could show me a couple of maneuvers. He showed me how he could use the suspension lines to pull in one wingtip of the glider, and cause the wingtip to collapse and deflate, but how the wingtip instantly re-inflated as soon as the steering lines were released. The point was obvious. The wing wanted to stay inflated and wanted to fly. Then Ralph pulled one of the steering lines down, and quickly put us into a spiral dive. The world whipped around us very quickly, but very smoothly. When Ralph released the steering line we immediately leveled out and resumed normal flight.

All too soon it was time to land. Ralph steered us over the forest at the south end of the LZ, hopped over the edge of the trees, and set us down on the grassy field. As we neared the ground, he pulled down both steering lines to flare the wing, greatly slowing our rate of descent as well as reducing our forward speed. As we touched down, I started running to eat up our remaining velocity. I ran a few steps with Ralph running right behind me, and then we quickly came to a stop. My first tandem flight was over. My first paraglider flight was over.

I was truly at a loss for words. I shook Ralph's hand and thanked him with all the genuine sincerity I could muster. It had been an incredible experience.

Forgotten was the hot sweaty session at the farm earlier that morning. All I could see were those cool, green, mountain forests. And me, soaring over them effortlessly. Like a bird.

It had been one of the most fantastic experiences of my life. Needless to say, I wanted more!

In Hindsight, What Would I have Done Differently?

My first day of flight training should have been my last. I should have gone elsewhere and found a safer operation. The failure of my instructor to check my harness, before my tandem flight, should have been the final straw.

But I was in the Previous Investment Trap. I had already paid my money and I hated to walk away from my investment. So I stuck around for some more training. Big mistake. I ended up paying for my poor judgment, both physically and monetarily (as we'll soon see).

Most dealers will tell you that if you buy your equipment from them, the training is free. It isn't, of course. They simply include the cost of the training in the price you pay for the equipment. This is called "Sucker Bait," and it's legal in all fifty states. Unfortunately if the dealer turns out to be a bad instructor, you've already paid for all of your training, and Good Luck Getting A Refund. So you either remain with a bad instructor, or else you pay all over again for training from another instructor/dealer. Either way, the first dealer has your money in his pocket.

If I had it to do over again, I'd separate the purchase of the flight training from the purchase of the gear. I'd shop around for the best deal on the equipment that included flight training, then negotiate a lower purchase price that did not include flight training.

Once I had settled on a discounted purchase price for my gear, without flight training, I would go shopping for my flight training. You want the very best instructor you can find. Your life may depend on it. Ask around. Get references and check the references. In particular, ask questions about the instructor's safety procedures. This is not the time to go looking for a bargain. You may end up spending an extra thousand bucks on training. So what? If good training saves you only one trip to the hospital, it will be more than worth it. Just an ambulance ride can cost $600. And don't hesitate to travel to another part of the country to get good training. It may be expensive, but I guarantee that a trip to the hospital will cost much more. In aviation you do NOT want the cheapest training that money can buy.

Of course there's nothing that says you can't be trained by the same dealer from whom you purchased your equipment. In fact it's preferable. But make it two separate deals; not one big package deal for both equipment and training. You can expect to hear a variety of arguments from the dealer as to why you should buy his package deal. Trust me. The dealer's real reason, his *only* reason, is to get all of your money up front.

Credentials for your flight instructor? Well, if your dealer has some credentials, that's a good sign. If he's a flight instructor with the United States Hang Gliding Association (USHGA) that's a good sign. But it doesn't mean he's a good, safe instructor. I've known flight instructors who were very highly credentialed, but who were also very unsafe. The only real protection is to use your common sense, and never buy a package deal for training. Pay for your flight training on a day-by-day basis. You may end up paying more than if you buy a package deal, but you'll retain your flexibility to walk away if the training turns out to be unsafe or just plain lousy. It's cheap insurance.

Remember, if the dealer has all of your money up front, then you're just another one of his sheep, waiting to be processed. He can readily leave you standing in the hot sun for an hour while he trains someone else. Why not? He's already got your money. If you walk away, it's *your* loss, not his. On the other hand, if he doesn't have all of your money up front, if you're paying him on a day-by-day basis, guess who's going to get the best treatment?

Should you find another flight instructor just because your instructor makes a mistake? Even a serious mistake? Not necessarily. Instructors are only human, just like the rest of us. They can, and will, make mistakes. Sometimes serious mistakes.

But what's important is how the instructor reacts when he makes a mistake. If he seems highly concerned or upset when he makes a mistake, and expresses great contrition (sackcloth and ashes would be about right), then you know that he takes the safety of his students very seriously. On the other hand if he has a casual, cavalier attitude toward the safety of his students, then find another instructor. If he reacts to a serious mistake by shrugging his shoulders and saying, "Oh well, these things happen," then find another instructor.

Some instructors seem to think that their titles and credentials are all the safety their students need. Don't patronize these people. This is aviation. You can get killed.

And finally, if you're still tempted to buy a package deal that includes your equipment and your training, be aware that until you have actually been trained by someone, you really have no idea how good, or safe, he really is. A dealer/instructor can sound absolutely fabulous on the phone before the sale. (Mine certainly did.) He can sound like the safest, most knowledgeable instructor in the world, and then turn out to be unsafe. So be smart and don't give him the money for your flight training up front. Pay as you go, and keep your options open.

Chapter 5

First Solo Flight

One week later it was time to fly again. Ralph told me to report directly to the Mount Wilson Landing Zone. My flying buddy, Mike, had decided to start his training as well. I think it was my glowing description of my tandem flight, with Ralph, that had convinced Mike to get started.

At the LZ, as we waited for the afternoon thermals to kick in, Mike was given some initial instruction in forward inflations. Ralph's assistant, Jake, tried to explain to Mike how to hold the risers and steering lines during a forward inflation. Mike has a degree in aeronautical engineering, has worked as both an aeronautical engineer and an air traffic controller, and is also a licensed pilot with an instrument rating, so it seemed unlikely that he would have any problem understanding the concept of the forward inflation. But as I listened to Jake, it was obvious that he simply couldn't deliver an intelligible explanation. So when Jake finally gave up, and left Mike on his own, I showed Mike how to hold the risers and steering lines. It took me about one minute to explain it. Ralph's organization dropped a few more notches in my estimation.

Mike then made several successful forward inflations. Unfortunately it was 85 degrees, sunny, and no wind. Mike very quickly overheated and nearly fainted. At one point he was forced to lie on the ground to recover. We decided that forward inflation practice could wait for a cooler day.

A short time later we headed up the mountain for some tandem flying. Mike was scheduled to fly first, with Jake. On top of the mountain, Jake handed a harness to Mike and told him to "put it on like a suit." Jake said he would check it later. Since Mike had no idea what it meant to "put it on like a suit," I helped him get into the harness and fasten the straps. As it turned out, we forgot to fasten the chest strap.

A short time later, Mike stood at the edge of the launching area with Jake right behind him, and the big paraglider wing ready to launch. I found out later that Jake had never checked Mike's harness. As they were about ready to launch, Ralph walked up and made a quick inspection of Mike's harness. He found that Mike's chest strap had not been fastened, and quickly secured it. I like to think that Mike and Jake would not have taken off until Ralph had made the final safety check of Mike's gear, but truthfully I think it was sheer luck that Ralph happened to come by when he did. It was beginning to look like safety violations were not an unusual occurrence in Ralph's organization. However Mike and Jake finally launched without incident.

Shortly after Mike and Jake took off on Mike's first tandem flight, I took off on my second tandem flight with Ralph. Once again the flight was simply fantastic. However this time the landing was really terrible. We touched down so fast that I couldn't run fast enough to stay on my feet. Ralph and I both fell down and rolled and skidded across the grass. Since I was wearing shorts and a T-shirt, I ended up skinning my knee and elbow. I noticed that Ralph wore a flight suit that covered him from head to toe, and protected him from abrasions. I was beginning to understand why the experienced pilots wore full-length flight suits, even in hot weather. I could not understand why the same safety gear was not offered to the student.

Ralph tried to explain the poor landing by saying that he was trying to avoid crowding other paragliding traffic coming in right behind us. This required him to make a fast landing that damaged his student? Ralph's explanation made no sense to me.

That evening Mike and I discussed what we had seen of Ralph's operation so far. Neither of us was very impressed. Basic safety violations had been made on both of our initial tandem flights, and I'd been injured by Ralph's bad landing on my second flight. We decided that we would have to watch out for each other, and pay very close attention to everything that was going on if we wanted to remain safe. I was very glad that Mike had not yet paid his $800 training fee to Ralph, and I was beginning to regret having paid mine, in advance, as part of the total cost of the engine and wing.

The next day was Sunday. Mike was scheduled to make his second tandem flight. Ralph told me that I could make my first solo flight off Mount Wilson with my new A5 Sport wing. *Gulp!* I hadn't really planned on being allowed to solo so quickly, even though I'd been bugging Ralph to let me do it. (Be careful what you ask for; you might get it.)

While I waited in the LZ, Mike went up the mountain with Ralph for another tandem flight. Less than an hour later, Mike and Ralph came sailing down out of the sky and made a perfect landing in the LZ. Then all three of us went back up the mountain for my first solo flight.

To say that I was nervous would be an understatement. I had never made *any* kind of solo flight with a paraglider before, not even a tow, and here I was making my first flight from the top of a mountain that was not the most beginner-friendly peak in the world. Against that, however, was the fact that I had made more than a hundred skydiving jumps with a ram-air canopy. As I had told Ralph earlier, "If I can get that thing into the air, I know that I can fly it and land it." Apparently Ralph had taken me at my word. I just hoped it did not prove to be famous last words.

I was concerned about my ability to launch the wing. I had made only a few forward inflation practices on the ground, and none of them struck me as being very successful. I could get the wing overhead, but I couldn't keep it there. Either it fell down, or else I managed to pull it down by holding onto the front risers too long. However gravity would be giving me a big assist on this launch. I would be running downhill, rather than trying to launch on flat land.

During the ride up the mountain I felt like a condemned man on his way to the guillotine. Suddenly a tandem flight, with an instructor at the controls, seemed like the easiest, safest thing in the world. At the top, I carried my gear out to the launch point and stood looking down at the ground, thousands of feet below. If anything, it looked even bigger than it did before my first tandem flight only a week earlier. I kept telling myself that Ralph wouldn't let me fly if he didn't think I could handle it. Now if I could only make myself believe it.

Since it was a hot day, I was wearing only shorts and a T-shirt. I realized that if I crashed into the trees, or fell onto the rocks and bushes below, my bare hide could get pretty badly chewed up. I decided that if I was going to continue in this sport, I would have to get myself a flight suit.

Slowly I put on my helmet and gloves. Ralph spread my wing out on the ground and gave me a radio to clip to the front of my harness so that he could transmit instructions to me during the flight. Ralph carefully explained to me how to perform the launch, how the flight would proceed, and how to land on the LZ, two thousand feet below. Jake was already down on the LZ, and would be talking me in for the landing via the radio. Ralph told me that if he wanted me to abort the launch, at any time, he would yell "Stop!" and that I should listen *only* for that word. I thought his instructions were clear and complete. Obviously Ralph could be a very good teacher when he took the time to do so. As we waited for flight conditions to optimize, there was a lot of annoying chatter over my radio from other airborne pilots on the same frequency. Finally Ralph reached over and turned down the volume of my radio.

"Whenever you're ready," Ralph finally said. I was standing about thirty feet from the edge of the launching area on the slope of a small, steep hill that rose a few additional feet above the regular launching area. Ralph had decided to let me take off from this "extra" hill to give me an even bigger gravity assist. The edge of the launching area looked like the edge of a cliff, but actually it was just a steep slope covered with thick brush. However the brush quickly degenerated into rocks and trees. Obviously if I was going to crash on takeoff, the quicker the better.

I took one last look around me. The risers and steering lines were in my hands, and my heart was pounding like a jackhammer. I yelled "Clear!" one last time, waited a few seconds, then started running down the hill. I took only a few steps before the big orange wing rose up behind me. The drag of the wing brought me to a complete halt. I tried to run, but my feet could not seem to get a grip on the ground.

The next few seconds were a meaningless blur. My brain was in total sensory overload. However I must have done something right, for I suddenly found myself flying through the air, away from the launching area. The trees were below me, the wing was directly overhead, and there was only the sound of the wind gently whispering around me.

My God, I did it! *I'm flying!!!*

According to reliable eyewitnesses, I let out a whoop and a holler that could be heard all over the mountain. Then I started giggling like a schoolgirl. I suppose it must be true. I couldn't say. I was too busy flying!

I looked back over my shoulder at the rapidly receding launch area. There were tiny little people moving around on it, and getting smaller every second. I looked down at the forest that covered the huge mountain below me. I was struck by the incredible amount of detail that I could see. The complex drainage patterns that covered the mountain like a spider web, the fallen trees here and there, the outcroppings of rock. In the past I had hiked over these very areas. I remembered huffing and puffing up the steep trails, every step an effort. Now I was effortlessly flying over them, like a bird! *I was flying!* If my first tandem flight had been merely fantastic, my first solo flight was completely off the scale.

I let go of the steering lines and reached down to push the harness seat under my butt. Ahh, much more comfortable! I was suddenly struck by the incongruity of flying over incredibly rough terrain; rocks, trees, and cliffs, dressed only in shorts and a T-shirt, and held aloft by a bundle of cloth and some string. It seemed impossible.

"Will you stop that infernal giggling?" said a faint voice over the radio. *"I know you can hear me, so the first thing I want you to do is turn up the volume on the radio."*

I was suddenly reminded that Ralph had turned down the volume on my radio before takeoff. I could barely hear him now. Obviously Ralph had forgotten to turn the volume back up before I took off. Sigh. What else was new?

Fortunately I had watched Ralph turn down the radio volume before launch, so I knew which knob to twist to restore the volume. No big deal. Of course it could have been a big deal. If I had not happened to see which knob to turn to control the volume, I would have had to guess, and I might have guessed wrong. I could have easily turned the radio off, or changed the frequency and put myself out of communication with Ralph. I could have been left in the air, on my first solo flight, without any communication, trying to land in a tight LZ without instructor assistance. Nor had I been given any instructions as to what to do if my radio failed in flight. Once again, safety was getting short shrift in Ralph's organization.

Not that I really cared at that moment. I was in my element. Thanks to my skydiving training, twenty years earlier, I knew how to fly this thing and I knew how to land it. And if there was no instructor to guide me into the LZ, I knew I could always land the wing in one of the nearby pastures where there was plenty of room for a beginner.

Over the radio, Ralph guided me though a series of turns as I zigzagged back and forth down the face of the mountain. At one point I suddenly felt a warm breeze envelope my body from below, causing the wing to rustle and sway a bit. *"That was a thermal you just flew into,"* said Ralph. *"If you had a vario, you could hang around and try to soar it, but today we're just going to concentrate on flying."*

Ralph guided me away from the mountain and out over the valley. I was descending at a rate of three hundred feet per minute. I had no altimeter, but I guessed that I was about five hundred feet in the air. The LZ looked mighty small from up here. I knew that without instructor assistance I'd never be able to make it into the LZ. I'd either undershoot, and end up in the trees, or overshoot and end up in the trees. It was like landing on an aircraft carrier. You really couldn't afford to miss. Once again I realized that this wasn't the best place in the world for my first solo flight.

Fortunately the radio was working properly. As Ralph was about to lose sight of me from the mountain top, he turned me over to Jake who was waiting down on the ground in the LZ.

"If you can hear me, kick your legs," Jake radioed to me. I signaled that I could hear him. *"Okay, we're going to set up your approach for the landing. Just do what I tell you to do."*

For the next two minutes I was a faithful puppet on a string. Jake had me fly downwind, past the LZ, and then turn left toward the mountain. Then I turned left again so that I was on course for a landing in the LZ. I thought I was flying much too far downwind and would never be able to reach the LZ. I was certain that I was going to land short, in the trees.

But my concern was based on my previous skydiving experience, and ram-air wings had vastly improved since then. My present wing had at least twice the glide ratio of anything I'd previously flown. I floated over the last of the trees and descended toward the grassy earth in the LZ. When I was about five feet above the ground, Jake radioed me to pull down the steering lines as far as I could. I did, and the wing virtually came to a stop. I stepped down onto the ground, ran a few steps to eat up the last of my forward velocity, and watched as the wing slowly collapsed to the ground in front of me.

For several seconds I just stood there, looking up at the lofty mountain I had just flown from. *I did it! I really did it! I soloed!!!*

As I stood there with a huge grin on my face, Jake came walking up to me. We shook hands and he congratulated me on my first flight. I felt ten feet tall and covered with hair. It was definitely one of the high points of my life.

That elation was to last about two hours. Little did I know what was about to happen next.

Having just made the most fantastic flight of my life, naturally I wanted to do it again. Ralph was agreeable, so we went back up the mountain.

About two hours later I was again standing at the edge of the launching area on top of the mountain. My wing was laid out behind me and there was a pilot ahead of me, preparing for launch. It was late in the afternoon and most of the flying was finished for the day. The parking lot behind the launching area was empty, except for Ralph's truck. The wind had also died. In fact it was dead calm. Something told me that the launch might not be quite so easy this time. Not only was there no wind, but I wasn't launching from the steep hill this time. Instead, my wing was laid out in the normal launching area, which was much flatter. I would have less assist from running downhill.

But I wasn't worried. I knew that Ralph was watching over me.

And then Ralph suddenly announced that he was leaving! He had to drive the truck back down the mountain, and he wanted to get started. He asked another pilot to see that I launched okay, then he left.

I didn't much care for this latest development. I felt like the rug had just been jerked out from under me. Ralph was my instructor. He was the one that I'd paid good money to teach me how to fly, and to keep me safe, and now I was being left under the guidance of a complete stranger. Was this stranger also an instructor? Or just a friendly pilot? I didn't know. All I knew for certain was that I didn't particularly like the new arrangement.

I could hear the sound of Ralph's truck leaving the parking area. What would happen if I was injured during the takeoff? How would I get down the mountain? Walk? How long would it take to get a vehicle back up to the top? Was it even possible to call for a vehicle? I realized that I was entirely at the mercy of a few strangers who were still on the mountain. It was not very reassuring.

But it was too late to call off the launch now. Not unless I wanted to walk down the mountain. Because everyone who was left on top of the mountain *had* to fly down. There was no other transportation available.

Oh well, I'd already done it once, and I was pretty certain that I could do it again. The pilot ahead of me suddenly launched. He made it look easy. Then my new "instructor" approached me and asked me if I was ready to launch.

I explained to my new instructor that if he wanted me to abort my launch, at any time, he should shout "Stop!" I explained that this was the word that Ralph and I had agreed on, to abort the launch.

It's important for the student and instructor to be perfectly clear on their signals. Launching areas for paragliders tend to be noisy, crowded places. With the student's attention totally focused on the launch, he cannot listen to, or process, every bit of idle chatter filling the air around him. He must train himself to listen for only one or two key words, and to react immediately if he hears them.

I took the steering lines and risers in my hands, got ready to run, and looked at my new instructor one last time. He nodded approval, and I ran forward as fast as I could. I felt the wing coming up behind me as I ran toward the edge. As I was about to go over the edge, I suddenly heard shouting in the distance, but since none of it contained the magic world *"Stop!"* I ignored it.

The next few seconds were pretty fuzzy, owning to the fact that I was totally hiked-up on adrenaline and in total sensory overload. I remember going over the edge of the launching area, into space, and suddenly being aware that the risers were twisted over my head. A split second later I realized that I was in the air, and facing backward toward the launching area! I was actually flying *backwards* off the mountain! Instinctively I tried to untwist the risers and get back to normal flight, but it was too late. The wing seemed to be suffering some sort of collapse, and was whipping around. I felt myself falling. A split second later I crashed into the side of the mountain. Fortunately I hit the brush-covered steep slope just below the launching area. The bushes absorbed most of the impact, but even so, the jolt was pretty severe. My head banged very hard into the side of the mountain. For several seconds I lay sprawled in the brush, trying to collect my senses. Thank God I was wearing a helmet! Thank God I had missed the rocks!

The slope was so steep that I was virtually standing up in the brush. As my head cleared, I slowly looked around. My worst fear had come to pass. I had crashed! Fortunately I still seemed to be in one piece. Cautiously I flexed my arms and legs. Everything seemed to be okay. Since I was only wearing shorts and a T-shirt, I was pretty scratched up, but nothing seemed to be broken. However a fine set of bruises was on the way, as well as a very sore neck.

I heard shouts from the rescuers about twenty feet above me. Was I okay? Yes, I was okay. A couple of the guys scrambled down the hill to help me untangle the wing and drag it back up the hill. It took us about twenty minutes to get both me and the wing back up to the launching area. Fortunately the wing was undamaged (which was more than I could claim). I questioned my new instructor. What had gone wrong?

He told me that the wing came up okay, but that I failed to release the front risers after the wing was overhead. Pulling on the front risers, during launching, helps to pull the wing into the air, but continuing to pull on them after the wing is overhead will cause the wing to collapse. Apparently that's exactly what I did. The wing was starting to collapse even before I went over the edge. During the collapse, the wing went into a spin, which would account for the twisted risers above my head and my subsequent backwards flight.

When I asked my new instructor why he didn't yell at me to stop the launch, he said that he did. He said that he shouted "Wait! Wait!" but that I didn't seem to hear him.

True. I didn't hear him. I was listening for "Stop!" Unfortunately my new instructor hadn't followed my instructions. But I really couldn't blame him. He wasn't getting paid to teach me to fly, or to keep me safe. And the guy who *was* getting paid, was nowhere around. The whole thing struck me as a perfect example of unsafe training.

True, I might have crashed anyway, even if Ralph had been present, but at least he would have been there. And I would have known that the crash wasn't due to the fact that I was under the supervision of a total stranger.

But regardless of how I felt about my training, I still needed to get off this damned mountain. What should I do? Send word down with another pilot, and wait for Ralph to come up and get me? No! I knew where I'd made my mistake. If I quit now, I might lose my nerve later. With my instructor's help, I quickly got the wing laid out again. I took the steering lines and risers in my hands, and ran forward.

This time the launch went flawlessly. Once again I found myself in the air, making another fantastic flight over the wooded slopes of the mountain. Almost immediately Jake's voice came over my radio. He guided me away from the mountain and out over the valley. I went though a series of turns, and then Jake told me to prepare for the landing approach.

I had almost forgotten my earlier crash. I was rather proud of the way I had run into trouble, had overcome it, and now was having another fantastic flight. I felt like I was home free.

Little did I know...

This was the second time that Jake had talked me down for a landing. However this time it seemed to me that I was coming in much higher than I should. I thought that I should be making a few S-turns to burn off some altitude before coming in to the LZ. However I deferred to Jake's radioed instructions. After all, he was the instructor.

I passed over the last of the trees with a great deal of altitude to spare. It just didn't look right. Not when compared to my earlier flight. I was flying down the length of the LZ. There was no wind, so my ground speed was at maximum. I passed over the middle of the LZ, and I was still high above the ground. The trees at the far end of the LZ were coming up fast, and I was starting to get nervous. I didn't see how I could possibly reach the ground before I ran out of grass.

I passed over the end of the LZ and I was still at least ten feet in the air. Now I was flying over long grass and brambles. Not a very inviting place to land. Jake radioed to start my landing flare. I looked directly ahead and saw an old concrete foundation among the weeds. If I flared now, I knew I'd land directly on the concrete. I could be badly injured. At the very least, I knew I'd lose a lot of hide if my bare arms and legs hit that rough cement.

I had no choice. I knew that I *must not* land on that concrete. I pulled the right steering line and swung to one side, barely missing the concrete. As I was about to touch down, I pulled both steering lines all the way down. There wasn't enough time left to do a complete landing flare. I hit the ground, still going fast. Too fast to run it out. I fell down and rolled. Fortunately it was mostly long grass, but there were a few sticks and brambles present, and I got even MORE skinned up and scratched up (as if the crash on the mountain wasn't enough). The wing wasn't so lucky. It fell onto a large bramble bush.

Slowly I got to my feet. I became aware of my fine new collection of bruises and scratches. At least I hadn't broken anything. I looked around at my surroundings. I had completely overshot the grassy LZ and was out in the bloody jungle! What the hell had happened? Why was I not sitting somewhere in the middle of the LZ, on the short grass, as I had managed to do on my previous flight?

Jake came walking up to me. He had a radio in one hand, and a can of beer in the other. I was dumbstruck. *A can of beer? My flight instructor is drinking on the job!?*

I couldn't believe what I was seeing. Perhaps this explained my god-awful landing. Was this Jake's first beer, or just the latest in a long line on a hot day? I found out later, from Mike, that it definitely was not Jake's first beer.

I asked Jake why I'd landed next to a concrete platform, in a bramble patch, instead of out in the grassy LZ. He said that the wind had died, and that I had overshot the LZ. I knew this was total bullshit. Pilots landed in that LZ all the time, in no wind. The truth was, Jake had royally screwed up. He had brought me in much too high, causing me to completely overshoot the LZ in the calm air. Could his judgment have been clouded by something?

I pointed out that I had nearly landed on the concrete. Jake told me that I had done a good job of avoiding it. That was all. No apology, no other explanation. Jake then walked away, presumably to get himself another beer. He didn't even offer to help me get my wing out of the bramble bush.

Mike arrived a few minutes later to help me. He could tell that I was mad enough to chew nails. Together we worked to get the wing out of the brambles without tearing it. It took us about forty-five minutes, but we finally managed to do it.

Later that evening Mike and I discussed what had happened. For me, the triumph of my first solo flight had turned to ashes. I had been abandoned on the mountain by my instructor, had suffered a crash that could have been very serious (even fatal), then had been guided down to a totally incompetent landing by a flight instructor who had been drinking on the job. In addition, my radio had not been properly checked before my first solo flight.

The conclusion was inescapable. Ralph was simply not running a safe operation. I had been very lucky not to have been badly injured or even killed.

Mike and I discussed what to do. Obviously buying my flight training from Ralph had been a mistake, but it was too late to do anything about it now. Obviously paying Ralph ahead of time, for my flight instruction, had also been a mistake. Fortunately Mike had not yet bought a training package from Ralph. We could still do something about that.

Mike and I decided that we were not going anywhere near Mount Wilson again. It was now obvious to me that novice pilots had no business flying there. So why was Ralph using it? For the same reason that all the other local instructors used it. It was all they had. But that didn't make it safe for beginners.

The real question was, should we continue training with Ralph? I was sorely tempted to find another instructor. One that ran a safe operation. But that meant forfeiting the $800 I'd already paid. It also meant a lot of long-distance driving to get trained. Ralph had the advantage of being local.

In the end I decided to continue my instruction with Ralph, but only under certain conditions. First, no more flying at Mount Wilson. In my opinion, the mountain was simply too dangerous for a beginner. And I felt that I had no need of mountain flying experience. I hadn't gotten into this sport to jump off mountains. I got into this sport to take off from a nice flat pasture with an engine on my back. So what in the hell was I doing risking my life by flying off the top of rugged mountains?

Second, I would continue my training out at the farm where I could be towed aloft. No mountains to run into. No trees to crash into. No cliffs to jump off. Mike agreed to postpone the rest of his training until we could see what happened to me. I would be the guinea pig.

I called Ralph up on the phone and told him that I was a little gun-shy about flying at Mount Wilson after my crash. I asked him if there would be any problem in confining my flying to the farm for the foreseeable future. He said he had no problem with that.

Mike and I talked it over. We decided to proceed as planned. As long as we stayed far away from the mountain, we thought we'd be okay. After all, how much trouble could we get into out in the middle of a cow pasture?

I was about to find out.

In Hindsight, What Would I have Done Differently?

Walked away. Forgotten about the lousy $800. If a flight operation isn't safe, then it isn't safe, and all the rationalization in the world won't make it safe.

Never be afraid to call a halt and walk away. It's your life on the line. Don't wait until you're injured.

And just because a lot of other people are doing it, doesn't make it safe. Mount Wilson was obviously no place for beginners to take their first solo flight. Yet virtually every instructor in the area used it. Why? Because it was available. Because it was the only place that was conveniently available for training. So once again, safety took a back seat to convenience. Such a thing is very common in the paragliding business.

But the fact is, training flights for beginners need not be conducted off the summits of rugged mountains. There are paragliding schools that give their students flight training off gentle, grassy hills, or even sand dunes (the best!). A beginning pilot needs room to make mistakes. He should not be taking off over tall trees or rocks. If he makes a mistake on takeoff, and collapses his wing, the worst that should happen is that he falls down on soft grass or even softer sand. He should *not* plummet down steep cliffs covered with trees and rocks.

Before you pay for your first lesson, go and visit the paragliding school. Watch how the beginning students are trained, and look carefully at the sites they fly from. If they're being launched from rugged peaks, or being maneuvered into tight LZs, go elsewhere.

It's your life. Remember that the sport of paragliding contains definite hazards, and is totally unregulated. If you fail to look after your own safety, no one else will. I had to learn this lesson the hard way. You do not.

Chapter 6

First Motor Flight Attempt

Three days later I was out at the farm. Except that it was a new farm. For some reason Ralph had to leave the old farm. But that was okay because the new farm was closer and bigger. Even better, it was just across the road from a public golf course where we could buy food and drink and use the restrooms.

It was time for my first tow flight. I was wearing my helmet and gloves, and the wing was spread out on the ground behind me. The tow line had been secured to the front of my harness. Ralph was sitting on the motor scooter, slowly taking up the tension on the tow line. When I felt the line go taut, I shouted, "Ready!" Ralph maintained tension on the line until I was ready to start my take-off run. I nodded my head and raced forward. That was the signal to Ralph to gun the scooter's motor. The tow line pulled me forward, I took a few steps, and was airborne.

Now for a man who had made over one hundred parachute jumps, and had twice flown solo off the summit of Mount Wilson, you'd think that a tow flight out of a flat cow pasture would be tame by comparison. But it wasn't. At least not for me. I was climbing awfully fast, and things were happening very quickly, requiring quick responses from me. When the wing started to drift to the right, I corrected it by pulling on my left steering line. I was trying to focus my attention strictly on the tow line, but it was difficult to do as I raced skyward at more than five hundred feet per minute, while simultaneously trying to remember the proper sequence of steps for releasing from the tow line.

At an altitude of about three hundred feet Ralph radioed that it was time to release. I acknowledged by kicking my legs. Then I put both steering line handles in one hand, grabbed the quick-release handle in front of my chest, and pulled it. Instantly I parted company with the tow line. Naturally I forgot to pull the steering lines down a bit to stop the wing from surging forward. It surged, and I lost about fifty feet of altitude. Oh well, no time to worry about that now. I needed to concentrate on flying this thing. I slid back into my seat and got comfortable for the ride down.

As instructed, I immediately turned one hundred and eighty degrees to the left and flew downwind along the edge of the pasture. The plan was to fly downwind to the far end of the field, then make another one-eighty turn to the left and land into the wind. Pretty simple. Just turn left when the instructor tells you to.

I was about halfway down the field, flying downwind, when suddenly I heard Jake's voice over my radio. The last time Jake had instructed me, he had a radio in one hand and a can of beer in the other. Hopefully he was sober for this flight.

After releasing from the tow line, my left turn had carried me to the far edge of the pasture. The pasture was now to my left, and the trees were to my right. It was just about time to turn left, back into the wind, and get set up for the landing.

Suddenly Jake's voice came over my radio. *"Turn right."*

Huh? For a moment I wondered if I'd heard correctly. A right turn would send me straight into the trees! What the hell was going on here? I hesitated, not knowing what to do.

"Right turn!" Jake shouted over the radio.

Now I was REALLY confused. Obviously I'd heard Jake correctly the first time. He really did want a right turn. But that would put me right into the trees! Or would it? I certainly didn't know everything about flying paragliders. Maybe this was part of some sophisticated maneuver for landing. Maybe I just didn't have the whole picture. But those trees were right under my feet! If I turned right, it seemed to me that I'd be committed to a tree landing. I'd never be able to make it to the grass. What should I do?

"Right turn!" screamed Jake over the radio.

Decision time. Common sense came to my rescue. There was no way I was going to deliberately fly into a stand of trees. I pulled down on the left steering line. The wing smoothly turned to the left, away from the trees, and flew out over the grassy field. I had just enough time to turn the wing into the wind and flare for the landing.

Touchdown. A perfect landing. Light as a feather. I didn't even stumble.

I was gathering up the wing in my arms when Jake came walking up to me. Uh-oh! Now I was going to catch it. I had disobeyed a direct order from the instructor.

"Nice landing," said Jake. "But why did you wait so long to make your turn?"

"You mean I did it right?" I asked, puzzledly.

"You did it perfect. Except that you waited longer than you should have before you finally turned for your landing."

I explained to Jake that I was confused by his radioed instructions. I told him that I was afraid that if I turned right, I'd end up in the trees.

"What are you talking about?" asked Jake. "I was shouting for you to make a left turn."

"No, no," I explained. "You were calling for a RIGHT turn."

Jake continued to deny having called for a right turn, but then a couple of other students stepped forward to confirm my story. Beaten by the presence of eyewitnesses, Jake merely shrugged his shoulders. "Oh. Guess I made a mistake. Well in that case you did the right thing. Don't ever let me get you killed."

And that was all he said. No contrition, no apology for endangering my life. What the hell kind of an attitude was that for an instructor? I could have been badly injured, or even killed, in a tree landing. And even if I had escaped unscathed, my wing could have been badly damaged. But Jake acted like it was no big deal. Happens every day.

If I had been a newcomer to this sport, with no previous ram-air canopy experience, I might very well have followed Jake's instructions and flown directly into the trees. I very nearly did.

Conclusion? This flight school simply wasn't safe. Not even away from the mountains. Not even in a flat pasture. The people in charge were simply too cavalier about safety.

Was I smart enough to walk away at that point? Did I have enough common sense to pack up and leave, and forget about the money I'd already paid?

No, I decided to remain stupid. I wanted to learn to fly in the worst way. And it was beginning to look like I'd managed to pick the worst possible way.

About an hour later it was time for my second tow flight. As Jake was checking my gear, I mentioned that my leg straps had seemed awfully loose on my previous flight, and maybe they should be tightened a bit? Jake responded by pulling both leg straps very snug.

My second takeoff, under tow, was still a bit scary but at least I could steer the wing okay. That was more than some of the other students could claim. Some of them were all over the sky during the trip up. One student very nearly managed to get the tow line over the nearby power lines, which gave us all a few anxious moments.

As I reached peak altitude, I again took the steering line lines in one hand and released the tow line with my other hand. This time I remembered to pull down on the steering lines so the wing didn't surge ahead of me at the moment of release. This was going to be a good flight, I thought to myself. Since I was still hanging in my leg straps, I tried to slide back into my seat and get comfortable for the flight.

But something was wrong. I couldn't move. I was stuck in the leg straps.

I quickly realized that there was nothing to do but finish the flight while hanging in the leg straps. It was quite uncomfortable, but I managed to fly the wing back to the ground and land it okay. After landing, I mentioned to Jake that I couldn't slide back in my seat; that my leg straps seemed to be too tight. Jake agreed. Then he laughed and admitted that he had been aware of the problem before I took off, but that he had only done what the pilot-in-command had requested.

I was flabbergasted. Jake seemed to have no idea that one of the duties of an instructor is to tell the student when he's doing something wrong. This flying school sucked!

After my two tows, Ralph told me to set up my motor and my wing to the right of the tow line. He indicated a spot about thirty feet from the tow line. After I had done so, I watched a student being towed aloft. Suddenly the student veered directly toward my engine. That's when I realized that my engine was sitting too close to the tow line. A student, under tow, could easily collide with my engine.

I figured that Ralph would see the problem and tell me to go move the engine. I didn't want to embarrass him by taking the initiative, so I waited. I waited while the student was towed aloft, released, and started back down. Ralph then proceeded to hook up a student for the next tow. Nothing was said about moving the engine. I decided that I would have to make the move.

I walked over to the engine, disconnected the wing from the engine, and started to drag the engine off to one side to get it beyond the reach of our peripatetic students. Before I could move the engine out of range, however, the next student launched. No sooner was she airborne than she promptly veered hard to the right, and flew directly over me and the engine. A few feet lower, and she would have hit us. I shook my head in amazement. Was Ralph completely lacking in common sense? (If so, it nicely matched my own lack of common sense for voluntarily remaining in such an unsafe environment.)

After my second tow flight, Ralph decided that it was time for me to practice forward inflations with the engine on my back. This puzzled me, because I hadn't yet mastered the forward launch *without* the engine. I thought it was too early to add the engine, but I yielded to Ralph's judgment. Although it was getting harder to make myself believe it, I figured that Ralph knew what he was doing.

Ralph told me to sit down on the ground, in the engine harness, and buckle up. I fastened both leg straps, and the chest strap, and zipped up the vest. It was a pretty tight fit. It was also a pretty hot day, and I was soon sweating profusely. I managed to get to my feet with sixty pounds of engine on my back. Unlike a backpack used in hiking and camping, the engine had no hip belt to place the load on my hips. It hung from my shoulders as a dead weight, and was very uncomfortable. I kept bending forward, trying to get the load off my shoulders and onto my back. I'm a big husky guy, but the load of the engine on my shoulders was rapidly wearing me out. I kept telling myself that I was having fun.

Under Ralph's instruction, I made three attempts to run forward and inflate the wing while carrying the engine on my back. None of my attempts was successful, and the effort was excruciating. Sweat poured off me in rivers. Was this really the best time of day for this sort of heavy exertion? With the hot sun directly overhead? Wouldn't the cool of the evening be much better? Then I could concentrate on what I was doing, rather than constantly wiping the sweat out of my eyes.

With the engine on my back, I couldn't stand up straight or raise my arms overhead. My efforts to run with the engine were pure agony. This was *awful*. I could only waddle like a crippled duck. I was so bent over that I looked like the Hunchback of Notre Dame. The harness simply wouldn't allow me to stand up straight. Was it supposed to be this way? Ralph seemed to be satisfied with it, so it must be right. But I couldn't see how anyone, bent over and half-crippled like this, could ever run forward fast enough to get this thing off the ground. This was starting to look like a sport suitable only for masochists.

After the first two inflation attempts, I noticed that I was trying to run in the long clover. The clover was about a foot long, and it made it more difficult to run, but this was where Ralph had told me to set it up. I asked Jake if it would be okay to move my rig over to where the clover had been recently cut. He agreed that it would be a good idea. Jake then admitted that he had seen the problem right from the start, but had decided to let me learn the hard way!

I was getting absolutely disgusted with this entire operation. I was paying money for this kind of instruction? I knew plenty of people who would be happy to abuse me for free!

At the end of the day, I went home badly discouraged. I'd made three attempts to inflate the wing while wearing the engine, and all three attempts had been unsuccessful. With the engine on my back, I simply couldn't run fast enough to get the wing overhead; let alone keep it up there. I'd spent a ton of money and waited months for this day. But instead of flying like a bird, I felt like I'd signed up for a torture session. If foot launching was this difficult, I'd never make it. And even if I managed to master it, who would want to work this hard?

Maybe I should have bought that PPC after all. Wheels were starting to look pretty good, compared to foot launching.

That evening, after a shower and some food, I re-examined the problem. I finally realized that I'd never be able to run with the engine on my back unless I could stand up straight. But I knew that I'd never be able to stand up straight, as long as the rigid seat was positioned under my butt. But unless the seat was pulled forward, under my butt, I couldn't even get into the harness! There had to be a better way.

I got out the instruction manual that came with engine, and studied the diagram of the pilot sitting in the harness. I couldn't see how either one of us would ever be able to stand upright in the harness. Suddenly I remembered that when I was wearing my training harness for my solo flights, the seat was always pushed up behind my butt, out of the way, before starting my takeoff run. I didn't slide back into the seat until after I was in the air. Could it be that the engine harness worked the same way? Could that be the answer?

I slipped on the engine, fastened all the straps, and stood up. As before, I was bent over like a crippled old man. I tried to pull the seat up behind me, but it wouldn't move. I decided to try lengthening the leg straps as much as possible. That gave the seat some wriggle room, and I was able to pull it up behind my butt. The retracted seat tucked in nicely between me and the engine frame.

It worked! Now I could stand up straight! With the seat pulled up behind me, the shoulder straps now went around my hips, instead of around my legs.

That freed me to stand up straight. Yay!

The problem, and the solution, was so obvious in hindsight that I wondered why Ralph hadn't told me about it earlier. Obviously I'd been wearing the harness all wrong, all day long. I could have been saved all that suffering!

This whole thing was looking more and more insane. My instructor was simply not teaching me what I needed to know in order to fly this thing. I was being forced to figure everything out for myself. So what was I paying Ralph for?

I had just about had it with Ralph and his entire incompetent organization. I was only a hair's breadth away from leaving, and finding another instructor. But at the same time I thought about how I was so close to flying! I actually had the engine on my back today. Ralph had said that I should be able to fly tomorrow. TO FLY!

I decided to give it another day. Especially now that I could stand up straight. Maybe now I could run with the engine on my back, and get the wing launched. I decided that it was worth another try. After all, even if I ended up sweating to death, and came home with nothing but aches and pains, how bad could it get?

I was about to find out.

The next day I was back at the farm. Ralph had brought his own motor and wing along. He carried his motor out to a clear spot, and attached his wing. Then he put on his motor, started it up, and let it warm up for a few minutes. Then he took the steering lines and risers in his hands, ran forward, and popped the wing overhead. He squeezed the throttle and the engine roared with power. A few more steps and he was in the air!

It was the first time I'd ever seen a powered paraglider actually fly. Oh, I had watched lots of videos, but this was live! God, it was beautiful! Ralph was actually going up! I watched, enraptured, as Ralph flew around the field. He climbed to several hundred feet of altitude and effortlessly soared over the nearby trees. Oh yes! *Yes!* This was what it was all about. This was what I'd come so far to find. Flying like a bird!

Ralph reduced the engine power to idle and drifted down toward the field. When he was about twenty feet away from me, and only about ten feet above the ground, he suddenly squeezed the throttle. The engine roared again, and Ralph started going up! That throttle in his hand was like a magic wand. And the engine was like a magic carpet. *This man could fly!*

After several more minutes of flying, Ralph finally killed the engine. He glided down to the field, just like a normal paraglider, and made a feather-soft landing. At that point I'd forgotten all my pain and suffering from the previous days. I just wanted to fly!

Ralph took off his engine and announced that it was time for me to fly. *Yes! Yes! Yes!* He told me to lay out my wing, start up the engine, and run it up to full throttle. Then he went back to supervising the tow flights.

I got the wing laid out, set the motor in front of it, and hooked the wing to the motor harness. I took the engine throttle in my hand and positioned my thumb over the starting button. I felt a little tingle of excitement. This was the first time I'd actually started my engine. I slid the choke to "on," took a deep breath, and pressed the starter button.

The electric starter spun the propeller for a moment, then the engine started almost instantly. I slid the choke off, and let the engine idle for three minutes. Then I braced my legs against the front of the harness, held the top of the motor frame with my left hand, and slowly began to squeeze the throttle with my right hand. The engine roared with power. It pressed hard against my legs. I knew that at full power my engine would be putting out approximately one hundred and fifteen pounds of thrust. I knew that I must be very careful not to let the engine get away from me. I was well aware that the spinning propeller, only inches away from my body, had been very appropriately described as the "Disk of Death." Anything that touched it would die.

Suddenly Ralph came running up to me. He snatched the throttle out of my hand and killed the engine. "Haven't you done enough for one day?" he shouted angrily.

For a moment I was puzzled. What was wrong? Then I suddenly realized what I'd done. The engine was pointing directly at the leading edge of the wing! The prop blast from the engine had been passing only inches above the wing. If the open cells in the wing had managed to catch that ninety mile per hour wind, the wing would have instantly inflated. The inflated wing could have caught any prevailing wind, and pulled the engine right out of my hands. The propeller would have hit the ground at full speed, and probably would have been destroyed. The wing suspension lines could also have been severed.

I hung my head in shame. I wanted to die from embarrassment. I knew better than to point a running engine at a wing lying on the ground. I apologized profusely to Ralph. I admitted that I'd just acted like a complete idiot.

Ralph seemed somewhat mollified by my display of penitence. He shook his head and walked back to the towing scooter. I turned the engine ninety degrees to the right, so the prop blast would miss the wing, and restarted the engine. As I was warming up the engine again, I berated myself for committing such a stupid lapse of safety. This was aviation. Safety must *never* be allowed to lapse.

But then something else occurred to me. Where was my instructor when I was doing my first engine runup? Oh yeah. He was off giving towing lessons. He wasn't standing next to me, watching over me and making certain that I was doing everything right. I was left alone to do my first engine runup on a flying machine costing ten thousand dollars.

Was there something wrong with this picture?

I slowly squeezed the throttle to give the engine full power. There was a tiny tachometer mounted on my harness, and connected to the engine. The tachometer was reading 6900 rpm, which was full power. Apparently my engine was working okay.

I shut down the engine and walked over to the scooter. Ralph told me to refuel the engine, then put the engine on and get ready to fly. I got goosebumps all over. This was it! (But would I be able to do it?)

I refueled the engine, sat down on the ground, and fastened the straps. This time I left the leg straps loose enough so that I could stand up straight, with the seat tucked up behind my butt. Then I managed to get to my feet. The engine felt very heavy. My tank was full of fuel for the first time, which added about ten pounds to the weight of the unit.

I took the throttle in my hand and prepared to start the engine. But before I could press the starter button, I suddenly noticed that gasoline was spilling onto the ground between my legs. Damn! I must have forgotten to put the gas cap back on. That's what can happen when you get excited, and fail to pay attention to what you're doing. There was nothing to do but take the engine off and put the gas cap back on.

Reluctantly I unzipped my vest and unfastened my chest and leg straps. Just as I was starting to slip out of the shoulder straps, Ralph came walking up. I told him that my engine was spilling fuel, and I asked him to check my gas cap.

Ralph shook his head. "That's not the problem," he told me. He explained that he'd seen me getting up from the ground with the engine on my back, and that I had bent over too far while I was getting up. This allowed some fuel to spill out of the overflow tube on the fuel tank. Nothing to worry about, but next time don't bend over so far. Then Ralph told me to buckle up and start the engine.

I refastened my chest and leg straps, and zipped up my vest again. Damn, but this engine was getting heavy! I either needed to make a takeoff attempt, or else take off the engine and take a break.

Ralph had given me an ordinary motorcycle helmet to wear. Since the helmet completely enclosed my head, and had no air vents, it was causing rivers of sweat to pour down my face. The sweat was even dripping onto the inside of my glasses, making it almost impossible for me to see.

Ralph clipped a radio to my chest strap, and plugged a small speaker into the radio. Then he shoved the speaker up under the ear flap of my helmet so that it rested against my left ear. There really wasn't enough room under my helmet for both my ear, and the speaker. It felt like someone was trying to jam his fist into my ear. At that point I think the only way I could have been more physically uncomfortable is if I'd been on fire (which turned out to be the next item on the list).

Just as I was about to press the starter button again, Jake came walking up. "Do you know your gas cap is off?" he asked nonchalantly.

I sighed, and tried to wipe the sweat out of my eyes. "Would you please put it on for me?" I asked. I looked at Ralph. His face was blank, and he said nothing. I wondered what would have happened if I'd tried to take off without the gas cap. Almost certainly the gasoline would have spilled out of the fuel tank. Could it have ignited, and set the whole rig on fire? I didn't know. I did know that having a blazing engine strapped to your back, with nowhere to go, was not a good idea. I knew that World War I pilots, having no parachutes, frequently chose to jump from their burning airplanes and fall to their deaths, rather than be burned to death in the air. I had no desire to emulate their example.

I wondered just how much more of Ralph's instruction I could survive. As I stood in the hot sun, with the engine on my back, Ralph gave me some last-minute flight instructions. They were pretty skimpy. He told me to fly for about half an hour, and don't skim the ground. There was no warning about flying downwind at low altitudes. Nothing was said about avoiding powerlines (probably the greatest hazard of all). I was given no instructions for aborting the takeoff if I failed to get into the air. Nothing was said about killing the motor as quickly as possible, or keeping the canopy lines out of the motor in case of an abort. I assumed that the netting over the prop cage would keep the lines out of the motor, even if I botched the takeoff. (Which turned out to be another false assumption on my part.)

It was time to fly. I hit the starter button, and the engine started almost instantly. With my gas cap firmly in place, and my motor running, I ran forward in an attempt to make my first powered takeoff. It was a dismal failure. The wing popped overhead, but then proceeded to collapse on top of me. Fortunately the prop cage netting kept the wing and the lines out of the propeller. This time.

I had failed in my first powered takeoff attempt, but I was doing much better than yesterday. At least I could now *run* with the engine on my back. At least I wasn't hobbling along like a crippled duck. But I still couldn't get my arms above my shoulders, which made it very difficult to control the wing.

I backed up and tried again. And once again the canopy collapsed on top of me before I could achieve takeoff. Damn! I was rapidly running out of steam. The weight of the engine was crushing me, and I was drowning in sweat.

I made a third attempt to take off, and again I failed. The problem was that I simply couldn't get my arms above my shoulders. This caused me to pull down on my front risers and collapse the wing when it was overhead. I was also having a lot of trouble holding the throttle, and the right riser, and the right steering line, all in my right hand. I'd never had to hold all three items at the same time. When I complained to Jake that I didn't see how I could hold everything, he held up his own hand and said, "Look, my hands are smaller than yours. If I can do it then you can do it."

How enlightening! What excellent instruction! I knew that I should just stop and walk away from this clown show, but damn it, I still wanted to fly!

After three failed attempts at launching with a running engine, Ralph told me to take a break. He and Jake returned to the towing operation. They offered no advice, encouragement, or explanation as to what I might be doing wrong. I shut off the engine and let it slide to the ground. I was exhausted, and dying of thirst. As I sat on the ground in the hot sun, gulping down cold water, I started to entertain some serious doubts about this sport. Was I really going to be able to do this? It was starting to look like only an Olympic athlete, or a circus acrobat, could do the necessary juggling to get a powered paraglider into the air. I was 46 years old. Maybe that was too old for this sport?

Except that I'd seen Ralph do it just a few minutes earlier, and he made it look effortless. Ralph was my size, and only a couple of years younger. If he could do it, surely I could too.

About twenty-five minutes later, with my strength somewhat restored, I was ready to try again. I put on the engine, got to my feet, and took the steering lines, risers, and throttle in my hands. I was wearing my safety helmet but had decided to skip the radio. I started the engine, let it warm up for a minute, and with Ralph and Jake watching me, made my fourth attempt to fly. The wing came up overhead and I squeezed the throttle.

The engine roared with power, but again the wing collapsed on top of me before I could take off. I simply couldn't keep that damn wing overhead long enough to get airborne. Also there were too many sensations and inputs, all bombarding my brain at the same time. I was trying to do too many new things at once. This just couldn't be how one learned to fly a powered paraglider!

I decided that I had one more attempt left in me today. Ralph told me that *this* time they were going to get me into the air! He and Jake were each going to grab a shoulder strap on my harness and drag me forward, like a puppet, until the wing was flying. Then I could squeeze the throttle and fly. It sounded like a plan born of desperation, but at that point I was ready to try anything to get into the air. Please! Just one flight! I've waited so long for this moment!

"Go!" Ralph yelled. With the last of my strength, I ran forward as fast as I could. Ralph and Jake were each pulling on a shoulder strap. The wing leaped off the ground and shot up into the air. I squeezed the throttle to go to full power, and the engine roared. I was going to make it! I was going to fly!

Alas, no. Just as I had done on Mount Wilson a week earlier, I held onto the front risers too long. This caused the wing to fly overhead, then collapse. Once again the wing fell on top of me, enveloping me in billowing clouds of fabric and a forest of suspension lines.

Then it happened. My luck finally ran out. There was a sound like a million pieces of paper tearing, and suddenly the engine stopped. Instantly I knew that something very bad had happened. Ralph and Jake were looking at me in tight-lipped silence. "Take it off," Ralph finally said. He muttered something to Jake about a "chopped line."

With a terrible feeling of dread, I slipped out of the engine and lowered it to the ground. Then I turned around and looked at it. One of the wing suspension lines had been sucked through the prop cage netting, and into the propeller. The line had been severed, and one end of the line was wrapped around the propeller hub. Then my eyes fell on the tips of the propeller, and my heart sank. All three tips of the propeller had been shattered. Shards of carbon fiber and resin hung like torn spider webs. The propeller had been destroyed, and for all I knew the engine had been destroyed with it. The prop cage had also been damaged. One of the velcro straps had been torn, and part of the netting had been pulled loose by the flailing suspension line. Good thing the suspension line hadn't been wrapped around any part of *me* before getting sucked into the prop.

"Get the line out of the prop," Ralph said. "Then take the prop off." He and Jake walked away to resume towing. Not a word of sympathy or condolence. It was like they didn't care. A hundred feet away, the rest of the students had been watching the drama unfold. Nobody said anything. It was like the crowd at the scene of a bad accident.

I knelt on the ground and stared at the wreckage of my once-beautiful engine. It had cost me seven thousand dollars to buy this engine. What would it cost to repair it? Could it be repaired? I didn't know. Ralph had made no comment.

I just wanted to sit in the dirt and cry, but there was work to be done. I felt sick to my stomach as I slowly unwound the end of the suspension line from the propeller hub. When the propeller was finally free, I got out the wrench and removed the six nuts that held the propeller to the engine shaft. With the shattered propeller off, the engine looked naked, but it also looked much better. It was like amputating a badly mangled limb. I gathered up the pieces of the propeller and carried them back to the towing area. Ralph was sitting on the scooter, getting ready to make another tow.

"I guess I'll need a new propeller," I said to Ralph. "How much are they?"

"Four hundred dollars," he answered.

I nodded sadly. "Go ahead and order one." I held up the pieces of my former propeller. "Want to buy a prop, cheap?" I asked.

"Leave the pieces with me," said Ralph. "It might be possible to repair them and use them for training flights. But you should still buy a new prop. Leave the cage with me, too. I can probably fix the velcro strap and the netting. I'll let you know how much it will cost to replace the line on the wing."

I nodded wearily, then I picked up my engine and headed for my car. I was thoroughly sick of the whole mess. I had never dreamed that my equipment could be destroyed like this, during my training. And I hadn't even fallen down! It was going to cost me at least four hundred dollars to get everything fixed. Was this normal for powered paragliding training? If so, then I couldn't afford it!

I tried to figure out how in the hell a suspension line could be sucked through the protective netting on the prop cage? Wasn't that what the netting was designed to prevent? I had a lot to think about during the long, miserable drive home. And I still had to tell Mike that I'd broken our new toy.

Sometimes life really sucks.

For the next several days I pondered what had gone wrong. Eventually I realized that a large part of the problem was due to the fact that I simply couldn't get my arms overhead while wearing the engine. This caused me to pull down on the front risers, and collapse the wing. Obviously I was doing something wrong.

I got out the engine and stared at it for a long time. There *must* be a way to get my arms overhead so that I could get the wing inflated, and flying, and not end up pulling it down on my head and into the propeller.

I got out the instruction manual and again read the section about adjusting the harness. The problem was that my engine was a later model, with some changes, and it didn't quite match what was shown in the instruction manual. The manual talked about adjusting the length of the shoulder straps, but I didn't even have adjustments on my shoulder straps. They were fixed in length. There was just some padding on the straps, held in place by a cloth cover. I idly ran my fingers over the padding and the cover.

Wait a minute! What the hell was this? There was a velcro seam under the cover! My fingers grasped the seam and gave a yank. The cover came off, and there was the shoulder strap adjustment buckle, in all its gleaming metallic glory. Well I'll be damned!

Instantly I pulled the cloth cover off the other shoulder strap. Yep! It had an adjustment buckle too. I hadn't even known the damn buckles were in there! And even more significantly, both buckles were pulled tight, which made the shoulder straps as short as possible.

I quickly loosened both buckles, put on the engine, fastened the straps, and stood up. It was amazing! I felt like someone had taken off my straightjacket. *I could now raise my arms overhead!* I walked around the living room with the engine on my back, raising and lowering my arms effortlessly. What a difference! With the longer shoulder straps, I could easily brush my fingertips against the ceiling. I felt like a crippled man who has just gotten the use of his legs back.

I also felt like a man who has been hit over the head so many times, that he finally gets the message.

Later that evening, I had a long talk with Mike. The shattered propeller, topped off by the unadjusted harness, was the last straw. I told Mike that I *would not* go back to Ralph for any further training. Ralph had never even shown me how to properly adjust my harness. Was he blind? Could he not see that I was jammed into a harness that was adjusted for a much smaller man? He hadn't shown me how to pull up the harness seat so that I could stand up, or how to let out the shoulder straps so that I could raise my arms overhead and control the wing. Maybe he was waiting for me to figure it out on my own?

I realized now that it would have been a miracle if I'd gotten airborne under Ralph's tutelage. I simply wasn't getting the proper training that I needed to safely participate in this sport. I'd been repeatedly injured, and now my equipment had been badly damaged due to lack of proper training. Enough was enough. It was time to find another instructor.

A couple of days later, Ralph dropped by with my new propeller and my repaired cage. The cage had been easy to fix, and there was no charge for that. Replacing the severed wing line only cost thirty dollars. The new propeller, however, cost $400. Ouch!

Ralph also told me that I owed him two hundred dollars in interest charges on my wing, for the time he had held it before I finished paying for it. Interest charges? Ralph had never told me that there would be interest charges for buying the wing on time. Not that I would have objected, but I should have been told, up front, that there would *be* interest charges, and what the rate of interest would be. Instead I was simply presented with the final bill. It struck me as a very unprofessional way to do business. Even though I would have been within my rights to refuse to pay the interest, I just went ahead and paid it. I just wanted to be done with Ralph.

When Ralph finally walked out the door, I felt like a great weight had been lifted from my shoulders, and that a great threat to my safety had finally been eliminated.

I picked up the repaired prop cage, and the new propeller, and headed for the garage. The engine sat on the concrete floor, looking very naked. I fitted the cage back on the engine frame, grabbed my torque wrench, and attached the new propeller to the engine hub. Then I grabbed the throttle, set the choke, and thumbed the starting button.

The engine started as though it was fresh from the factory. I breathed a big sigh of relief as the engine idled at just under two thousand rpm. Apparently the engine had not been damaged internally. I braced myself against the engine frame and squeezed the throttle. The rpm quickly rose to seven thousand, and the engine pushed against my body with over one hundred pounds of thrust. The engine seemed to be running perfectly. Yes! I was back in the flying business.

Now all I needed to do was find someone to teach me to fly.

In Hindsight, What Would I have Done Differently?

I should have walked away before I managed to shatter a $400 propeller. I should have walked away as soon as I realized that my instructors were too cavalier about safety. I thought that I could compensate for their lack of safety and incompetent training. I learned the hard way that I could not.

In hindsight, it's obvious that I had no business attempting to fly with the motor until I had learned to do proper forward inflations. If you can't handle the wing without the motor, I guarantee that putting on the motor will not suddenly improve your skill level.

What should my instructor have done differently? First he should have taught me to do forward inflations without the motor. Once that skill had been mastered, I should have put on the motor and practiced forward inflations until I had demonstrated that I could do them consistently and reliably.

Of course my instructor should also have taught me how to adjust the motor harness before I started practicing forward inflations with it. And the only way to properly adjust a motor harness is to hang it up from a tree branch, overhead beam, or swing set, with the pilot in it, and adjust the straps until the pilot is properly fitted.

Why Ralph failed to do any of this, is a mystery. He virtually guaranteed my failure to get airborne. I also feel that he was directly responsible for the damage to my equipment. It was as though he was only interested in getting me airborne, once, in whatever fashion, so that he would then be able to claim that he had fulfilled his obligation to "train" me to fly. Then he would not need to waste any more time on me. I don't know for certain that this was Ralph's plan, but there are powered paragliding schools that seem to operate pretty much in this fashion.

Granted, every instructor is different. Every instructor has his own peculiarities when it comes to training, and "different" does not automatically mean "inferior." But there are some things that simply must be done during training, or else the student will not be able to fly. My experience is a perfect example of dealers who sell the equipment, get the money, and then skimp on the training.

And finally, trying to master an intricate skill while drowning in sweat, just doesn't work. Not only does it quickly take all the fun out of the sport, not only is it physically exhausting, but the student's mind quickly becomes so numbed and fatigued that he is unable to focus on the task at hand. He quickly becomes a safety hazard.

Take it from me. Don't try to run around on a hot summer day with a heavy engine on your back. Don't spend hours in the hot sun trying to learn to do forward inflations of a paraglider wing. Remember, this is supposed to be fun. You're not doing this because you have to; you're doing it because you want to. Running with an engine, or learning to launch a paraglider wing, especially in no wind, is hard work. Insist that such training be done in the early morning, or early evening, when it's much cooler. You simply can't learn to fly, or learn to handle your wing, when you're drowning in sweat. So either wait for cooler weather, or else go to an instructor who is considerate of his student's comfort and well being.

Remember, a good instructor pays close attention to his student's comfort level. If he doesn't, then find another instructor.

The best way to evaluate an instructor is to visit his training school and watch him in action for a day or two. You will very quickly learn whether or not you want to hire him to teach you to fly.

A Note On Towing:

Towing is a fine way to learn to fly a paraglider wing. You don't need a training hill, and the students need not waste precious energy gathering up their wings after each flight, and trudging back up the hill in the hot sun.

Nevertheless, I personally prefer training hills to towing. Why? Because there is less to go wrong with a training hill. There is no tow line to break, entangle, or fail to release. Towing can be extremely dangerous if not done by a trained, competent towmaster. Plus there is always the life-threatening hazard of the lock-out if the student steers the wing too far to one side. This hazard does not exist on the training hill.

I would not hesitate to go to a good school that used towing, but I would personally prefer to use a training hill; preferably one covered with soft sand.

Chapter 7

Finding A New Instructor

I couldn't afford to keep breaking $400 propellers. Obviously the brute-force method of learning to fly by putting on the engine, running forward, and hoping that everything somehow works out okay was not a good idea.

I tracked down several powered paragliding schools in the United States and talked to their owners. Two individuals, Francesco DeSantis from Florida, and Hugh Murphy from California, stood out. Both men were very free with their information, and they obviously loved the sport of powered paragliding. Both agreed that it was essential to learn to fly the wing before adding the motor. Both men agreed that damage to the student or the equipment during training was simply unacceptable. They both felt that in a proper training environment, damage or injury should almost never happen.

Some schools offered motor training in only a day or two. Others recommended up to a week of training. It was a bit confusing, but I finally realized that "quick" and "cheap" were not attributes of a good training program. In aviation, it's unwise to pay too much, but it can be fatal to pay too little.

My hard-won experience told me that it was best to learn to fly the wing first. Most of the experts recommended getting a P2 paragliding rating, then adding the motor. A P2 rating is a novice rating, and indicates only that you know enough to fly a paraglider, unpowered, without being under the direct supervision of an instructor. Basically, to get a P2 rating you make about two dozen flights and demonstrate that you can land within fifty feet of a target. It seemed logical that I should first get a P2 rating, then learn to fly the motor. Also, I wouldn't have to travel as far in order to find a good, unpowered paragliding school.

I finally narrowed my choice to two paragliding schools. One of the schools also offered powered paraglider training. But at this stage I only wanted to learn to fly the wing. In that respect, both schools looked equally good. I decided to visit both schools. Although I wasn't exactly sure what I was looking for, my experience with Ralph had certainly taught me what I *wasn't* looking for.

On September 9, I visited North American Paragliding in Ellensburg, Washington. Washington State is really two different states, separated by the Cascade mountains that run north and south. Western Washington is wet and forested. Eastern Washington is mostly dry desert, just like parts of Arizona or Nevada, only a little colder. Crops require irrigation to grow in much of Eastern Washington. It's hard to believe that a chain of mountains can cause weather patterns to be so different.

Ellensburg was in the heart of cattle country. The town sat on a flat plain, surrounded on three sides by mountains. The town was a curious mixture of the old and the new. The downtown area made you feel like you'd stepped back in time about eighty years, while a modern university sat on the edge of the town. I liked Ellensburg.

North American Paragliding operated out of a small storefront, just off the main drag in downtown Ellensburg. I had told the owner, Mike Eberle, what I was looking for, and he gave me permission to observe one of his classes.

The class started at eight o'clock in the morning, and had only a single paying student (which was very unusual). It was taught by a very likable fellow named Marty. He started with a couple of hours of classroom instruction. Marty stood in front of a blackboard and sketched out a cross-section of a paraglider wing, and explained how it flew. What a difference from my earlier training! Immediately I started to feel very comfortable with this operation, particularly since Marty included me in the instruction and discussion, even though I wasn't a paying student.

Eventually it was time to go flying. We threw some gear into a four-wheel drive Suburban, and headed out of town. Soon we entered a notch in the mountains that had been carved by the Yakima River. We followed the river for about half an hour, and finally pulled up in front of the infamous Yakima Bowl.

I'd heard horror stories about the Yakima Bowl. Stories about climbing long distances through the rocks, dirt, heat, and cactus–all while carrying a heavy wing on your back. Although the stories were somewhat exaggerated, they did contain an element of truth. The Yakima Bowl was just a big amphitheater, scooped out of the side of the mountains. It was something less than a mile in circumference, and about five hundred feet high. Several trails snaked up the sides of the Bowl. There were windsocks positioned around the top of the Bowl. With binoculars you could easily determine the wind direction at the top of the Bowl. To fly the Bowl, the wind had to be blowing up the slope. Marty said the wind typically blew up the slope in the morning, and down the slope in the afternoon.

With its relatively flat floor and gently sloping sides, the Bowl was nice for training students. It was fairly steep near the top, but the beauty of the Bowl was that a student could climb just high enough for short training flights, and move higher as his skill level increased. I could see that it would be a long haul to the top of the Bowl, carrying a paraglider, and I didn't look forward to making such a climb.

The three of us unloaded the equipment and set off across the floor of the Bowl. Even though it was a September morning, the desert climate was already heating up. In the middle of the summer it could easily reach 120 degrees. Fortunately I had my new Hydrapak™ drinking bladder strapped to my back. It contained nearly a gallon of ice water. A drinking tube allowed me to drink as often as I liked. For the first time in my life I was hiking in a hot climate, but staying fully hydrated. Nice!

The floor of the Bowl was covered with sagebrush that grew about two feet tall. On Marty's recommendation I had worn shorts for comfort in the heat, and gaiters to keep my bare legs from being scratched. Before I'd come to Ellensburg, North American Paragliding had sent me a brochure that explained their various courses, costs, and what equipment to bring with me. Because of the desert climate, they recommended bringing water, hat, and sunscreen. What a wonderful change of pace! A paragliding school that was concerned about the student's comfort and well-being!

We trekked about a thousand feet across the floor of the Bowl, and climbed a short distance up the side so the student could make a training flight. He'd already made a couple of flights, and was eager to make another one.

We finally arrived at a small clearing near the base of the steep portion of the Bowl. At this point we were about a hundred feet above the lowest portion of the Bowl. The plan was for the student to fly down the gentle slope of the Bowl, staying airborne as long as possible. The flight would probably last only thirty or forty seconds, never getting more than ten feet above the ground, but the student would get to practice launching, flying, steering, and landing.

Marty laid out the wing and lines, and explained the function and purpose of each part. I was receiving a flood of useful information, and learning things about the wing that I had never known before. This was exactly the sort of training that I had expected to receive from Ralph, but never did. I was picking up so much useful information from Marty that I started to feel guilty that I wasn't a paying student.

After the wing was laid out, Marty showed the student how to put on the harness and adjust the straps properly. I paid close attention, since I'd never been taught any of these things. The differences between this *training* facility, and Ralph's *processing* facility, were very evident.

Even though this was only a short hop, on a bunny hill, Marty insisted on checking every strap and buckle to insure that the student was properly prepared for his flight. What a difference! The constant attention to detail, and the ceaseless emphasis on safety made a deep impression on me.

Marty explained exactly how the student should run, and how to handle the wing. The student ran forward with the risers and steering lines in his hand, and the wing leaped overhead. A few steps later he was airborne. It looked easy! Best of all, no white knuckles, and no fear.

As the student flew down the gentle slope of the Bowl, Marty radioed instructions for making gentle turns to the left and right. It was so simple! No complicated towing instructions, no flying over powerlines, and no trees to run into. As the ground finally flattened out, and came up to meet the student, Marty radioed landing instructions. The student pulled down on both brake lines, flared, and touched down lightly on the ground. Marty turned off his radio and smiled in satisfaction. "Good flight," he said simply.

"You are an excellent instructor," I told him, with all the sincerity I could put into my voice. I really meant it. I felt like I'd found my home.

I bombarded Marty with questions during the drive back to Ellensburg. I learned that while the initial training usually took place in the Yakima Bowl, the student quickly moved on to other flying sites, and these other sites didn't require the hike across the Bowl and up the hill. That was nice to know. I decided that making a few climbs to the top of the Bowl was a cheap price to pay for such excellent instruction. Then I asked Marty about the student/teacher ratio. He explained that he never trained more than three or four students at a time. Another point for North American Paragliding.

Back at the store, I thanked Mike Eberle for permitting me to observe a class. I was really impressed by Marty's professionalism and dedication to safety. I also decided that I much preferred learning to fly the wing by flying off low hills, rather than being towed into the air by a scooter. Hill launching was much simpler. I could concentrate on the wing, rather than on the towing process. I could safely abort the takeoff at any time. I was in total charge, rather than being played like a fish on a line.

All in all, North American Paragliding looked like a winner. I nearly signed up for lessons on the spot. But first I wanted to check out the other paragliding school before I paid my money.

The next morning I was sitting in the empty parking lot of an abandoned restaurant, waiting for a man I'll call "John" to show up. John was the proprietor of another paragliding school, and he was scheduled to teach a class of students today. John and the class were an hour late, and I was beginning to think I'd missed them. It was not a good beginning.

Finally I got out of my car and walked around to the other side of the empty restaurant. I spotted several people milling around a few cars across the highway. I went back to my car, grabbed my gear, and started across the street to join the others. Just as I was crossing the street, a large van bearing the name of John's paragliding school pulled up. Yeah, this was the place.

I quickly identified John, and introduced myself. Then we all piled into the van and headed for John's school. The gravel road that we followed was so rough and washed out that it was closed to the public. John had to ferry his students to his school in his van. As we climbed up into the foothills, John laughed and chatted and seemed friendly enough.

John was very well known in the paragliding community. He had been active in paragliding for many years, and had trained many students. I had also heard that he could be quite a character. It was said that if you looked in the dictionary under "Prima Donna," you would find a picture of John. (This claim turned out to contain more than a grain of truth.)

We parked in front of a converted farmhouse that served as John's center of operation. The students gathered up their wings and equipment, piled into a large truck, and soon we were headed up the canyon to the launch point.

John's paragliding school covered quite a few acres of grassy foothills in a canyon that had once been a hay farm. The whole valley was one gigantic sheet of grass. There were no trees or rocks. I learned that there were several launching sites, depending on the pilot's skill level. John liked to boast that no matter which way the wind blew, there was always a hill facing into the wind. Not many paragliding schools could make that claim. It was one of the most perfect spots for learning to paraglide that I had ever seen.

Shortly after we arrived, as if on cue, the wind began to flow up the valley, giving us perfect launching conditions. John processed the students like cattle in a chute, but he did not cut corners or skip basic safety procedures. He worked quickly, but efficiently. One by one, the students pulled their wings into the air, turned around, and launched off the lip of the canyon. Drifting out over the valley, the students would sometimes be as much as one hundred feet above the valley floor. They flew down the length of the valley, trying to get as far as they could before finally being forced to land. During the entire flight they were under John's radio guidance.

I was surprised to see that every student did a reverse inflation. This involved turning around and facing the wing, with the lines crossed, then grabbing the risers and pulling the wing up into the air. Then the student turned around and started running down the hill until he lifted into the air.

The reverse inflation was obviously much easier to do than the forward inflation. The pilot could watch the wing as it was pulled into the air, so he could make immediate adjustments as required. I had been told that the only disadvantage of the reverse inflation was that it required a wind of at least four miles per hour. It could not be done in calm conditions.

I asked John about forward vs. reverse inflation. I found that he was quite opinionated on the subject. As far as he was concerned, reverse inflations were the only way to go. He considered forward inflations to be obsolete, and taught only by incompetent instructors. He said that the only reason he even taught forward inflations was to enable his students to meet national paraglider pilot certification requirements.

Once all the students had landed down the valley, John and I got in the van and went to pick them up. I commented to John that it was nice that the students didn't have to walk up the hill, carrying their equipment. John told me that he thought it was stupid to make a student walk up a hill. All that did was tire the student out, and sour him on the sport. I had to admit, he had a point. I liked the idea of not having to walk up a hill during training. I was starting to think that John's paragliding school was even better than North American Paragliding. The quality of instruction seemed equally good, but John's school had the advantage of better location.

We drove down the length of the valley, picking up the students and their gear. If a student had not finished packing up his wing, John and I helped him to finish. Then we drove back up the hill and the launchings started all over again. After several rounds of flying, John called a halt and we returned to the farmhouse for a bite of lunch.

I had told John that I was interested in getting a P2 rating, but that I really wanted to ultimately learn to fly a powered paraglider. Since John was also a dealer for paraglider engines, I did not tell him I had already bought a machine. I asked him if he could teach me to fly a powered paraglider. I was really surprised when he told me that he didn't recommend it for me. I thought this was a rather odd attitude, coming from a PPG dealer.

John explained that at my present weight of 210 lbs., I was too heavy for any of the DK Whisper engines. He said that I would only be able to get off the ground by running down a hill, and that I would be grounded on a hot day. He said that I would need to fly one of the more powerful engines, like the La Mouette, and that such a heavy machine, for a man of my age and condition (46 years old and decidedly out of shape) would not be an enjoyable experience. He recommended that I buy a powered parachute, such as a Buckeye.

I finally realized that John was not much of a PPG enthusiast. I knew that the DK Whisper Plus engine was quite capable of getting me off the ground, even on a hot day (although I might have to run a few extra steps). I thought I was better informed about the DK equipment than John. Obviously I would not want him for a PPG instructor, but he would probably make an excellent unpowered paragliding instructor, and that's what I was currently looking for.

After lunch, John announced that the more advanced students were going up to one of the high launch points on a nearby mountain and that the rest of us were welcome to come along and observe. However he cautioned us that the road did not run all the way to the top of the mountain, and that we would have to walk the last twenty minutes or so. I decided to go, even though I wasn't keen on walking.

For almost half an hour our van switchbacked its way up through the foothills. Finally we topped out on a high, windswept ridge, a couple of thousand feet above the valley floor. In front of us, a wooded peak rose several hundred feet higher. The pilots who were scheduled to fly, slung on their packs and we started to hike.

The trail was rough, and the climb was a bit steep in places. Very quickly it separated the men from the boys. The boys ran on ahead, while the men brought up the rear, huffing and puffing in the high altitude air. The "twenty minute stroll" turned out to be more like a "forty minute hustle." If I wasn't one of the first to arrive at the summit, at least I wasn't the last.

The peak was covered with trees except for a small opening to the east. The clearing didn't look large enough to launch a paper airplane, let alone a paraglider. Nevertheless, several pilots immediately started laying out their wings on the soft pine needles that covered the forest floor. The slope was fairly steep. There wasn't a breath of wind, and the September sunshine was pleasantly warm.

I watched three pilots launch. Since there was no wind, they all did forward inflations as I had expected. Two of the pilots made it into the air on the first try. The third pilot allowed his wing to overshoot, and ended up tumbling down the hill. He was unhurt, and climbed back up to launch successfully on his next attempt.

When it was John's turn to launch, he announced that he would be flying a tandem wing and carrying a passenger. I asked him, "Since there's no wind, you'll have to do a forward inflation, won't you?"

John stopped fussing with his wing, walked up to me, and stuck his face about two inches from mine. He seemed angry. "What did I tell you earlier when you asked me the exact same question?" From the tone of his voice he sounded furious, and seemed to be about two seconds away from punching me in the nose. Since I couldn't tell if he was joking or not, I measured my response carefully. Even though John was only about half my size, I didn't want to start a fight with him.

"You said that you always do reverse inflations," I answered evenly, trying to keep any emotion out of my voice.

"That's right!" John snapped. "I said that I *always* do reverse inflations. I *never* do forward inflations. When you ask the same question again, it sounds to me like you're questioning my honesty!"

"Oh no," I quickly demurred. "It's just that I was always told that a forward inflation was always required in no wind." Then I gave John my best goggle-eyed look of amazement. "You're *really* going to do a reverse inflation here?"

"That's what I said!" snapped John. "And I don't like to repeat myself!"

With that, John spun on his heel and went back to work on his wing. I looked around at the rest of the group. The place had suddenly become very

97

quiet, and all eyes were on me and John. I answered the silent stares with a shrug. In my mind I was thinking, *Crackpot Alert!*

A few minutes later, John was hooked into the big tandem wing. A student was clipped into the front of John's harness exactly as I had flown tandem with Ralph. I still couldn't believe that John was going to do a reverse inflation. Hell, I thought he'd be lucky to be able to do a *forward* inflation, given the limited running room and the complete lack of wind.

When John was ready, he turned halfway around, grabbed both front risers in his right hand, and pulled. The big wing rose off the ground and hung momentarily in the air. Before it could fall out of the sky, John shouted, "Run!" and he and the student went racing down the hill. They only got a few steps before the wing lifted them away from the hillside. Both of them soared off into space.

I could only shake my head in admiration. John had done it. And he had done it exactly the way he said that he would. That arrogant little sonofabitch was *good!*

The other pilots had quickly sunk out and landed back at the farmhouse. Not John and his student. John carefully worked the available thermals and climbed an additional six thousand feet into the sky. Then he pointed his wing toward a nearby town about six miles away, and flew toward it. He and his student finished their flight about an hour later by landing in the town park. Any way you looked at it, it was a very impressive performance.

A couple more pilots flew off the peak, and then the rest of us wandered back down the mountain to ride back to the farmhouse in the van. I shook hands with John before I left. He seemed to bear me no ill will. He just told me to let him know when I was ready to start my lessons.

As I drove back to my motel, I thought about what I'd seen during the last two days. John charged $800 for his P2 paragliding course, whereas Mike Eberle charged $1300. On the other hand, Eberle's course lasted almost twice as long. Both schools had good reputations, and both seemed to offer competent instruction, so it basically came down to personal preference.

In the end, I decided to go with Mike Eberle and North American Paragliding. His course was more expensive, took longer, and would require me to walk up some hills, but Marty's instruction was first rate. Even more important, Marty was one of the friendliest guys I had ever met. He had been willing to answer endless questions and explain every answer, whereas John had thrown a bit of a hissy fit when I questioned one of his claims.

And that's what finally decided it for me. In aviation you must understand what's going on. And if it's necessary to ask a question several times, then that's what you do. I did not want to be so intimidated by my instructor that I failed to ask a question a second time, if necessary. It's important to be relaxed and comfortable with your instructor, and I thought that would be difficult to do around a Colorful Character like John.

A couple of weeks later I called Mike Eberle at North American Paragliding and signed up for his lesson package.

In Hindsight, What Would I have Done Differently?

Not much. This time I did almost everything right. I checked out the paragliding schools as much as possible, and then went to visit them. I actually observed the quality of their instruction.

I only made two mistakes. My first mistake was to sign up for a lesson package and prepay the whole thing up front. Bad idea. I should have paid for my lessons on a day-by-day basis. However, as it turned out, I didn't suffer.

My second mistake was to go for a P2 paragliding rating. That was really overkill. I went from not enough training, to too much training. I let the pendulum swing too far in the opposite direction. I spent a lot of time and money getting my P2 rating, and as it turned out, it wasn't really necessary. There was certainly nothing wrong with getting a P2 rating, but much of what I learned would prove to be unnecessary for powered paragliding. Furthermore, what I learned that was useful for powered paragliding could have been learned much more efficiently at a good powered paragliding school. More on this later.

Chapter 8

Flying With The Dustbuster

Just over two weeks after my first visit to Ellensburg I was back to take my first lesson from Mike Eberle and North American Paragliding.. I had hoped that the hot weather would be gone by this late September date. It was still warm; getting up into the high 70s and low 80s every day, but at least the thermometer was no longer breaking 100.

It was 8:00 a.m. in the morning, and still chilly. This high desert country, although very warm during the day, got cold at night. We were all gathered in North American's storefront. Mike was at the blackboard, delivering his lecture on basic aerodynamics and the mechanics of paraglider flight. I'd heard some of this before, but it never hurt to go over it again. And Mike was a good teacher.

I was joined by four or five other guys from Seattle who had come for the standard, two-day introductory course to paragliding. They were friendly, high-spirited guys, and I was certain I was going to enjoy flying with them.

After about two hours of classroom instruction, we headed out with Marty to do some flying. Marty said the wind was wrong for the Yakima Bowl, so we were going to Watt Canyon instead.

Actually, I was surprised that we were heading for either place. I was under the impression that the first lesson normally took place in the Ellensburg city park, where the students learned to inflate their wings on level ground before moving out to the hills.

When I questioned Marty about this, he explained that the school used to do it that way, but they found it was more efficient to have new students practice their inflations while running down a hill. Remembering how much easier my own inflations had been, while running downhill, that made sense to me.

Watt Canyon was a small hill that rose about fifty feet above the flat farmland of Ellensburg. We parked at the bottom, and carried our equipment up the hill, following a fence line. Marty was young, and in excellent condition, but the rest of us were middle-aged baby boomers. Although we struggled to keep up, none of us was going to be the first to ask Marty to slow down. What's a lousy heart attack, compared to looking like a wimp!

We arrived at the launch point before anyone could drop dead. While we were waiting for the wind to arrive and start blowing up the hill, Marty gave us a simple game plan. We would take off from the top of the hill, fly down to the bottom, and land. Each flight would last about thirty seconds, after which we would gather up our wing and hike back up the hill for another flight.

After two solo flights off the top of Mount Wilson, you'd think that I would have no fear of flying off a mere hill only fifty feet high. That's when I discovered just how badly my confidence had been shaken by my crash on the summit of Mount Wilson, my crash in the Mount Wilson LZ, and the shattering of my propeller. This little bunny hill looked positively terrifying! For starters, it looked incredibly steep. It was steep enough that a wing collapse, or other mistake on takeoff, would almost certainly cause an injury. Wasn't there some nice, long, gentle hill we could launch from? Something with a twenty degree slope where I couldn't possibly get hurt if I fell?

In other words, I had no confidence in my ability to do a proper forward inflation. I was convinced that my successful forward inflations at Mount Wilson had been sheer luck. So I hung back and let the other guys launch first. Two of them launched just fine. The other two were having trouble keeping their wings in the air. I discovered that one of the guys had a bad leg from a motorcycle accident that prevented him from running very fast.

Finally it was my turn to fly. And I didn't want to. I told Marty about my concern, and described my problems. To my utter amazement, Marty fixed both of my problems in about sixty seconds! He showed me how to release my front risers when the wing was overhead, so I didn't pull down the leading edge and collapse the wing. He also showed me how to pull down on the steering lines (also called the brakes) when the wing was overhead, to keep it from surging ahead and striking the ground. I hadn't even known that I could use the steering lines as brakes to control the wing like that!

Marty urged me to give it a try. Not to launch, but to just try pulling the wing up and keep it flying overhead. I tried it, and it worked like a charm! I could keep it flying overhead! I finally let the wing drop to the ground and stood there in open-mouthed amazement. I was looking at Marty like he was some kind of Sky God. In only one minute he had completely repaired the damage done by hours of incomplete and incompetent instruction. Remarkable!

Suddenly I was feeling a whole lot better about this sport.

I made a few more perfect practice inflations. Then it was time to fly! I laid out my wing and took the steering lines and risers in my hands. The five to seven mile per hour wind made for perfect launch conditions, but I was still nervous. With the ghost of Mount Wilson hovering nearby, I ran forward. Instantly the wing leaped off the ground and shot overhead. I added a little brake, and the wing stopped dead in its tracks. I tried to run forward, but I'd applied too much brake, and the wing was almost picking me up off the ground. I couldn't get any traction with my feet. I eased off the brakes slightly, and suddenly I could run again. I went racing down the hill, gaining as much speed as I could.

Suddenly I was airborne! Like magic, I swooped out away from the hill. I heard myself shrieking with delight. It worked! I had done a successful launch, *and I was in control!* What a difference!

I followed Marty's radioed instructions to make a few shallow turns, then was forced to land as my altitude finally ran out. As my feet touched the ground, I held the brakes down as the wing slowly collapsed to the ground behind me. What a wonderful flight! I wanted to do it again!

As I started back up the hill, carrying my wing, I was hot and sweating, but I didn't care. Finally I was learning how to fly this damned thing!

At the top of the hill, Marty told me that I'd been a little slow to release the front risers after the wing was overhead. He suggested that instead of grasping the front risers with my hands, I simply allow the front risers to rest loosely on my open palms, between my thumb and index finger. He told me to use my open palms to *push* the front risers up into the air, rather than grasping them and pulling them. That way I would automatically release the risers at the correct time.

I laid out my wing again, and started to launch. The new "open-palm" riser technique worked perfectly! It made it impossible for me to forget to release the front risers after the wing was overhead. The result was a perfect launch and a perfect flight.

I made two more perfect flights that day. My confidence level increased about five hundred percent. Marty was a fantastic instructor. He was exactly what I'd been looking for.

At about noon, the thermal activity became too great for students to safely fly. The smooth, early-morning air was starting to get bumpy and turbulent, and the wind speed had picked up a little. While the rest of us took a break, Marty put on an aerial ballet. First he pulled his wing into the air, stabilized it overhead, then started to play with it. He pulled the brakes slightly, and was instantly lifted several feet into the air. He released the brakes and slowly settled back onto the ground. For several minutes he literally leaped and soared like a gazelle, with a performance that a Russian ballet dancer couldn't have matched. With the wing making him virtually weightless, Marty looked like Peter Pan in the air. The rest of us watched in open-mouthed amazement. We had no idea that this sort of aerial acrobatics was even possible! I thought I'd been doing good to keep the wing flying overhead for several seconds. But Marty could keep his wing flying overhead, under total control, for as long as he liked! This was a skill I wanted to learn!

I slept very well that night. A load of problems and a ton of self-doubt had all been erased in the space of a couple of hours. So far I was very, very pleased and impressed with the quality of instruction I'd received from North American Paragliding.

The next morning we returned to Watt Canyon. But now there was a problem. The wind was blowing in the wrong direction. It was flowing down the east side of the hill, rather than up.

"No problem," said Marty. "We'll simply fly the west side."

The west side of the hill was steeper than the east side, but after my excellent flights yesterday, I had no fear of it. We laid out our wings, and one after another we launched. The wind was a little stronger, and the flights lasted a little longer, but everything was fine.

No sooner was the last man safely down on the ground, than the wind finally switched direction. We gathered up our wings and trekked over to the east side of the hill. The previous day the Watt Canyon hill had looked like a vertical cliff, roughly the size of Mt. Everest. Now it looked like a speed bump in the road. What a difference a day of good instruction had made!

I turned around to look at Marty who was checking the wind speed. "We can't fly here," I told him.

"Why not?" he asked.

"There ain't no hill!"

Marty just shook his head in disgust, and muttered something about "student pilots."

We laid out our wings and started flying. I managed to make three good flights before the wind started to pick up. Then we packed up our gear and returned to the store where Marty delivered some more information on basic paragliding theory. Now we had some practice to go with our theory. I was very pleased.

It was the end of the two-day introductory course for the Seattle guys, and they were going home. They planned to return the following spring to continue their instruction. I bid them good-bye. They had been a great bunch of guys to fly with. Since I had signed up for the complete lesson package, I was eager for my next lesson.

Four days later I was back at the North American store, looking at half a dozen new faces; one of them female. It was 8:00 a.m., and Marty told us that we were going to Saddle Mountain for a high flight. I asked Marty how high. "Two thousand vertical feet," he answered. Damn! That was as high as Mount Wilson. Immediately some of my old fear came seeping back.

It was a longer drive out to Saddle Mountain. The mountain was actually a very long ridge, rising from the sand and scrub. The treeless ridge climbed almost two thousand feet above the surrounding plain. And it was steep! In many places it was nearly vertical, with numerous rocky spires that rose from the side of the ridge like gigantic teeth. The wooded slopes of Mount Wilson looked harmless by comparison. One would definitely not want to crash into the side of Saddle Mountain.

On the other hand, the landing zone was a dream come true, consisting of at least fifty acres of soft sand, with very few trees or bushes. Before we started the drive up the mountain, Marty put out a blue panel marker, and traced a circle, fifty feet in diameter, around the marker. This would permit us to practice our spot landings. Five spot landings were needed for a P2 rating, and a landing inside the circle would qualify as a spot landing.

The front face of Saddle Mountain was much too steep for roads. We returned to the main highway and drove for miles until we turned onto a road that switchbacked up the back side of Saddle Mountain. The gravel road was rough and unimproved. In places it was washed out. I doubt that anything other than a four-wheel drive vehicle could have made it. Except for sagebrush, there was no vegetation.

After a long drive, we approached the top of the mountain. There were several communications towers that took advantage of Saddle's commanding view of the area. Finally we topped out on the ridge, and all that I could see directly ahead of us was thousands of feet of empty space. Just as I was about to yell a warning, Marty suddenly swerved to the left and pulled to a stop.

We climbed out of the vehicle and beheld a spectacular view of the Columbia River and its basin. The land seemed to stretch away for a hundred miles in all directions. The view alone was worth the long trip.

The top of Saddle Mountain was bare rock and loose rubble. Easy to lose your footing. I was glad that I had worn my heavy-duty paraboots.

Although Saddle Mountain was smoothly rounded on top, and sloped away gently to the south, to the north it steepened very rapidly. If a paraglider pilot were to crash into the steep face of Saddle, it was very unlikely that he would survive. After the crash, he would likely tumble for hundreds of feet down the near-vertical rock face.

Were we really ready for this, I wondered? I'd had eight good flights on the training hill at Watt Canyon. True, I was starting to wish for something a little higher, but this was FORTY TIMES as high, and seemed much more treacherous.

Still, a flight was a flight. Once you were airborne, did it really matter if you had fifty feet, or five thousand feet, beneath you? It was actually safer to be higher. Also, I'd already made two flights from Mount Wilson, and in terms of vertical feet, it was just as high as Saddle Mountain.

The difference was that Saddle Mountain looked about ten times higher than Mt. Wilson. Probably due to the absence of trees. We started to lay out our wings. I was getting pretty good at layout, but I still liked to have Marty give my layout his blessing before I launched. Marty reminded us to take our wing sacks and water bottles with us when we launched. We'd need the sacks to pack up our wings on the ground. Since it would take about an hour for the van to return to the LZ, and pick us up, we'd need water to drink while we were waiting.

As I was stuffing my wing sack and water bottle into the back pocket of my flight harness, I noticed that the guy next to me, a fellow named Jerry, was stuffing a battery-powered Dustbuster into the back pocket of his flight harness. Since that was a rather odd piece of equipment to take flying, I asked him why he was carrying it.

"Comes in handy after landing," was all he would say. I tried not to laugh.

Why in the world would anyone want to carry a vacuum cleaner on a paraglider flight? What in the world could he use it for?

As some of the other students launched ahead of me, I studied them very carefully. With the wind blowing almost ten miles per hour, they lifted off after only a few steps. They didn't even get close to the part of the mountain that dropped away steeply. Still, if an abort was necessary, it would be better to do it as soon as possible.

As I prepared to launch, I realized that I wasn't the same pilot that I'd been, only a month earlier. Although I was still pretty scared, my eight good launches had made me confident that I could do it.

When I was ready to launch, Marty asked me if I was confident that I could land safely even if my radio failed during the flight. I told him that I was. I backed up a few steps, then started my run forward. The wing snapped up. As I'd done earlier, I pulled a little too much brake trying to prevent a wing surge, and it stopped my forward progress as though I had run into a brick wall. I eased off the brake a bit, and found that I could run again. I plunged forward into the abyss. The ground very quickly started to steepen, and I was airborne after just a few steps. I soared out into empty space.

I flew straight out from the mountain, and waited several seconds before trying to slide back into my seat. I wanted to put plenty of distance between myself and the mountain before I even thought about taking my hands off the steering toggles. When I was certain all was well, I let go of my steering lines and used both hands to slide back into my seat. Much better! Then I re-acquired the steering line toggles and got down to the business of flying my wing.

What a view! There was just me, hanging in my harness, with the whole world spread out at my feet. I heard Marty's voice over my radio, instructing me to make a right turn. I gently pulled the right steering toggle, and the big wing swung to the right. That left me flying parallel, along the gigantic ridge that was Saddle Mountain. It was such an incongruity to be flying effortlessly over terrain that was so rough that no human being on foot could traverse it. Several hundred feet below me, the wreck of an old car clung to the side of the mountain. How in the world had it gotten there?

Then Marty instructed me to make a left turn. I pulled the left toggle and held the turn until I had completely reversed direction. Now Saddle Mountain was on my left. Far below me I could see the colorful wings of the other pilots who had launched before me. One of them was in the process of landing. He was trying to land within the circle, to qualify for a spot landing, but missed the edge of the circle by just a few feet. Better luck next time. I wondered how close I would get?

Marty radioed for me to make a 360 degree turn. I did so. "Very nice," Marty radioed back, then he moved on to the next student. Unless I started to do something stupid or dangerous, Marty would let me make the rest of the flight on my own.

For the next six minutes I zigzagged back and forth down the face of Saddle Mountain. Although I still had my heart set on learning to fly with my engine, I decided there was something magical about unpowered paragliding. Except for the whisper of the wind in the rigging and an occasional rustle of fabric from the wing overhead, the only thing that broke the silence was the joyful shout of a distant pilot.

At approximately five hundred feet, I started setting up for my landing . I headed away from the mountain and across a small creek, then turned around to start my final approach. There were two wings ahead of me, and two more in the sky above me. Damn, but they were beautiful in flight!

There were patches of small scrubby trees at the far end of the LZ. I wanted to make certain that I didn't land in them, so I flew over them with plenty of altitude. The landing circle was now dead ahead. I made sure both brakes were fully released so the wing was flying at top speed (the safest way to land). As I got near the ground, a strange thing happened. Some lift seemed to come out of nowhere, and I suddenly realized that I was going to pass over the landing circle about fifty feet higher than I had wanted. Could there be warm air rising from the sand, giving me extra lift? Or had I simply misjudged the approach angle? Oh well, no harm done. There was plenty of open space beyond my original target. Maybe next time I would be able to land inside the circle.

I swooped down over the surface of the sand, and pulled down both brake lines to flare the wing. Suddenly I realized that I was still about twelve feet in the air, and that was much too high for a landing. Instantly I eased off the flare a bit, and waited for the wing to lose some more altitude. A couple of seconds later I flared again, and touched down with only a small bump.

As I stood on the sand, congratulating myself on a wonderful flight, I made the mistake of simply releasing my brakes. Instantly the wing dived forward, ahead of me, and plunged its nose into the sand.

"Nice going, Hotshot," I told myself. I was supposed to keep the brakes pulled down, spin around, and collapse the wing onto the sand, on its tail. Now it was lying on the ground, nose first, and those open cells had each just scooped up a big load of sand. Damn!

I gathered up my wing and started to carry it over to the packing area that had been set up on a nearby grassy strip. The pilots who had launched ahead of me were busy folding up their wings and stuffing them back into their sacks. We spent a few minutes swapping experiences, then I got busy on my own wing.

First I had to get the sand out of the cells. I picked up the trailing edge of the wing and gave each cell a good shake. That got rid of most of the sand, but the curved nose of the wing prevented some of the sand from falling out; even when the wing was held upside down. There was nothing to do but shake the sand down into the nose of the wing, then brush each cell out by hand. I knew it was going to take some time. I'd never counted the cells, but I knew there were a lot of them. Somewhere around thirty.

The job was slow going, and the sun was hot. Now I knew why pilots were careful not to let their wings dig into the sand, nose first. Next time I'd be paying attention to the wing, even after I landed. Another valuable lesson from the School of Hard Knocks.

As I was scooping the sand out of the cells, I heard a throat being cleared behind me. I looked over my shoulder to see Jerry. He was holding up his Dustbuster and grinning at me. "Wanna borrow my vacuum cleaner?" I gave Jerry my most sincere nod. He cheerfully handed over his little battery-powered Godsend. In only a few minutes, the job was done. "I see why you carry that thing," I told Jerry as I returned his miniature vacuum cleaner.

"Yep," said Jerry. "They laugh when they see me putting it in my pack, and then they're very happy to use it later."

About an hour later, Marty and the van pulled into the packing area. We loaded up and went up the mountain for another flight. This time I was second in line to launch. It was another fantastic flight, and it lasted about eight minutes. During this flight, Marty had me make a turn by pulling on the rear riser instead of the normal steering line. It was a backup technique, in the unlikely event that my regular steering line got detached, leaving me with no way to steer. Good tip to remember.

Even though my second flight lasted as long as the first, it seemed much shorter. Already I was starting to crave more airtime. Of course that was one of the reasons why I'd bought the motor; so I could stay up as long as I liked.

Once again I tried for a spot landing. Since I'd overshot the landing circle the last time, I figured this time I'd go farther out before turning to land. Naturally I overcorrected, and landed about one hundred feet short of the landing circle. This was obviously going to take some practice. But at least this time I kept my wing under control after landing. The instant I touched the ground, I spun around and carefully collapsed the wing onto the sand, tail first. From the top of Saddle Mountain, Marty radioed his congratulations.

Eighteen long days passed before I got to fly again. The wind and weather just didn't want to cooperate. But finally, on October 12, I was back in Ellensburg again. The nights were getting colder. Winter wasn't far off. I wondered if I would have time to finish my P2 rating before North American Paragliding shut down for the winter.

As before, we were all gathered together in the store, waiting for Mike Eberle to tell us where we were going to fly today. We were all hoping for Saddle Mountain again. Finally Mike came out of his office where he'd been checking the weather on the Internet. Saddle Mountain was a no-go, he said, because of the wind direction. Instead, we were going to the Yakima Bowl. *Yuck!*

Less than an hour later we were all standing next to the van, looking out at the broad expanse of the Yakima Bowl. Mike distributed the radios, then we slung on our packs and headed out. Even though the summer heat had faded, climbing the Bowl was still hard work. The first half of the climb wasn't too bad. We retraced the steps that I'd taken on my first visit to the Bowl. But then the Bowl got much steeper. Most of the other students were in better shape than me, and they soon passed me on the trail. I was still struggling up the trail, just a few minutes from the top, when I heard a shout directly overhead. The first student had already launched, and I saw a giant shadow passing overhead. I stuck out my thumb in the time-honored tradition, asking for a lift, then resumed trudging up the trail.

When I arrived at the top of the Bowl, I was breathing hard and covered with sweat. This was exactly the sort of exertion I'd hoped to avoid. I dropped my pack on the ground, and flopped down after it.

The view was quite nice from the top of the Bowl. The huge, open amphitheater lay at my feet, with the swiftly flowing Yakima River as a lovely backdrop. I enjoyed the view for about ten minutes until my breathing returned to normal.

I started to lay out my wing. Not only was I eager to fly, but it was positively chilly up here. I wanted to get back down to the sheltered bottom of the Bowl, where it was warmer and out of the wind. I put on my helmet and gloves, switched on my radio, and clipped my radio to the side of my helmet. I clipped into my wing, made sure I was centered on my wing, and got ready to run.

The launch went okay, except for one moment when the wing seemed to twist a little bit sideways. But after just a few steps, I was airborne, and flying out into the open expanse of the Bowl. I waited until I was about one hundred feet away from the side of the Bowl, then I released my steering line toggles and slid back into my seat.

At that moment Mike Eberle's voice came over my radio. "I didn't want to alarm you earlier, and I don't want to alarm you now, but you're flying with a collapsed wing tip. Look overhead."

I looked up in surprise, to see my right wingtip folded under the rest of my wing. Only about three feet of the wing was folded under, and it was having virtually no effect on my flight performance. Undoubtedly it had happened during takeoff.

"You could ignore it," said Mike, "and it would probably pop out on its own, but why don't you go ahead and pump it out?" I grabbed my right steering line and give a long, quick pump. Instantly the wingtip straightened out and reinflated. My flying machine had been restored to 100% functionality.

I had hoped to catch some rising air near the edge of the Bowl, and maybe get in a little soaring, but the time I'd spent pumping out the collapsed wingtip had caused me to lose too much altitude. I was now below any possible source of lift, so there was nothing to do but ride down to the bottom and land.

But the trip down did not have to be dull. I flew along the side of the Bowl, following the contours of the land. I was seldom more than fifty feet from the swiftly moving earth, and it gave me a very heady sensation of speed. It was extremely enjoyable. Near the end of the Bowl, I turned and flew back along my earlier route. Mike radioed a warning not to get too close to the side of the Bowl, so I pulled away a bit.

As I came in to land, I headed for the middle of the Bowl and the blue marker panel that Mike had laid out in the middle of a fifty foot circle. Once again I managed to overfly the spot landing area. In fact I was so busy trying to land on the spot that I forgot to flare in time. I ended up making a rather fast touchdown. Even though I ran as fast as I could, it wasn't fast enough. I ended up making a slow forward fall, and rolled a few times in the dirt and sagebrush. Nothing was hurt, except for my pride.

I packed up my wing and started the long climb back up to the top of the Bowl. Now that the students were scattered all up and down the Bowl, I felt no peer pressure to keep moving toward the summit. Every few minutes I stopped and rested.

Eventually I regained the summit of the Bowl. Mike and his girlfriend, Kristin, were huddled under a tarp to shield them from the cold wind. I sat down to catch my breath, and managed to put my hand into a small cactus plant. Ouch!

Kristin spent the next twenty minutes pulling cactus spines out of my hand. When the last of the spines were out, my hand still stung. Kristin then told me to rub my hand across some rough lichens that were growing on a nearby rock. I did so, and was amazed to feel the stinging sensation instantly vanish! I looked at my hand, and it was like it had never touched the cactus. Remarkable! I have no idea how the lichen treatment worked, but it did.

With the wind increasing in strength, and the clouds rolling in to hide the sun, it was really getting cold up here. I felt myself starting to get chilled, and a bit dull-witted. I just wanted to get off this windy summit. I quickly got set up, and attempted to launch.

The wing came up fine in the high wind, but then, like a rookie, I forgot to apply some brake to keep it from overshooting. As I started to run downhill, the wing got completely ahead of me and crashed into the ground. Fortunately it happened very quickly, so I was able to stop my run before I had picked up much speed. Otherwise I might have fallen and gotten hurt.

I dragged my wing back to the top and prepared to launch again. Only now I was pumped up with adrenaline, and was much more alert. Mike helped me to lay out my wing, reminded me of the need to brake, and told me not to be in such a hurry. It was good advice.

My second launch attempt went much better. I soared out away from the summit, then turned and flew along the face of the Bowl. What a wonderful ride! If only I could make it last longer. But about three minutes later, the last of my altitude had been used up. I made a good landing at the bottom of the Bowl, but once again managed to miss the spot landing area. Maybe next time.

I dragged my wing and weary carcass back to the top of the Bowl for a third flight. This was going to be my last flight of the day. Some of the more energetic students had managed to get in five or six flights. One macho jock had managed to bag *seven* flights! He must have had legs and lungs like a steam locomotive.

At the summit of the Bowl, I surveyed the expanse of land below me with great satisfaction. Not only had I managed to get in two flights at the infamous Yakima Bowl, but I was also done with Bowl climbing for the day. I was looking forward to flying down, eating a sandwich, and sinking into the soft cushions of the van for the ride back to Ellensburg.

The wind had dropped to about seven miles per hour and had shifted direction slightly. I realized that I would need to make a crosswind launch. Fortunately I'd already had one experience with a crosswind launch at Watt Canyon, so I didn't expect to have any trouble with this one.

And I didn't. In fact, I seemed to catch some lift as I flew along the face of the Bowl, because this flight lasted nearly five minutes. Unfortunately, without a variometer, I couldn't pinpoint the exact location of the lift, and eventually I sank out below its level. Still, it was a fine ride. If only we could drive to the top, the Yakima Bowl would be a really nice place for training flights. But the landowner wouldn't permit driving, so it was necessary to hike if you wanted to fly.

With my altitude nearly exhausted, I once again headed for that elusive spot landing circle. I slid out of my harness and hung in the leg straps, preparing to touch down.

These last few flights had greatly increased my familiarity with my wing. It was starting to feel like a part of me. I was starting to develop a real "feel" for what the wing could do. As I looked ahead, I realized I was heading straight for the spot landing circle. In fact, I appeared to be heading directly for the bullseye!

What a way to end my flying day! I decided to go for it. I started feeding in slight corrections to my course and speed, keeping myself lined up on the blue panel marker. A couple of other students were on the ground, cheering me on. Finally I was only about twenty feet up, and just outside the perimeter of the circle. I let off the brakes to go to full speed for the landing. As I swooped down into the circle, I could almost touch the blue panel marker with my foot as I flared for my landing. I finally touched down about ten feet from the panel marker, but well within the circle.

I did it! My first spot landing! It was my thirteenth flight with North American Paragliding. Who said thirteen wasn't a lucky number?

Unfortunately, little did I know that it would also be my *last* lucky flight at the Yakima Bowl.

In Hindsight, What Would I have Done Differently?

If I had it to do over, I wouldn't have gone for my P2 paragliding rating. Mike Eberle's training was really excellent, and he ran a very safe operation, but my experience with North American Paragliding illustrates some of the fundamental differences between powered paragliding and unpowered paragliding.

The little training hill in Watt Canyon, and the lower slopes of the Yakima Bowl, were excellent places to learn to fly the wing. If I screwed up during the takeoff, there really wasn't much danger of serious injury. Bruises and scrapes were about the worst thing that could happen.

However all of that changed when I started flying at Saddle Mountain. This was NOT a gentle training hill. Not only was it nearly two thousand feet high, it was almost like flying off a cliff. The top of Saddle Mountain was a gentle rounded ridge, but the top very quickly fell away to a near-vertical slope of pure rock. If a student screwed up on the takeoff, he'd better hope that he hadn't yet reached the steep portion of the mountain, because a crash-landing on the steep portion of Saddle Mountain would almost certainly be fatal.

Of course this is the sort of risk that goes with unpowered paragliding. You must launch from high mountains, and these mountains are frequently very steep and rugged, with little room for error. By contrast, powered paragliding takes place from flat pastures, beaches, and other Very Safe Launching Areas. If you screw up a launch with a powered paraglider, falling down on the grass, and into a cow pie, is about the worst thing that can happen to you.

The point that I want to make is that if you go for your P2 paragliding rating, there are certain risks that you will have to take. On the other hand, if you forget about the P2 rating and simply learn to fly the motor, you will never be faced with risks such as Saddle Mountain. Why expose yourself to the very real dangers of unpowered paragliding if you don't have to? For the truth is, most injuries and fatalities in unpowered paragliding occur during takeoff. Powered paragliding completely avoids the risks associated with the rough terrain and bouncy air conditions that unpowered paraglider pilots are forced to face.

Chapter 9

I Get Ribbed

Nine days later it was time to fly again. Mike Eberle announced that the winds were favorable for Saddle Mountain, so that's where we were going to fly. Yay! We packed up the van and took off for Saddle.

An hour later, when we finally pulled into the parking area on top of Saddle Mountain, we discovered there was no wind, which was unusual for Saddle. We laid out our wings and got ready to launch. One pilot launched ahead of me, and then it was my turn. I grasped the steering lines and risers and started running. I could definitely feel the difference in the wing as it came up. With no wind, there was much less resistance. I stopped the wing's forward surge with a little brake, then eased off the brake and started running down the rocky slope.

I was not lifting off nearly as quickly as I'd done in the past. That was because there was no wind this time to give me free airspeed. ALL of the airspeed had to come from me. In the excitement and adrenaline of the launch, my time sense was greatly stretched. Seconds seemed like minutes. It felt like I was running endlessly down the mountain, waiting for the wing to pick me up. I could hear myself muttering, "Come on you sonofabitch! Fly!"

After what seemed like an eternity, I had run at least fifty feet down the mountain with no sign of lifting off. The mountain was getting very steep. If I ran much further, I'd quickly reach the point of no return, where the mountain would be so steep that stopping would be impossible. Then it would be fly, or fall. Suddenly I remembered a piloting tip that I'd gotten from someone. Pulling a little brake could give the wing extra lift during takeoff. I tugged on the brakes, and instantly felt myself lifting from the ground. It worked!

I flew out and away from the mountain, and slowly released my brakes for maximum flying speed. Then I let go of the steering toggles and slid back into my seat to get comfortable for the flight down to the LZ. Suddenly I heard Mike Eberle's voice in my helmet radio.

"We do not swear at our wing to make it fly. We do not call our wing a 'sonofabitch.' We *love* our wings, and we only say nice things to them, since our lives depend on them."

Hmm. Maybe he had a point.

We must have had some buoyant air the last time we flew at Saddle Mountain. Then the flights were lasting up to eight minutes. Now we were lucky to get five minutes. I came down for a fine landing, but still managed to miss the spot landing circle. Damn! Guess I needed more practice.

Later, as several of us were packing up our wings, Marty came in for a landing. Instead of landing out in the LZ, he appeared to be going for a landing right in the packing area. There was a gap, just big enough for a paraglider, between my wing and the wing of another pilot. As I watched in admiration (and amazement), Marty landed right between the two wings. He did it so perfectly that when his wing fell to the ground, it was lying exactly between the other two wings. I was impressed! Someday I hoped to be that good.

About an hour and a half later, we were back up on top of Saddle Mountain, ready for another flight. These flights were almost starting to seem routine. This time I made a perfect no-wind takeoff, and didn't even have to swear at my wing to get it to fly.

During my sled ride down to the ground, I heard a slight rustle in the wing fabric overhead, and looked up. Obviously I'd just flown through a bit of minor turbulence, just enough to give the wing a little shake. Nothing to worry about, except that I was suddenly aware that I was two thousand feet above the earth, with absolutely nothing to keep me there, but my wing. It was always important to remember that a paragliding wing was not a parachute, nor could it serve as one. It was a *flying wing*, and if it ceased to be a wing, then the pilot was going to fall like a rock.

It was very unlikely that my wing would collapse in the smooth air that we were flying in. Mike wouldn't let us fly if conditions were too turbulent. Nevertheless, it was possible, under rare circumstances, for a wing to collapse and be unrecoverable. In which case, only a reserve parachute would likely save the pilot's life. It was something to think about. Maybe it was time for me to get a reserve.

As it turned out, I barely got off the mountain in time. Less than ten minutes later, as I was standing on the ground in the LZ, watching the last of the wings launch, I saw a wing rise up into the air, hang there momentarily, then collapse. I watched intently for about fifteen minutes, waiting for the wing to rise again. It never did. Had the pilot fallen? Had he been injured?

Over an hour passed, and there was no sign of the wing or the van. Could Mike be rushing an injured pilot to the hospital? If so, we might be here for a while. We started to joke about sharing food and water, and building huts.

But finally the van arrived. We learned that the wind had suddenly reversed direction as the student began his takeoff run, forcing him to abort the launch. Mike and the student had waited a while for the wind to become favorable again, but finally were forced to give up. It was a poignant reminder of how the wind conditions could change in an instant, and why a paraglider pilot must always be aware of what the wind is doing.

I returned to Ellensburg three weeks later, but was greeted by bad weather. The whole Ellensburg valley was socked in with heavy fog. We drove up to the top of Saddle Mountain, hoping that the fog would lift as the morning wore on, but no such luck. The summit of Saddle Mountain was surrounded by an ocean of unbroken fog. It was like being on an island in the middle of an ocean. It was an eerie, beautiful scene, but it was also quite unflyable. Launching would be easy enough, but soon the pilot would descend into the heavy fog layer and would become hopelessly disoriented. He could easily end up flying into the side of the mountain.

In a spirit of helpfulness and goodwill, I offered to drive the van to the bottom of the mountain and honk the horn to provide a beacon for the other fliers to home in on, just like a foghorn for ships at sea.

My suggestion was brutally rejected.

Defeated, we returned to the store in Ellensburg. Mike announced that since we couldn't fly, we'd hold a reserve clinic instead. This would give us training in how to properly deploy a reserve parachute. It was part of the training for a P2 paraglider rating.

Throwing a reserve parachute while paragliding wasn't quite like throwing a reserve while skydiving. The paragliding reserve had no pilot chute to help pull the reserve canopy out. That's because paragliding reserves were normally deployed at very low speeds where pilot chutes would probably do little good. Instead, the reserve canopy was packed inside a deployment bag. When the pilot pulled the reserve handle, the nylon container opened, and out came the deployment bag with the reserve still packed inside. The pilot then threw the deployment bag away from him, to permit the lines to deploy. When the lines were fully stretched, the deployment bag popped open, and the reserve canopy came billowing out. It was a proven system that had saved many lives over the years.

We took turns hanging in a suspended harness from the ceiling and pulling the handle on a reserve trainer. The reserve trainer was just like a real reserve, except that the deployment bag was stuffed with rags, and didn't pop open when you threw it.

Before I left the store, I purchased a reserve parachute. It cost me $858, but it was a big reserve chute, and it would be large enough to lower both me and the PPG engine to the ground.

Four days later, on November 15, I was back at Ellensburg for some more flying. I now had fifteen flights with North American Paragliding, and I was getting close to the magic number of flights to qualify for my P2 rating. Of course I also needed four more spot landings to qualify, so I was eager to bag a couple of spot landings today.

We were all gathered in the store at 8:00 a.m., waiting for Mike Eberle to decide on our flying destination. The weather was much colder now. Shorts and tee shirts had given way to hats, gloves, and warm coats. Finally Mike came out of his office and announced that the winds were coming from the south, which meant that neither Saddle Mountain nor the Yakima Bowl would be suitable for flying today. Instead, we would try a place called Uptanum, where none of us students had ever flown before. Mike said that Uptanum had a good southern exposure, and frequently had good ridge soaring conditions. After launching, we might be able to stay aloft for an hour or two, before landing. *Yes!* We were all very excited at the prospect, since most of us had never soared before (at least not on solo flights).

Uptanum was to the west, in the foothills of the Cascade Mountains. We loaded up the gear and headed out of town in the van. It was a long winding drive up a network of Forest Service roads. In no time at all I was completely lost. But it was beautiful country, and the day was sunny and pleasant, even if a trifle cold. Several times we passed large, flat pastures that would be ideal launch sites for a powered paraglider. I was reminded again that all of this was just a means to an end. As soon as I got my P2 rating, I was going to learn to fly my engine.

The top of the ridge at Uptanum was rocky, but not as rocky as either Saddle

117

Mountain or the Yakima Bowl. The sides of the ridge were mostly grass. It looked like a great launching area, and the soaring conditions looked good. Even as we watched, a flock of crows were soaring and playing in the upwelling air.

There was just one little problem. During the time we drove up, the wind had done a complete reversal and was now coming from the north! Mike told us that it was not unheard of for the wind to do that at Uptanum. I asked Mike if this meant the wind would now likely be blowing from the north, in general, which would make Saddle Mountain flyable. He answered that Saddle was most likely still getting its wind from the south. Damn!

It was quite impossible to fly from Uptanum when the wind was blowing from the north. All we could do was wait, and hope that the wind would switch direction. So we waited. And waited. And waited. A couple of hours passed. Occasionally the wind would suddenly switch to the south, and our hopes would rise, but the wind always returned to the north a few minutes later. I felt like the sky gods were playing games with us. This was Parawaiting in its purest form. Waiting for the winds to cooperate.

Finally the wind eased around to the southwest. If it held, we might be able to launch from the far end of Uptanum ridge. We drove down to the end of the ridge and surveyed the scene. Yes, it was quite launchable here. The only problem was that we were now too far away to glide down to the regular Landing Zone for Uptanum. However we could easily land in a farmer's pasture, directly below the end of the ridge. Unfortunately we didn't have permission to land in the pasture. Kristin volunteered to fly down and ask permission. She would take a radio with her and let Mike know what the farmer said. If the farmer was agreeable, the rest of us would follow Kristin. If not, then all we could do was drive down and fetch Kristin back to the summit, then hope that the winds would change.

Kristin quickly laid out her wing and got into her flight suit. But just as she had the steering lines and risers in her hands, and was ready to launch, the fickle wind suddenly shifted back to the north! Launching from the ridge was once again impossible. Damn! Sadly we folded up Kristin's wing and put it away.

Finally Mike decided that we'd waited long enough. We piled into the van and said goodbye to the fickle winds of Uptanum. Maybe next time.

We spent a couple of hours driving all over the Ellensburg valley, looking for a place to fly. There were several other possible flying areas that Mike wanted to check. He admitted that they were long shots, but we were getting desperate.

Everyone wanted to fly!

But our luck remained bad. Every place that we visited was either fogged in, or else the wind was blowing from the wrong direction. In one spot, the clouds and temperature had combined to cover the entire area in a layer of thick frost. It looked like something out of a Christmas card, but it was quite unsuited for flying.

Finally our wandering course took us back though the Yakima River canyon. We followed the winding road along the Yakima River. Mike announced that we would stop at the Yakima Bowl and see if the wind had changed. Maybe we could get in a flight at the Bowl, just before sunset. *Ugh!* Another climb to the top of the Bowl. I thought I was done with that place forever.

At exactly 4:00 p.m. we rolled up to the Yakima Bowl, and everyone piled out. Mike checked the wind, and used his binoculars to check the windsocks on top of the Bowl. The north side of the Bowl had a favorable wind. If we hurried, we could get in one flight before sunset.

Now I was faced with a real quandary. I wanted to fly, but I didn't want to fly so badly that I was willing to race up the side of the Yakima Bowl, carrying my paraglider on my back. I'd rather wait for another day, when the winds were favorable for flying at Uptanum, or Saddle Mountain, where there was no need to hike. In other words, I was really spoiled.

On the other hand, I was paying $150 a day for instruction, and today counted as a paying day, whether I flew or not. If I didn't fly, then I would have completely wasted my money.

And then there was my macho male pride. Our group consisted of about half men and half women. All of the men were preparing to hike to the top. All of the women, except one, were staying behind. I didn't blame the women who had elected not to fly. It was going to be a fast, strenuous climb, carrying a heavy load. I could go up the hill with the men, or stay behind with the women. It was entirely my choice. No one was pressuring me in any way.

Once again, testosterone triumphed over common sense. I slung on my pack and struck out across the floor of the Bowl with the rest of the Macho Brigade. Meanwhile, the smart women remained back at the van, warm and comfortable, watching the latest installment of The Male Idiot Show.

All of us who were going to fly were in a big hurry. The sun would be setting soon, and as soon as it did, the wind would do its evening reverse, and the Bowl would quickly become unflyable.

Unfortunately the north side of the Bowl was not well suited for a high-speed ascent. Unlike the center of the Bowl, there was no well-worn trail. We had to pick our way over rocks and through sagebrush. Very soon I was dripping with sweat and panting hard. Several other students who started up after I did, passed me less than halfway up. How embarrassing. Oh to be twenty years younger!

Finally, after much heavy breathing and a gallon of sweat, I reached the top of the Bowl. The other pilots had already spread their wings and were preparing to fly. "Hurry up and get laid out and clipped in," Mike advised everyone. "The sun will be setting in just a few minutes, and anyone not in the air will have to walk down."

Oh no! There was *no way* I was going to walk back down this miserable pile of rock! I'd worked too hard to get up here. I was a pilot, and I was going to fly down! So even though I was still breathing hard, and my heart was pounding, I started to lay out my wing and get into my flight gear. I felt utterly exhausted, and just wanted to sit down and rest, but I was running out of time. So I forced myself to hurry. Big mistake. When you get in a hurry, that's when accidents happen.

One by one, the other pilots started to launch from the top of the Bowl. There was no wind, so it was necessary to run fast to get airborne. No problem. I'd already done two no-wind launches from the summit of Saddle Mountain. I knew what I was doing. Yeah, right.

Finally I was ready to launch. Only Mike and I and the lone female pilot were still on the summit. I was still out of breath, but in a few seconds I knew I would be relaxing in the air. I took the risers in my hands. I was trying to keep my rapid breathing from fogging my glasses. I glanced at the sun. It was just touching the horizon. Not much time left.

I started my takeoff run. The wing popped overhead, just as it always did. I started to feed in some brake to stop it from surging ahead of me. That's when I suddenly realized that I'd forgotten to put the brake lines in my hands! The brakes were still snapped into their keepers, on the risers. I was in the middle of launching, and I had no brakes!

Did I exercise my good training and common sense, and immediately abort the launch? No way! The testosterone had already taken over, and I was determined to get airborne on this attempt. Like a demented mountain goat, I went plunging down the side of the Bowl, trying to keep up with the unbraked wing, while at the same time struggling to get my brakes unsnapped from the risers. It was no good. The wing got ahead of me and dived toward the ground. I lost my balance, fell down, and rolled to a stop. The force of the fall knocked the wind out of me for a few seconds.

Slowly I sat up, covered in suspension lines, and feeling like a complete idiot. I had been in such a rush to launch that I had forgotten to put the brake lines in my hands! Then in a doubly stupid move, I had failed to abort the takeoff as soon as I realized that I didn't have hold of my brakes. Instead, like a complete idiot, I continued to run, trying to salvage the launch, until I fell down. I was lucky that I hadn't broken anything. The combination of forgetting the brake lines, and not aborting when I should have, easily qualified as my dumbest paragliding stunt of all time.

Fortunately there was still time for me to be an even *bigger* idiot.

About fifty feet above and behind me, still on the summit, Mike was shouting down to me to ask if I was okay.

Yes, I called back. Nothing broken. I just forgot my brakes. Mike told me to drag my wing back up to the top. As I gathered up my wing, our lone female pilot took to the air. It was a perfect no-wind takeoff. I was quite jealous.

I managed to stagger back up to the top of the Bowl. Mike was eager to get launched himself, so he helped me prepare quickly for my next attempt. The sun was starting to slide below the horizon. We were almost out of time.

If I had thought I was exhausted before, it was nothing compared to what I was feeling now. The launch attempt, and crash, had drained the last of my energy reserves. I felt like a walking zombie. My brain felt like it had shut down. I was simply going though the motions of getting ready for the launch. All I wanted to do was get off this damned pile of rock!

With my risers and my brake lines in my hands, I started my takeoff run again. Once again the wing came up and shot overhead. I pulled some brake to stop the wing from surging ahead of me, and once again went racing down the rocky hillside as fast as I could run, waiting for the wing to pick me up.

I almost made it.

But my brain was so fuzzed from fatigue that I failed to pay sufficient attention to my wing. I failed to pull enough brake. Once again the wing got ahead of me and dived toward the ground. I tried to stop my headlong plunge down the hill, but I was going too fast. Before I could slow down, I tripped and fell. My left side smashed heavily into the rocky ground, and I fell on a small rock about the size of a baseball. Instantly I felt a sudden, stabbing pain in my lower left rib.

I lay on the ground, dazed. This time I couldn't get up. When I tried to move, my chest hurt. I tried to wish the pain away, but it refused to leave. I realized that there would be no more flying for me today.

Mike was at my side just a few seconds later. "Are you okay," he asked.

I nodded. "Just had the wind knocked out of me. But that's it. I'm walking down."

Mike nodded. "I think that's a good idea. But you need to get packed up as quickly as possible or you'll get caught by the darkness." He was right. Neither of us had brought a flashlight. Once the setting sun had faded, that was it for the light. Negotiating a descent of the Yakima Bowl, in the dark, would be extremely difficult, if not impossible.

Slowly I gathered up my wing and trudged back up to the top. Mike helped me pack up the wing. His own wing was still spread out on the ground. He was ready to take off. "Can you make it down okay?" he asked.

"I think so," I answered. "I'll take it slow."

Moments later, Mike was in the air. As he soared out over the Bowl, he even managed to locate some lift, and soared for several minutes. The Stinker!

I was now completely alone on the summit. The sun had slid out of sight, and it was getting chilly. It was also getting dark and I still had to climb down the side of a five hundred foot high amphitheater. I slung on my pack and started picking my way down through the rocks and sagebrush. Not only did I feel like an abject failure, but every time I took a step I felt a stabbing pain in my lower left rib. I was starting to suspect that I'd broken a rib.

Slowly I worked my way down the side of the amphitheater. I was starting to get some strength back, but my rib was still hurting. Half an hour later I was about two thirds of the way down. At least I was now past the steepest portion of the descent. If I lost the light now, I could probably find my way out to the road without falling down and breaking something else.

Suddenly I saw a figure coming through the sagebrush toward me. It was Mike Eberle. "Can I give you a hand?" he asked. I gratefully relinquished my pack to him. Now I only had to carry myself. We discussed my accident as we made our way toward the van.

It was my own damn fault, of course. In perfect hindsight I could see that I should never have rushed my takeoff preparations. In aviation there is *never* a reason to hurry (unless you're being shot at). I should have stopped to rest after I reached the summit. And if that left me insufficient time to launch, then so be it. Better to walk down than to risk an accident.

But what was really disgusting was that I had screwed up *twice*. After blowing one launch and falling down, I didn't have enough sense to quit while I was ahead (and uninjured). Oh no! I had to go back up and try again! I had to keep trying until I got hurt and was forced to quit. Stupid! Really stupid!

At the van, the rest of the gang was sympathetic to my accident. There was a lot of good-natured teasing about my unorthodox launch technique. I acknowledged my mistake, and advised the rest of them to learn from my bad judgment.

Back in Ellensburg, everyone went to a local restaurant for dinner. Lots of good food and good fellowship. But not for me. All I wanted to do was return to my motel room, fall into bed, and be thoroughly miserable. My rib was really starting to hurt.

Back in the motel, I stretched out on the bed, trying to find a position where it didn't hurt. For the next four or five hours I lay on the bed in an animal-like torpor, only partly conscious. I could hear the sound on the television, but the words made no sense. I was probably in shock from the accident.

That night was pure hell. I would get to sleep, then be awakened by a stabbing pain in my left rib when I rolled over. Later the next day, a visit to a medical clinic confirmed my own diagnosis–a broken rib. Fortunately the x-rays showed that the rib was not out of place, and there was no danger of a punctured lung. The doctor said he could prescribe some pills for the pain, but that was about it. Strapping ribs had proven to be mostly useless, and had largely fallen out of favor. About all I could do was wait for my rib to heal. The doctor said it would take about six to eight weeks. By the time my rib had healed, the flying season would be over. There was nothing to do now but go home.

Postscript: The rest of the gang went flying the next day. They went back to Uptanum, where the wind and lift were perfect. Naturally everybody got to soar. Some flights lasted for more than an hour. And I had to miss it. All because I didn't know when to quit. Damn! Damn! Damn!

Sometimes Life really sucks.

In Hindsight, What Would I have Done Differently?

During the next two months I had plenty of time to think about what had happened. Obviously, in hindsight, I should have skipped the last flight. It wasn't worth it. There just wasn't time to make a slow, leisurely climb up the Bowl, and fly. So I rushed it, and I got hurt. I can't even say I wasn't warned. After falling down once, and surviving, I tried it again, and this time I did get hurt. I should have known better than to try to fly in a state of exhaustion, with my brain fuzzed and fogged from fatigue. Stupid!

Another hard-won lesson from the School of Hard Knocks.

Chapter 10

California Dreamin'

My accident at the Yakima Bowl had been a wake-up call. The real question was what to do once my rib had healed. Was there any point in going back to Ellensburg for more flights in an unpowered paraglider? One of the reasons I'd bought the engine was to avoid having to make risky takeoffs from rough, rocky mountains. I'd mastered the art of forward launching the wing (at least while running downhill). I knew how to fly, and how to land. I needed a few more spot landings for my P2 rating, but did I really need to keep spending time and money, just to get my P2 rating? I didn't think so. The P2 rating was for unpowered paragliding. In the last few months I'd learned that powered paragliding, and unpowered paragliding, were two very different animals. Much of what I'd learned in unpowered paragliding did not really transfer to powered paragliding. Unpowered paragliding primarily teaches you to fly off mountains, and I wouldn't be doing that with my engine.

One problem with the P2 rating was that it didn't give the student very much ground handling time. I'd learned just enough to get the wing off the ground, and to keep it airborne long enough to run down a mountain and take off. That's about all an unpowered paragliding pilot really needs to know about ground handling. But a powered paragliding pilot's ground handling skills must be much more highly developed. In fact, a PPG pilot needs to have damn-near perfect ground handling skills if he is to be able to inflate a wing on level ground, in calm air, while carrying a seventy pound engine on his back. It's not a difficult skill to learn, but it *is* demanding. You had to do it right, or you'd never get airborne.

Another problem with the P2 rating was that it took a long time to get. Good flying days could be few and far between, especially in the non-summer months.

To make an unpowered paraglider flight, the weather has to be good and the winds must be blowing in just the right direction, within a certain speed range. Many variables have to come together at the same time. Parawaiting and Paradriving are two very real facts of life in the unpowered paragliding world. I could spend an entire weekend away from home, and I was lucky if I got in two flights. Thus my flying progress had been very slow and expensive. Flying my engine, I could get in more flights in two *days* than I could in two *months* going the unpowered PG route. With a powered paraglider, any flat stretch of ground was a launching area, and it didn't matter which way the wind was blowing because you could always take off directly into the wind.

I decided that it was time to learn to fly the motor. I didn't regret my unpowered PG flight career. I had learned a lot. I had learned how to launch, fly, and land my wing. I'd gained a lot of confidence in my flying abilities. But it was time to move on.

While my rib was healing, I took a long, hard look at the various powered paragliding instructors who were available. I now had a much better idea of what I was looking for, and what questions to ask. There were several good instructors, but one in particular had caught my attention several months earlier. He was Hugh Murphy, of San Luis Obispo, California. He ran a PG/PPG school called Surf The Sky Paragliding. I gave him a call and we talked for a long time.

It was obvious that Hugh loved the sport of powered paragliding. That was the first thing I was looking for; someone whose interest went beyond just making a buck. Hugh answered all of my questions, and I couldn't trip him up on anything. He knew his stuff. Hugh explained the importance of good ground handling for successful powered paragliding. Since San Luis Obispo was located on the shore of the Pacific Ocean, and was blessed with gentle, consistent winds, Hugh told me that he would have me spend a week on the beach doing nothing but learning to ground handle the wing. Yes! That was the approach I was looking for. It had become obvious to me that good ground handling was everything when it came to successful powered paragliding.

Hugh explained that we would take my instruction one step at a time, moving on only when I was thoroughly comfortable at the current level. He pointed out that the worst thing you could do with a new student was to load him up with several new tasks to master at once. Yes! That exactly agreed with my own unfortunate experience the first time I had tried to fly with the motor. This guy was sounding better all the time! Hugh also pointed out that the ocean beach was the best place in the world to learn to ground handle a paraglider wing. The wind on the beach was steady, reliable, and smooth. Hugh explained that it was like standing in a wind tunnel. You could kite the wing overhead and keep it there for as long as you liked. You could get hours of good ground handling time, instead of mere minutes elsewhere, where the wind was not so steady.

Hugh also pointed out that if I needed some additional flight training, there were sand dunes nearby that were perfect for the job. True, you had to walk up to the top, but the dunes were only about a hundred feet high. And best of all, if you fell down, the sand was very soft. No rocks! My broken rib immediately voted yes!

I discussed my paragliding wing with Hugh. He agreed that the A5 Sport was a good wing, but was a bit too much for a beginner. My broken rib agreed with him. Hugh suggested that I buy a Pro Design Compact wing. The Compact was very easy to inflate, and it did not need to be braked during launching. It just shot up overhead, and stayed there. This was very surprising to me. I thought all wings had to be braked during launching to keep them from overshooting and *whumping* into the ground in front of the pilot. Apparently this was not true. If I had been flying a Compact, I wouldn't have had to worry about braking the wing during launching. I could have just pulled it into the air and launched. With a more suitable wing, I probably wouldn't have broken my rib at the Yakima Bowl.

Hugh said that none of his students had ever gotten hurt, or even damaged their equipment, while under his instruction. I liked the sound of that. His opinion was that if one of his students got hurt, then he hadn't done his job properly. That sounded mighty good, coming from an instructor!

Hugh suggested that I hang on to my A5 Sport wing. It was a faster wing than the Compact, and I could use it on windy days to get better wind penetration. But the Compact would be better for learning, and would function like a rock-solid tugboat for those days when the air was a little rough. The Compact would be more resistant to collapse than the A5.

It didn't take me long to decide that Hugh Murphy was the man I wanted to teach me to fly my powered paraglider. By the end of the year, my rib was pretty well healed. I started making plans to travel to California to train with Hugh. But El Niño had other plans. Storm after storm pummeled the state of California. It looked like half the state was washing away, and the other half was a disaster area. Since I didn't want to sit in an expensive motel room, day after day, waiting for the weather to clear, I decided to wait for the cycle of bad weather to end. Finally, near the end of February, Hugh reported a good weather forecast and I immediately made plans to leave for San Luis Obispo.

Which, of course, caused the Practical Joke Department to take a renewed interest in me.

On March 4, I left for California. My new Pro Design Compact wing was in the trunk of the car. Next to it was my engine, chained to one of the trunk hinges for added security. I had removed the cage and propeller, and had carefully packed them away.

But while the equipment was ready, I wasn't. About a week before I was scheduled to leave, I got hit with a mild case of the flu. Although it only lasted a couple of days, it caused me to start my trip to California in a weakened condition.

It was a long drive to California. When I stopped at a motel, I always parked the car directly in front of my room. If anyone tried to break into the trunk, I would hopefully wake up and hear them. It wasn't really practical to unpack the engine from the trunk and take it into the room with me. I'd found it impossible to get any kind of traveling insurance on my PPG engine. At home, the engine was sort of protected by my homeowner's insurance, but out on the road it was fair game for any freelance Socialist who wanted to share my wealth.

I finally arrived in San Luis Obispo, late at night, after about fourteen hours of hard driving. I had managed to misplace the main highway while coming over the last stretch of mountains, and had ended up wandering for some time over a very lonely mountain road, hoping that my gasoline would last long enough to get me back to civilization. Fortunately it did.

After a bit of searching, I found the Howard Johnson motel where I planned to stay for the next two weeks. The room was small, but comfortably furnished. There was just enough room, in one corner, to hold the PPG engine. I often wondered what the maid thought of that weird-looking contraption as she tidied up the room every day.

I was scheduled to meet with Hugh Murphy at 10:30 the next morning, at the motel. I woke up at 8:00 a.m., and made some coffee. I felt very peculiar. My body seemed to weigh a ton. I hadn't slept very well the night before. I was still shaking off the last of the flu, and my lower back was giving me some pain. It was a major effort even to stand up in the shower.

After getting dressed, I walked to the restaurant next door to get some breakfast. The waitress brought me an enormous plate of fried eggs and hashbrown potatoes. Normally I would have relished them, but today I could hardly eat a bite. Something was very, very wrong. Sweat was pouring down my face, and my heart was starting to race. I was having trouble catching my breath. I couldn't figure out what was wrong with me. This certainly wasn't the flu. In fact it was like nothing I'd ever experienced before.

Unable to eat, I paid the bill and made my way back to my room. I lay down on the bed, hoping that whatever was afflicting me would go away. It seemed to be coming in cycles. I would start to feel better, and then the terrible sensation would wash over me again. All I knew for certain was that something was terribly, terribly wrong with me. It felt like some fundamental part of me was no longer working.

Could I be having a heart attack? I didn't know. I was 47 years old, about twenty pounds overweight, and not in the best of physical condition. All I knew was that I was starting to get pretty scared. Finally I decided that if I was going to have a heart attack, the best place to have it was in the Emergency Room at the local hospital. I walked down to the front desk and told the desk clerk that I needed to go to the hospital. Immediately one of the hotel workers, a fellow named Michael, offered to drive me there. Fortunately the hospital was just a few miles away.

On the way to the hospital, Michael told me that a bunch of first-class heart surgeons had recently fled Los Angeles and had opened up a practice in San Luis Obispo. He told me how he had recently had open-heart surgery and was now doing just fine. I suppose his words were about as reassuring as anything could be, given the circumstances.

At the hospital emergency room I handed over my insurance card and told the desk attendant that I thought I might be having a heart attack. Zip! Off with the clothes, on with the gown, and into the Emergency Room. A doctor immediately checked my heart with his stethoscope, asked me some questions, and ordered an EKG. While the orderly was hooking up the wires to my chest, another nurse hooked me up to a heart monitor.

The digital readout on the heart monitor indicated that my pulse was 120 beats per minute. The sweat was now pouring off me in rivers. Although I was still badly frightened, I was reassured by my hospital surroundings. If I was really going to have a heart attack, this was certainly the best place in the world to have it!

The nurse who was hooking up the heart monitor asked me what I was doing in San Luis Obispo. I told her, and she asked me some questions about paragliding. I told her how I'd broken my rib in a paragliding accident several months earlier. She told me about a hang glider that had recently crashed, farther down the coast, killing the pilot. I reflected on the irony of having come to San Luis Obispo to learn to fly my PPG, and ending up in the hospital before I could even start my training. Obviously I wasn't going to be doing any flying for a long, long time. Instead of training with Hugh Murphy, I was simply fighting to stay alive. Was there a curse on that damned PPG engine? First a broken propeller, then a broken rib, and now a damaged heart. Was something trying to keep me out of the air?

But I wasn't thinking too much about learning to fly my PPG. When you're convinced that you're staring Death in the face, it tends to reorient your thinking. You start to think about all the things you haven't done yet.

It's not fair! It's too early for me to check out! There's still so much I want to do! If there is a God, please get me out of this!

The EKG machine started to spit out a strip of paper covered with squiggly lines. The doctor studied the paper, asked me some more questions, then leaned back in his chair.

"Good news, Mr. Wolf. You're definitely not having a heart attack."

At that moment, I learned a whole new meaning for the word "relief."

"The problem is," the doctor continued, "I don't know what *is* wrong with you. So we're going to take some blood and urine, and do all the usual tests. Meanwhile I just want you to relax. Try to get your heartbeat down below 100."

For the next hour or so, I lay on the bed in the Emergency Room, thinking about what had just happened. I had plenty of time to think about what I'd done with my life so far, and what I still wanted to do with it. It's amazing how a brush with death can clear your mind and focus your perspective.

I watched the digital readout on the heart monitor. My heartbeat was slowly returning to normal. I had stopped sweating and was starting to feel more like my old self. It was the most wonderful feeling in the world! Whoever said that if you have your health, you have everything, wasn't kidding. I asked a nurse for something to read, and she brought me a copy of *Glamour* magazine. It was all they had. Sigh.

Finally the doctor returned with the lab test results, all of which were normal. Other than being a few pounds overweight, the doctor told me that I was in excellent physical condition for a man my age, which surprised the hell out of me. Apparently those workouts on the exercise bike were finally paying off.

So what was wrong with me? The doctor had no idea. He recommended that I take it easy for a day or two, and see my own doctor when I got home if any of the symptoms ever returned.

After the doctor had left, the nurse spoke privately to me. She was convinced that I'd simply had an anxiety attack. She pointed out that I hadn't flown a paraglider in five months, and the last time I'd flown, I'd broken a rib and suffered a lot of pain. "I think your subconscious was revolting against the idea of flying again," said the nurse. "The fear of flying caused your heart to start racing, you started sweating, and since you had no conscious reason for these symptoms, you thought you were having a heart attack and you started scaring yourself to death."

Actually, that seemed like a pretty good explanation to me. Amazingly enough, I now felt fine. I called the motel and asked Michael to come and pick me up. Back at the motel, I tipped him twenty bucks for giving me a ride to the hospital. Michael had saved me a very expensive ambulance ride. I returned to my motel room, called Hugh Murphy, and told him I was ready for my first lesson. If my subconscious had earlier fought the idea of going paragliding again, it now seemed to have changed its mind.

The human mind is a strange and wonderful thing. I had just gone through the weirdest (and scariest) three hours of my life.

Hugh arrived about twenty minutes later. He was a thin, wiry little guy, but I'm over six feet tall, and almost everyone looks little to me. Hugh was very friendly, and in excellent shape. He'd be an easy man for a couch potato like me to hate, if he wasn't such a likable guy. We chatted about my temporary heart attack for a few minutes, then I grabbed my wing and we headed for the beach.

Now that I was back among the living, I had time to examine my surroundings as we drove to the beach. San Luis Obispo was a California coastal town, about halfway between Los Angeles and San Francisco. It still had a small-town atmosphere and flavor, but the wealthy refugees from Los Angeles were starting to discover it, and were flooding in. The town was set among gently rolling, grass-covered green hills, and was separated from the hot desert climate of the interior of the state by a range of mountains. The city was home to Cal Poly University (where the coeds were known as the Cal Poly Dollys). With all the hills and mountains nearby, San Luis Obispo was the perfect place for paragliding, as well as a nice place to live. As Hugh liked to put it, "When it comes to paragliding, we are fat, contented cows down here."

After a short drive, Hugh and I arrived at Montana Del Oro State Park, on the shore of the Pacific Ocean. We parked the car and walked down a sandy bluff to the water's edge.

I've always loved the ocean. It has a soothing, calming effect on me. I think I must have been a clam in a former life. The air temperature was about sixty-five degrees, and a gentle breeze blew onshore. It was perfect. As we hiked along the beach, with the waves breaking just a few feet away, I felt the last of my tension and anxiety evaporate. No more rocks, no more cactus, no more rugged mountains, and no more heart attacks. Just soft sand and gentle waves. There was something about this place that seemed incredibly right. As my Indian friend would say, it was a "good medicine spot."

After about fifteen minutes of walking along the ocean, we reached Hugh's training area. It was a gently sloping sand dune about one hundred feet high. As the wind blew in off the ocean, it flowed up the face of the dune, creating lift. The higher up the dune, the faster the wind blew. You could basically pick your wind speed by moving up or down the dune. Nice!

Hugh and I hiked about halfway up the dune, and then he had me unpack my wing. It had never been out of the bag until now, so I got my first look at my purple and white Pro Design Compact wing. Hugh put on his own harness, clipped into my wing, pulled it up into the air, and proceeded to run it up and down the sand dune. At the top of the sand dune, he stood on the summit, wing flying overhead in perfect control. Then he stepped into the air and floated around for a few minutes, just a few feet off the sand. Finally he drifted back down to the beach to a soft landing. Just as I had been impressed with Marty's total control of the wing, so I was equally impressed with Hugh's expertise. I vowed to become as good.

Finally Hugh told me to put on my harness and clip into the wing, facing backwards. Then he had me demonstrate what little ground handling technique I'd acquired over the past few months. Hugh showed me how to pull the wing overhead, using a reverse inflation technique. Unlike my A5, the Compact had absolutely no tendency to overshoot after it was pulled up into the air. It simply rose up into the air, and stayed there. As Hugh promised, it was much more suitable for a beginner.

Since I had clipped into the wing, facing backwards, it was fairly easy to pull the wing overhead and keep it there. Hugh was an excellent teacher, and I was soaking up his ground handing instruction like a dry sponge. We had moved about halfway up the dune, and I was managing to keep the wing overhead for several seconds at a time.

"I want to see you fly," said Hugh.

"Okay," I said. I started to bring the wing down so I could unclip, turn around, and clip back in facing forwards. But before I could do so, Hugh suddenly pushed me off the dune, going backwards! I found myself flying backwards through the air!

"Are you nuts?" I yelled at Hugh as I floated in the air a few feet away. He just laughed and waved. "Show me what a good pilot you are!"

And that's when I discovered just how gentle and benign an ocean breeze could be. We would not have dared do such a thing at an inland flying site. But the wind coming off the ocean was as smooth as whipped cream. And the fact that there was nothing but soft sand underneath, didn't hurt either. I slowly drifted down the face of the sand dune, brushing the sand with my feet, occasionally glancing behind me to see where I was going, until I finally touched down gently at the bottom of the dune. Sand dunes make the perfect training hill. If you fall down, it doesn't hurt.

Flying backwards was also a great confidence builder. As Hugh said, "Now that you know that you can fly this thing backwards, think how much easier it will be to fly forward." I couldn't argue with that logic.

I made several trips back up the sand dune, launched, and flew to the bottom of the dune and landed. Hugh was able to quickly determine that I knew how to handle the wing in the air, and was competent at landing it. What I needed was instruction in handling the wing on the ground, and launching it. I returned to the motel that evening, feeling quite good about Hugh's teaching skills.

The next day we went about twelve miles up the coast to Moro Strand beach. This was a flat beach, with no dunes. It was perfect for learning to ground handle the wing. About three miles down the coast, the giant Moro Rock rose from the bay, a few hundred feet offshore. Reaching almost five hundred feet into the sky, it looked like a miniature Rock of Gibraltar. It was actually the core of an extinct volcano.

The first thing Hugh taught me was How To Build A Wall. The idea was to lay out the wing, hook into it backwards, grab the steering lines in one hand and the front risers in the other, and pull gently on the wing until the cells were inflated. The wing should sit on its tail, pointing straight up into the sky, forming a wall about three feet high.

Once the wall had been built, a sharp tug on the risers would cause the wing to shoot straight up into the sky, flying overhead like a huge kite. After about an hour of wall building, I was pulling the wing up into the sky as if I'd been doing it all my life. Since I was facing backwards, it was very easy to look up at the wing and control it with the steering lines.

The beach was the perfect place to learn ground handling. With a steady, onshore wind, with no turbulence, I could kite the wing overhead and keep it there for as long as I wished. I had time to get a feel for the wing in a way that a land site simply couldn't match. If I had it to do all over again, I would take all of my PG/PPG training at an ocean beach. It's really that good.

At first I could only keep the wing flying overhead for a few seconds, but after a couple of hours of practice I learned to keep the wing flying for as long as I wished. It became a matter of skill, rather than luck. The trick is to keep yourself centered under the wing. The wing always wants to face directly into the wind, but the wind constantly shifts a bit from side to side. That means the wing wants to shift from side to side, as well. I learned to take short, quick sidesteps to keep myself centered under the wing. It was a balancing act, like learning to ride a bicycle. At first it seemed impossible. Then suddenly it clicked, and after that it seemed like the most natural thing in the world.

The next day Hugh taught me to walk up and down the beach while keeping the wing flying overhead. Just a little bit of brake would cause the wing to drift to one side or the other, and I simply walked along, staying centered under the wing. I learned to pull the wing up in a reverse launch position, kite it overhead, and then bring it back down onto the sand, always under my control. I learned to stand under the wing, spin around 180 degrees with the brakes still in my hand, and resume controlling the wing with the risers and brake lines crossed above my head. Then a few minutes later I would spin back around to my starting position, all the time keeping the wing under my control.

Eventually I started hooking into the wing normally, facing forward. I would then turn to stand facing the wing, with the risers crossed in front of me. I would take the steering lines in one hand and the front risers in the other, and build a wall in the gentle breeze. When the wall looked good, I would pull on the front risers to cause the wing to shoot straight up into the air. When I had the wing perfectly stabilized overhead, I would spin around, facing forward, and yell "Full Power!" That was Hugh's signal to act as the motor, pushing against my back as

I ran forward. With Hugh pushing as hard as he could, I would run about a dozen steps and slowly rise into the air; just as if I was wearing the motor. Hugh would push me along like a giant kite, then stop and let me settle back onto the sand. The idea was to practice and rehearse every aspect of powered flight, so that when I finally added the engine, that would be the only new variable.

For that was Hugh's teaching philosophy. One step at a time. Practice that step until you can do it in your sleep. Practice it until you're bored with it. Then add another step and practice that step until it's also second nature. Break the learning curve up into small, easily mastered steps. That's the best way to learn to fly. Never any pressure. Never any rush to fly. Never any "white-knuckles." Never any doubt about your ability to do it. I loved it. As Hugh liked to say to me, "You'll tell me when you're ready to fly."

After three days of ground handling at the beach, Hugh decided that it was time for me to do a couple of unpowered flights off the local mountains. Cayucos Peak was 736 feet high, and about half a mile from the beach. It overlooked the small beach town of Cayucos, and was just within view of Moro Strand beach where I'd done all of my ground handling training.

The peak itself was covered in green grass, as were many of the hills in the area. Cattle grazed along one side of the hill. A deeply-rutted, dirt road wound its way to the top, up from the town of Cayucos, home of some really good fish and chips, and an excellent clam chowder.

The view from the top of Cayucos Peak was fantastic. All of Moro Bay was spread out from one end of the horizon to the other. Halfway down the Bay stood gigantic Moro Rock, like an armed fortress ready to repel attacks from the sea. Directly out to sea, opposite Cayucos Peak, oil tankers were loading oil via an underwater pipeline from a tank farm directly across the valley, sitting atop another high range of hills.

The plan was for me to take off from Cayucos peak, fly down the hill, across the busy coastal highway, then land on the beach near an access trail. The trail led up to a convenient pull-off area alongside the highway where Hugh would pick me up. The whole flight would last only about five minutes.

The wind had been blowing steadily all day, but began to die as we neared the top of the hill. By the time I got my wing laid out, my boots on, and my harness ready to go, the wind was only blowing at 1-2 miles per hour. This was too little wind for a reverse inflation, so I suggested a forward launch. Hugh agreed.

I was more than a little nervous. It had been almost six months since my last flight, and that flight had ended with a broken rib. Also, this was my first actual flight on my new Pro Design Compact wing. Although I'd been kiting the wing and ground handling it for several days, and had flown it off the sand dune several times, I felt like this would be my first, real, honest-to-God flight with it. At least if I fell down this time, my fall would be cushioned by soft grass rather than hard rock.

I put on my helmet, took the steering lines and risers in my hands, and started my takeoff run. The wing popped overhead, and after just a few steps it lifted me away from the earth. Once again, after months of absence, the exhilaration of pure flight returned in a rush. Once again I was flying like a bird!

I flew away from the hill, looking down at the homes built at the bottom of the hill, the cattle wandering across the grassy slope, and the cars racing down the coastal highway. For a couple of minutes I wondered if I would have enough altitude to make it across the highway to the beach. I knew that I could always turn back and land in the pasture, but I ended up crossing the highway with plenty of altitude to spare. In fact, I still had a couple of hundred feet of altitude left when I finally arrived over the beach.

The beach was miles long in both directions, but I wanted to land near the access trail that would take me back up to the highway. Unfortunately, right in the middle of the stretch of beach where I wanted to land was a big hunk of rock. It stretched from the water's edge, to the bluff, and was about twenty-five feet high. I told myself that the smart thing to do was to fly over the rock and land on the open beach beyond. But that would require me to walk back to the access trail, carrying my wing. Being inherently lazy, I decided to burn up some altitude and land short of the rock.

I did a series of S-turns as my altitude slowly melted away. Finally, when I was only about fifty feet up, I decided to get lined up for the landing. I flew down the length of the beach, parallel to the water. Suddenly I realized that I was either getting some extra lift off the warm sand, or else I had misjudged my height. I was going to hit that damned rock! I no longer had enough altitude to get over the rock, and I was too low to turn around and land in the opposite direction. So I did a couple of shallow S-turns to burn up a little more altitude, and then turned back toward the rock so that I could land into the wind, hopefully just short of the rock.

The beach was quite flat at this point, and when the waves broke, they ran quite a distance. I touched down lightly on the dry sand, and immediately ran away from the water, pulling the wing after me, but it wasn't quite enough. About six feet of the left wingtip managed to fall into the puddled seawater left lying on the sand by the previous wave. Not only did the wing fall into the water, but several of the open cells managed to scoop up a load of wet sand. *Yuck!*

I quickly pulled the wing up onto dry sand before the next wave arrived. I was in no personal danger, but I felt sick to my stomach. On my very first flight, with my brand-new wing, I had managed to dunk the end of it in the ocean! Had I ruined it by getting it wet with salt water?

I shook the wet sand out of the cells as a small crowd of people gathered around me. Apparently they had never seen a paraglider fly before, and wanted to admire me and ask many questions. Even though my heart wasn't really in it, I smiled and answered their questions, letting the young girls admire the Brave Pilot Who Had Just Cheated Death. Any other time I would have eaten up this sort of attention with a spoon, but now all I could think about was my poor wing.

Finally I managed to excuse myself from the crowd, gathered up my wing, and carried it up the trail to the parking area. I started packing it up, and shortly Hugh arrived. I told him what had happened, and he told me not to worry about it. We would go back up the mountain, get the wing dried out, and it would be flyable once again. He recommended that I rinse the end of the wing with fresh water when I had a chance, assuring me that the material would not be harmed by a quick dunking in salt water. I was greatly relieved.

By the time we arrived back at the top of Cayucos Peak, the wind had started to blow again. It was a perfect seven miles per hour for a reverse inflation. However before I could fly again, I needed to dry out my wing. I put on my helmet and harness, clipped into the wing, and did a reverse inflation to get the wing flying overhead.

The damp end of the wing quickly popped open and flew with no problem. I kited the wing overhead for about half an hour until it was thoroughly dry. Then I shook the remaining dry sand out of the cells and got ready to launch.

This time I faced the wing with my steering lines in one hand and the risers in the other. When I felt ready, I gave the front risers a sharp tug and the wing leaped into the sky. I steered it for a few seconds until everything looked and felt just right. Then I spun around and ran forward.

After only a couple of steps, I was airborne. It was my first reverse launch and it had been incredibly easy. I could see why many pilots preferred reverse launches. Unlike the forward launch, the reverse launch permitted you to see exactly what the wing was doing. You could guarantee that it was properly inflated, inspect it for any problems, and then when everything was perfect, turn around and launch. Nice!

My second flight from Cayucos Peak was pretty much a repeat of the first, except that this time I flew farther down the beach before turning to set up my approach and landing. This time I had plenty of beach between me and the rock, and landed effortlessly on the dry sand.

After the flights from Cayucos Peak, I spent several more days practicing my ground handling skills at the beach. By then it had become second nature for me to lay out my wing, build a wall, pull the wing up into the sky, and fly it overhead as I walked up and down the beach, all under perfect control. Hugh set up a couple of small pylons, about thirty feet apart, and I steered the wing around the pylons in a figure eight course, keeping the wing directly overhead and completely under my control. I could now fly the wing overhead for as long as I wished. The wing was fast becoming a part of me. Instead of an unruly whale that I could barely control, it now did what I wanted it to do, and went where I wanted it to go.

It was time to start ground handling with the engine on my back. We left the cage and propeller off, so there would be nothing to break if I fell down, and I started kiting the wing while carrying fifty pounds of engine on my back. I figured that I would have to learn to kite all over again, and that I would spend the first day falling down a lot.

To my amazement, I never fell down once! I never even came close to falling down. Very quickly I became used to handling and controlling the wing with the extra fifty pounds on my back. Hugh's teaching method was really starting to pay off. When I finally put on the engine, I could concentrate on handling the weight of the engine because I already knew how to handle the wing. It had become second nature. It was like learning to ride a bicycle before you try to eat an ice cream cone while riding.

As I worked out with the engine on my back, I made the pleasant discovery that the wing was generating lots of lift while flying overhead. And the first thing it did was to lift some of the engine's weight off my back. This meant that I could spend hours learning to control the wing while wearing the engine, without having to actually carry the engine. I also suddenly realized that I would not need to carry the whole engine during my takeoff run. As soon as I got the wing overhead and flying, it would be generating lift and making the engine feel much lighter. All I would have to do was run! *I didn't have to try to run while carrying the full sixty pounds of engine on my back, because the wing would carry part of the engine weight for me!*

I just might be able to do this!

After spending a day kiting with the wing and the engine, I added the engine throttle to the equation. It was quite a handful. I now had the right steering line, the engine throttle, and both front risers in my right hand. It took a little practice to hold the risers without squeezing the throttle, but after a few hours I was successfully launching the wing with the engine throttle in my right hand. I also learned to kite the wing with the steering lines crossed, so that when I spun around for the launch, the steering lines would already be in the proper hands. I would not have to drop the steering lines as I spun around for the takeoff, then waste precious moments grabbing for them again.

After seven days of instruction, and many hours of practice on the beach, I was wearing the wing and the engine, launching the wing with the engine on my back, controlling the wing, spinning around, squeezing the throttle, yelling "Full Power!" and having Hugh push me into the air for a short flight across the beach. Hugh told me that I had now mastered every ground aspect of powered flight. All that was left was to put the propeller and cage back on the machine, put some fuel in the tank, fire it up, and launch. I told Hugh that I was confident in my ability to handle the wing and the engine, and that I felt ready to take the plunge.

The moment of truth had arrived. It was time for my first powered flight.

But in spite of my newfound confidence, I was scared to death. The ghost of that shattered propeller, and the multiple crashes in the mountains, were still very much present. Would I be able to fly, or would I simply break another expensive propeller?

I was about to find out.

Postscript: It took me about a year, but I finally figured out what had sent me to the hospital in San Luis Obispo. It wasn't a heart attack, and it wasn't anxiety. It was an artificial sweetner. Honest to God!

I had recently started using one, to help lose weight. Unfortunately this particular sweetner can cause weird side effects in some people. Too much of the sweetner caused me to be short of breath, feel heavy in the chest, and to sweat profusely. When I stopped using the sweetner, the "heart attacks" vanished. If I started using it again, the "attacks" quickly returned. So I stopped using it. No more problems.

Sometimes life is just Totally Weird.

In Hindsight, What Would I have Done Differently?

Just one thing. I should have been carrying a hook knife every time I clipped into a paragliding wing at the beach. Actually, it's always a good idea to carry a hook knife whenever you fly, but it's especially good to have one at the beach. As my own experience demonstrates, it's possible to get your wing into the water. It's also possible to get caught in the surf, get pulled out to sea by the wing, and drown. It's happened to others.

A hook knife is a little gadget with a razor-sharp blade hidden away inside a plastic sheath. The sheath keeps you from cutting yourself. An open slot allows a line or piece of nylon webbing to slide into the blade, and to be instantly severed.

The hook knife is very cheap (about $10), but it's worth its weight in gold. You should never leave the ground without one.

Chapter 11

Running into the Sky

I was sitting in my motel room, staring at my PPG engine on the floor in front of me. I'd been training with Hugh Murphy for exactly one week. Hugh felt that I'd mastered all of the necessary skills for my first motor flight. I felt exactly the same way, except that I thought another six months of intensive training would be about right.

In my head, I knew that Hugh was right. I'd become quite adept at handling the wing on the ground. I knew how to lay it out, how to center myself in the wing, how to build a wall, how to pull the wing up into the air and inflate it, and how to steer and fly it once it was overhead. I'd practiced spinning around after the wing was overhead, squeezing the throttle, and running forward with fifty pounds of engine on my back. I'd even lifted off and flown a few feet while wearing the engine, with Hugh providing the thrust. So now it was time to put some gasoline in the engine and fly it.

But emotionally, I was still scared stiff. I was still thinking about that broken prop and my broken rib. I felt like I was being asked to juggle chainsaws.

For a week, the engine had sat in the corner of my motel room. Twice it had gone out to the beach for ground handling training. But this was different. This time the engine was going to the beach to *fly*. I picked up the engine, sat it on the edge of the bed for support, and slipped my arms through the shoulder straps. I stood up, turned sideways, and carefully eased out through the doorway. As I strode down the hallway I passed one of the Hispanic motel maids. She was probably thinking "What's this crazy gringo up to now?" I smiled and nodded, just as though this sort of thing was a common sight in a Howard Johnson motel.

I carefully walked down the steps, eased out through the last door, and headed for my car. I unlocked the trunk, slipped off the engine, and packed it away in the trunk, next to the disassembled cage and prop.

Ten minutes later, Hugh arrived in his car. I followed him to the local city park, where we stopped in front of a single large tree. As Hugh tossed a couple of nylon ropes over a sturdy branch about seven feet off the ground, I sat on the ground and strapped myself into the engine. I got to my knees and managed to stagger to my feet. The engine on my back felt like it weighed a ton. It seemed impossible that this thing could ever fly.

Hugh maneuvered me under the branch and attached the ropes to the main carabiners on my harness. Slowly I transferred my weight from my feet to the tree limb. I didn't want to fall to the ground with fifty pounds of engine on my back. Hugh showed me how to release the footbar from the bottom of my seat, catch it with my foot, and push the bar forward to drag the seat forward and under me. When I was sitting comfortably in the seat, Hugh began to adjust the harness straps.

Getting the harness properly fitted was basically a balancing act. Both the machine and I were hanging from the overhead tree branch. I was hanging from the front, and the machine was hanging from the rear. The straps needed to be adjusted until we were in balance, and the propeller was approximately vertical. This would cause the thrust from the propeller to be horizontal while I was in flight.

Hugh worked on the straps for several minutes, searching for just the right combination. The seat and side straps were easy to adjust. Then Hugh began to tighten the shoulder straps, slowly pulling the machine and propeller into an upright position. Finally the machine was vertical. "Perfect," said Hugh. "How do you feel?"

The truth was, I wasn't very comfortable. The last few adjustments on the shoulder straps had caused them to press uncomfortably down onto my shoulders. If I sat up straight, my shoulders ended up carrying the weight of the machine. Not good! The only way to get the weight of the machine off my shoulders, was to hunch forward; to make myself less tall.

When I told Hugh, he simply shook his head. "This is as good as it gets. The shoulder straps have to be tight enough to hold the machine vertical."

I understood Hugh's point. The needs of the engine had to come first. The pilot's comfort was secondary. And I could fit into the harness if I hunched forward. Nevertheless, I felt a stab of disappointment. Obviously this harness was simply too small for a person of my height. It wasn't designed for pilots much over six feet tall. I should have tried on the machine, like this, before I bought it. Perhaps I could have the harness modified to make it more comfortable.

With the harness adjusted as well as we could get it, we packed up and headed for the beach. The parking lot was almost empty when we arrived. It took several trips to haul all our equipment out to the beach. Hugh had brought a plastic tank of gasoline, some oil, and a Ratio-Rite measuring cup. The Ratio-Rite was just a fancy measuring cup to make it easy to mix oil and gasoline. The 2-cycle engines that power most PPGs require the lubricating oil to be mixed with the gasoline. The Ratio-Rite had numerous marks on the side of the cup that showed how much oil was required to get the desired gas/oil ratio for different amounts of gasoline. It made it very easy to determine the proper amount of oil to mix with the fuel.

Hugh watched as I measured out the oil. It was nice having an instructor supervise my actions instead of going off to instruct other students. I put the cap on the tank and shook the tank for a few minutes to thoroughly mix the gas and oil. Then I replaced the tank cap with a long pouring spout, and dumped the mixture into the fuel tank of my PPG engine. I felt like I was arming a bomb.

We filled the DK's fuel tank about two-thirds full. A full tank would allow me to fly for about an hour, but since I wouldn't be flying that long on my first flight, there was no need to carry the extra weight.

The unspoken question in my mind was, "Will I fly at all?"

With the engine fueled, I used my torque wrench to attach the three separate propeller blades to the engine hub. After the propeller was installed, I assembled the four-part propeller cage and then attached the cage to the motor frame with Velcro straps. Finally I put the starter battery in place and attached the wires from the starter.

It was finished. The engine was ready to fly. And my stomach was trying to climb up my throat.

I sat the engine on the trunk of the car, slipped my arms through the shoulder straps, and headed out for the beach. I only had to walk a few hundred feet, but the sixty pound engine grew quite heavy on my shoulders. This was not the first time I'd carried the engine out to the beach, but this time it seemed much heavier. If I lived through this day, I vowed to find a better way to transport the engine from the car to the launch site.

On the beach, Hugh told me that he wanted to take the engine up for a short flight to check out the wind conditions. I readily agreed. If he had asked to fly the engine for the next two hours, I probably would have agreed.

Hugh laid out the wing while I went to warm up the engine. I held on to the motor frame with one hand, and the throttle in the other, and flipped the master switch. Then I slid the choke to the 'on' position and pressed the starter button. The propeller rotated several times, and I heard the first exhaust "note" as the cylinders started to fire. I released the starter button, slid the choke to the 'off' position, and then hit the starter button again. The engine started almost instantly. There was a lot of vibration and clanking noise as the engine idled at just under two thousand rpm.

After letting the engine warm up for about three minutes, I hit the stop button to kill the engine. Hugh had finished laying out the wing and was putting on his helmet. I flipped the master switch to "off" to prevent an accidental start, carried the engine over to the wing, and set it down next to Hugh. Hugh quickly attached the wing risers to the harness, sat on the ground, and strapped himself in. He declined my offer of a helping hand, rocked forward onto his knees, and slowly stood up with the engine on his back.

I helped Hugh lift the left riser and lines over the top of the motor cage as he turned around to face the wing. He took the throttle and steering lines in his hands, and signaled me to flip the master switch to 'on.' He pressed the starter button, and the engine roared to life. Hugh let the engine run for a few seconds, then took the front risers in his throttle hand and glanced around to make sure everything was clear. He glanced at me, and I gave him the thumbs up signal. Hugh gave a sharp tug on the risers and the wing shot up into the air. It stabilized overhead while Hugh took a couple of steps backward as he steered the wing with the brakes. Suddenly he spun around, went to full throttle, and started running forward. The engine roared at full power, blowing a cloud of sand across the beach. Hugh took only about six steps, and then he was airborne. He made it look so easy. I could only shake my head in envy.

Hugh flew around for about fifteen minutes, making several low passes over the beach. Finally he touched down in a feather-soft landing on only one foot. What a show off! As I helped him to take off the engine, Hugh told me that conditions were perfect for flying. We had a steady, seven mile per hour breeze that was smooth as silk. It just didn't get any better.

Hugh rested one hand on the propeller cage and looked me in the eye. "What do you think?" he asked gently.

I thought I wanted to run back to the car, drive back to my motel room, jump into bed, and hide under the covers. I was still scared to death. I had this horrible sick feeling in the pit of my stomach that I was about to die. But I found that it's sometimes easier to be a brave man than a coward. I glanced down at the engine, and then up at Hugh. Somehow I managed to find my voice.

"Let's get this sumbitch in the air," I said, with all of the phony confidence I could muster.

Hugh nodded agreement and started laying out the wing for another flight. My flight. My first motor flight.

I was already wearing my windbreaker, but I knew it would be colder aloft. I pulled out my Gore-Tex rain jacket and slipped it on. It made for a rather handsome flight jacket. Then I dug out my soft foam ear plugs. I rolled them between my fingers to compress them to the size of matchsticks, and stuck one in each ear. The soft foam expanded to fill my ear canals, and suddenly the outside world got much quieter. I slipped on my helmet and fastened the chip strap, then pulled on my gloves. I was already wearing my paraboots.

I was ready to fly. And my legs were ready to turn to jelly.

The wind was blowing directly onshore, so I would have to take off directly toward the ocean. Damn! Why couldn't the wind have been blowing parallel to the beach? Then I would have had a runway several miles long. Which is what I figured I might need. The hundred feet to the water's edge seemed to shrink to about twenty feet. Or less. Hugh had gotten off the ground in only a few steps, but I weighed almost twice what he did. What if I couldn't get airborne in time? What if I reached the edge of the sea and I was still on the ground? I certainly didn't want to run into the sea wearing my engine, so I asked Hugh how far I should run before aborting the takeoff.

Hugh suggested that I forget about aborting the takeoff. "Just squeeze that throttle, and run, and you'll fly. I guarantee it."

God, but I wanted to believe him! But the last time I trusted an instructor to take care of me, I ended up with a shattered prop. I decided that I didn't have much choice. I'd either fly, or I'd get wet. If I couldn't fly the damned thing, maybe I could turn it into a motorboat.

The engine was sitting in front of the wing, all hooked up and ready to go. I sat down in the sand, slid the seat under me, and hooked up my leg straps. There was beach sand clinging to the ends of the straps, and I slapped them against my leg. I slid my arms through the shoulder straps and fastened the chest strap. I was so nervous that I forgot to zip up the vest.

It was time to stand up. I drew my legs under me, rolled forward onto one knee, and slowly staggered to my feet. God, but this engine was heavy! I made yet another vow that I would find an easier way to put on the engine.

I brushed off the sand and turned around to face the wing. Hugh helped me lift the risers and lines over the motor cage. The lines were now crossed in front of me in the familiar reverse-inflation pattern. I unsnapped my brake lines and took both brake handles in my left hand. I strapped the throttle to my right hand

Everything was ready. I quickly thumbed the starting button before I could lose my nerve. The electric starter whined for a moment, then the engine caught. I braced my feet and slowly squeezed the throttle to full power. Thanks to my helmet and ear plugs, the engine sound was quite modest, even though the engine was screaming at nearly seven thousand rpm. The engine was developing full power, and tried to push me over. I eased off the throttle, and the engine returned to idle.

I grabbed both front risers and squeezed them between my thumb and the plastic throttle housing in my right hand. It worked, but it felt incredibly clumsy. I would definitely have to find an easier way to hold the front risers during reverse inflations.

With the front risers in one hand, and the brake lines in the other, I gently tugged on the wing to begin building a wall. All those hours and days of training started to pay off. This was now routine stuff. I had done it repeatedly with the engine on my back. The only difference now was that the engine was running. The engine was just as heavy as ever, but now the adrenaline was flowing so strongly that I barely noticed it.

I got the wing fully spread out, every cell open and inflated, and I was perfectly centered on the wing. "*Now!*" a voice whispered in my head. I tugged sharply on the front risers. The wing shot off the ground and rose overhead. I released the front risers and transferred the right brake handle to my right hand. With a brake handle in each hand, I took a step backwards, steering the wing in the smooth ocean breeze. I was in complete control of the wing, and it was flying perfectly.

It was time for both of us to fly. This was it!

I spun around to face the ocean and squeezed the throttle. The engine roared, and I started to run forward. I kept my head tilted back, and my eyes on the wing. As I ran forward, I kept myself centered under the wing.

All my senses were in complete overload, and the adrenaline was flowing in buckets. I think I could have lifted a car with one hand. The rest of the world had dissolved into a meaningless blur. There was just me, the engine, and the wing overhead. I couldn't tell you if five seconds or five hours had elapsed since starting my run. All I could hear was a voice in my head shouting *Run! Run! Run!*

Suddenly there was a new sensation. My feet were slipping on the sand. In fact, they were just lightly slapping the ground. I was running across the sand like Peter Pan, and each step was a massive stride, about six feet long. I was bounding across the ground like a giant kangaroo. Was something wrong? Then the truth managed to filter into my sensation-soaked brain: *The wing was trying to lift me into the air!*

The ocean abruptly loomed into view, just ahead. I was certain that I was about to run into the water. But I wasn't stopping now! I squeezed the throttle for all it was worth. I wanted every ounce of power that engine had. We'd either fly, or hit the water together. As I'd done on top of Saddle Mountain, months earlier, I tugged on the brake lines to give the wing some extra lift.

And then one of my footsteps missed the ground. Suddenly there was nothing under my feet, but air. I looked down, and the only thing still on the sand was my shadow. *The ground was dropping away!* The waves were breaking on the sand just a few feet below me. I was out over the ocean, suspended in an ocean of air. I was flying! *I did it! I did it! I did it!*

The engine was turning at seven thousand revolutions per minute, the tips of the propeller were traveling at several hundred miles per hour, the air was blasting out of the propeller at almost ninety miles per hour, and one hundred pounds of thrust was shoving me forward at twenty miles per hour. *I was flying!*

I pulled on the right steering line. Overhead, my wing slowly turned to the right. I swung away from the ocean and flew over the breaking waves as they collapsed onto the sand. As soon as I was flying parallel to the shore, I eased off the steering line and returned to level flight. But I kept the throttle squeezed tightly, and the engine continued to roar at full power. And we were lifting! We were climbing into the sky!

A wild shriek filled the air. It nearly drowned out the noise of the motor, and it was coming from me! I think it was a cross between the Rebel Yell, Tarzan's jungle battle cry, and the mating call of a deranged moose. It was two years of waiting and suffering and training for this moment. It was the sound of a man who had just discovered that he could fly. It was the sound of a man who had just run into the sky.

147

I think they heard it in San Francisco. And Los Angeles. And probably Seattle.

I was flying!

I kept the throttle squeezed, and continued to climb into the sky. I wanted altitude. Altitude was my friend. With plenty of altitude I would have time to react if something went wrong. I was determined not to make any stupid mistakes that could spoil one of the greatest moments of my life.

I glanced up at the wing. It was just hanging up there, like it always did. Every cell was open, and was fully inflated, and all of the lines were straight and taut. Only now, instead of merely slowing my descent, the wing was lifting me into the sky. With a little help from the engine, of course. I glanced behind me at the shiny aluminum of the propeller cage, and the bright yellow of the safety netting. Inside the aluminum cage, the propeller was a barely visible, whirling disk, giving me the power that I needed to defy gravity

My dream had finally come true. *I was going up!*

As I flew down the beach, I realized that I was still hanging in my leg straps, and they were starting to get uncomfortable. I let go of the steering lines, grabbed the seat on either side, and tried to slide back into it. I couldn't budge it. My own weight was pressing me deeply into the leg straps, and was preventing me from sliding into the seat. I realized that I needed to use the footbar. I felt around under the seat, trying to find the footbar. No good. I couldn't find the damned footbar, and my efforts to find it were distracting me from my chief job of piloting this contraption. I decided to forget about the footbar and the seat. I would just hang in the leg straps for this first flight. What's a little discomfort to a man who can fly!

I had traveled about a quarter of a mile up the beach since my takeoff. I estimated my altitude at about two hundred feet. I would need to get an altimeter. I was passing over an RV park on the beach. There were lots of old folks sitting outside their campers and trailers and motor homes. I don't think they'd ever seen a powered paraglider before. They were all waving at me, with that incredulous look that I would see frequently over the next few months.

I decided to fly back to my point of takeoff. I pulled the right steering line, and slowly the wing started to turn to the right. In just a few seconds I was heading back the way I'd come. Ahead of me was a small stand of trees at the edge of the beach. I'd been looking at these trees every day for the last week while practicing my ground handling on the beach. But today I was looking at the trees

148

from a new perspective. I was looking *down* on them. A short distance away, Hugh was standing on the sand, waving at me.

And at that moment it really hit me. *I was flying like a bird!* As if on cue, a couple of seagulls suddenly rose up in front of me, banked hard to the right, and disappeared behind me. I realized that I could go with them, if I wished. I no longer had to stand on the ground, looking wistfully up at the birds. I too, could fly! I could spread my wing, run across the sand, and fly away.

And a sense of exaltation washed over me like an ocean wave, and soaked deeply into the marrow of my soul. A whole new world lay at my feet. Literally.

I cruised up and down the beach for several more minutes. With several hundred feet of altitude, I felt safe enough to ease off the throttle and cruise in level flight. The engine slowed down to 5800 rpm. The view was simply spectacular. It was the same view that I had seen before, of course, during my unpowered flights, but there was something different now. Now I was not constantly descending. Now I could go up, as well. Now I could fly around as long as I liked, take my time, and enjoy the view. Like a bird, I had the power to remain in the air. At least until I ran out of gas.

I eased off the throttle, descended about fifty feet, then squeezed the throttle to go back up. That was the most fun of all. To feel the engine increasing in power, to see my descent suddenly *stop*, and then feel myself climbing back up into the sky. That throttle was like the control for a magic carpet. It gave me complete mastery over my environment. I was no longer at the mercy of gravity.

But I was still at the mercy of those damned leg straps, and they were starting to get very uncomfortable. Even though I'd been flying for only about ten minutes, I decided to land. I think I could have stood the discomfort for a bit longer, but this first flight had been so absolutely perfect that I didn't want anything to go wrong to mar it. I wanted to land while it was still perfect.

The land behind the beach was hilly, with beach grass growing across the top of the dunes. I flew over the dunes, turned to face the ocean, eased off the throttle, and started my descent to the beach. Hugh had planted a wind streamer in the sand, so I could easily determine the wind direction.

I let the wing fly forward, unencumbered, as it slowly penetrated the wind blowing in from the ocean. That's when I discovered the beauty of having power for landing. Any time I thought I would land short of the beach, I simply applied a little power and shifted my landing spot back to the beach. Having power made landing a piece of cake.

About fifty feet above the ground I eased off the engine, eyeballed my glide slope, and realized that I would land right in the middle of the beach, halfway between the dunes and the ocean. Right where Hugh was waiting for me. Perfect. I thumbed the kill switch on my throttle control, and the engine suddenly fell silent. I could hear only the whisper of the wind as it swirled around my helmet and hummed among the lines of my wing.

With a seven mile per hour headwind, I slowly drifted down onto the sand. At about three feet off the ground, I gently pulled the brake lines down about one foot; just enough to bring the wing to a complete stop in the air.

I settled down onto the sand as softly as a snowflake. The instant my feet touched the ground, I spun around and pulled both brake lines down as far as they would go. The wing promptly stalled, quit flying, and started to fall out of the sky. The weight of the engine slowly settled down onto my back. Then the wing collapsed to the ground in a little pile of fabric and line.

I had landed. My first powered paraglider flight was over. And my feeling was indescribable.

Hugh snapped my picture, and then came running up to me with a big grin on his face. I still had the brake lines in my hands, and I just stood there, looking at the wing as it lay on the sand. I could not believe that I had done it. I was afraid that I would suddenly wake up in the emergency room at the hospital, still hooked up to that heart monitor.

But this was no dream. I had flown. Hugh clapped me on the shoulder. I dropped my right brake line, turned to face him, and gave him a hug with my right arm, which is not easy to do while wearing sixty pounds of engine on your back. For a few seconds we simply luxuriated in the sense of Mission Accomplished.

When I looked down to unfasten my chest strap, I realized that I'd forgotten to zip up my vest before taking off. I hadn't notice it before takeoff, and neither had Hugh. Guess we were both a little nervous. I lowered the engine to the ground and sat down next to it. God, but the world was beautiful!

Hugh sat down next to me, and together we reviewed my flight. He told me that my takeoff and landing had been textbook perfect. It was a flight that I could be proud of. I was now a powered paraglider pilot!

Hugh told me that he wanted me to go up again, right away, to really nail down my new set of skills. That way I wouldn't start thinking that I had just gotten lucky on my first flight. I agreed, but first I wanted to call my flying buddy, Mike, to give him the good news. I wanted to tell him that our ten thousand dollars had been money well spent.

I walked back to the parking lot, got my cell phone out of the car, and sat down at a nearby picnic table. I punched in Mike's number and waited while the phone rang. It seemed like an eternity before Mike finally answered the phone. And when he did, I could not speak. I literally could not find my voice. Finally I managed to croak into the phone, "I flew!" I could hear Mike grinning from ear to ear. "Well tell me all about it," he said.

And so I did. Every single detail. About eighteen times.

I flew again about an hour later. This time I remembered to zip up my vest before I took off. It was a very good flight; almost a carbon copy of the first flight. But as every pilot knows, there is only one First Flight.

On my second flight I was able to find the footbar after takeoff, and used it to pull the seat under me. Much more comfortable! Now I had a comfy seat in the sky, albeit a little on the small side. I flew up and down the beach for about twenty minutes, drinking in the view and loving every minute of it. With that magic throttle I could drop down low to examine something in detail, then climb back into the sky when I was finished. It was magnificent!

I didn't sleep much that night. I had buried a lot of demons out on that beach, today. And I had a new mind tape to play, over and over. Mentally, I examined every detail of my two flights, extracting as much useful information as possible. And I wallowed in the emotional stew that I brewed up from playing the tape in my head as I watched the ground drop away, again and again. I luxuriated in every exhilarating second of each replay. It was quite a night.

Of course, as the months and years have passed, other flying memories have largely replaced the memory of that first powered paraglider flight. Sometimes I go as long as two or three hours without thinking of it.

Life is very good.

In Hindsight, What Would I have Done Differently?

I would have had someone videotape my first flight. I would give almost anything to be able to actually see that magic moment when I finally lifted off the ground for the first time.

But of course I can replay that first flight in my mind, any time I like. And

I do have the still pictures that Hugh took of me. I especially like the one he took of me right after landing, as I stood on the beach with my brake lines and risers still in my hands. I can't decide whether to title that picture "Conquering Hero," or "Deer Caught In Headlights."

Needless to say, I wouldn't take ten thousand dollars for those pictures.

Life is very good.

The first step in learning to fly a powered paraglider is to learn to control the wing. And the beach is the very best place to learn.

Hugh demonstrates how to fly with the motor. The showoff!

Finally it's time for me to put on the motor and fly.

Run! Run! Run!

Yeeeehaaaa!

A seat in the sky.

Powered Paragliding: The Next Generation

It just doesn't get any better.

The end of a perfect landing. The wing comes down.

My instructor, Hugh Murhy.

The world's smallest manned airplane.

Chapter 12

A Seat In The Sky

The next day was perfect flying weather, and I was ready for my third powered flight. This time Hugh wanted me to make a cross-country flight up the coast to the beach town of Cayucos, where I'd landed after my unpowered flights off Cayucos Peak. The round trip distance would be about twelve miles. This would be my first trip away from the immediate vicinity of Moro Strand beach, but I wasn't worried since the beach itself would always be available for emergency landings.

The wind was blowing about seven miles per hour as I laid out the wing, warmed up the engine, and got into my flight gear. I'd like to be able to claim that my two perfect flights on the previous day had left me calm, collected, and supremely confident in my new flying skills.

Hah!

I can honestly say that I was *less* nervous and scared than I'd been on the previous day, but not much. I guess my subconscious mind still wasn't convinced that I wasn't trying to commit suicide. As I sat on the sand, fastening the straps of my harness, I still had a hard time believing that I could actually heft this heavy machine onto my back and run it into the sky. It just seemed impossible that this unlikely conglomeration of parts and fabric could actually fly.

But it did fly. With my steering lines in my left hand, and the throttle in my right, I grasped the front risers and once again built the wing into a perfect wall. Then when everything seemed just right, I tugged sharply on the front risers, causing the wing to shoot up into the sky. I stood there for several seconds, keeping the wing steered into the wind while I inspected the lines and cells for proper inflation.

Once again there was that magic moment that whispered *"Now!"* in my brain. It was the moment when my training took over, and I knew it was time to fly. I spun around, went to full power, and started to run. This time I didn't have to worry about getting close to the water. The wind was blowing parallel to the beach, so I literally had miles of runway in front of me. In only a few seconds I was once again lightly slapping the sand with my feet, and a moment later I was running into the sky.

On my second flight, the previous day, I'd remembered to zip up my vest before I took off. As soon as I was in the air, I had found it very difficult to breathe. The vest was simply too tight for my big barrel chest. Today was no different. It was almost impossible to breathe with the vest zipped up. I groped for the footbar beneath my seat, released it, and caught it with my foot. A quick shove with my foot, and the seat slid forward, taking the harness with it. That moved the vest forward a bit, until I could once again breathe normally. The harness was still too short for my height, and I was forced to hunch forward to keep the weight of the machine off my shoulder straps. Hugh had mentioned a vest extension that could be purchased from the manufacturer, but I was still going to have to work on the height problem.

At full power I climbed to several hundred feet, then eased off the throttle to achieve a level cruise. I was following the beach, but the wind had shifted direction and was now blowing about thirty degrees from the left. This was causing me to slowly drift inland, so I turned a bit left, into the wind. By crabbing the wing into the wind, I was able to stay directly over the beach. I could already see the town of Cayucos, off in the distance. Since I couldn't possibly lose my way, there was nothing to do but settle down for a fantastic flight.

And fantastic it was. There's something extra-special about the third flight. On the first flight you're utterly overwhelmed by the experience. The fact that you got into the air, is quite enough. On the second flight you're amazed by the fact that you were able to do it again. You start to think that maybe the first flight wasn't just dumb luck. Maybe you really *can* fly this thing!

But on the third flight, you know that you're really a pilot. Now you know that your first two flights weren't just dumb luck. You *really can* fly this thing! Now it's time to settle back and take in the whole experience of the majesty of flight. It's time to enjoy flying like a bird!

With a seven mile per hour wind blowing, I cruised up the beach at about ten miles per hour, or about three times as fast as a person normally walks. Not very fast, but I was loving it every foot of the way. Walking along the ocean is great fun, but sometimes the sand is very soft and deep, and the walking can be difficult. Also there are rocks and logs that have to be stepped over, and puddles of water that must be negotiated. And when you've walked as far as you wish to go, you still have to turn around and walk back, which can quickly turn into a long, hard grind.

But *flying* up the beach gave me the best of both worlds. I could cover the territory three times as fast, but not so fast that I missed things. Since I was only flying a couple of hundred feet high, I could see everything. But I didn't have to walk! I simply sat in my skyborne chair, and flew effortlessly above it all. It was wonderful!

Flying a powered paraglider is nothing like flying an airplane. You don't even have that much sensation of flying. It's more like drifting across the landscape in a balloon; except that this balloon will go where you want it to go. In my opinion it's the best kind of flying in the world. Just imagine sitting in your easy chair and drifting across the landscape. That's what it's like to fly a powered paraglider. (At least the flying part. The launch part is kinda like running with another guy on your back.)

A few minutes after I'd taken off, I'd covered about half a mile of beach and was passing into new territory. The first thing I noticed was a couple of horses and riders ambling down the beach. A small crowd of people was nearby, watching them ride. That's when I learned that horses don't like strange noises coming from the sky. As I drew closer, the horses started to buck and rear. The riders were having trouble controlling them, and the crowd of people was looking up at me and yelling. I couldn't hear them, but I knew they weren't yelling "Welcome to the beach!"

When several people started throwing sticks and rocks into the air, I got the message. I squeezed the throttle and started to climb. I gained several hundred feet of altitude as I continued to travel down the beach, away from the horses.

Hugh had mentioned something to me earlier that now stuck in my mind. He'd said, "When you start flying, there's about twenty-five important things that you'll learn that you didn't know before." I decided that this would be Important Lesson Number One: "Don't fly near the horses."

As I continued down the beach, I moved out of the public park area and started flying over expensive beach homes. I felt like an aerial Peeping Tom. Many of these costly homes had inner courtyards where the inhabitants thought they were completely private, and could engage in various adult activities, safe from any prying eyes. I tried to wave and smile, but my intrusions were not always well received (although one couple just smiled and waved). Ah well. Even the Rich have their troubles.

At least no one shot at me.

The beach was an incredibly rich visual environment. There was always something to see. People strolling along, dogs romping in the surf, swimmers and surfers paddling around in the waves, small children playing in the sand. Just about everyone, except the horse lovers, waved at me.

Suddenly I caught a movement out of the corner of my right eye. For an instant I felt a stab of panic. I thought an airplane was headed toward me on a collision course. Then it suddenly snapped into focus.

It was a box kite! A big, brightly colored box kite about five feet tall, with several long wind streamers hanging from the base. The kite was hovering about twenty feet off my right wingtip. For a few seconds we seemed to be flying in formation, then I started to pull away from it.

The sight of the box kite was fascinating. I had met a fellow denizen of the air! But what mesmerized me was the fact that the kite was just floating freely in the air, with no visible means of support. On the ground there's always something holding up everything; a support, or stand, or chain, or rope. Up here there was nothing! The kite just hung out there, in space, exactly the way a brick doesn't (with apologies to Douglas Adams).

Before I flew away from the box kite, my eyes traveled down the almost-invisible string to the tiny figure on the beach below. I waved, and he waved back.

I noticed that the beach was getting smaller and rockier as I flew on. Occasionally the beach would be entirely interrupted by a rocky headland. Whenever I saw one of these coming, I increased power and gained altitude so that I would be able to safely glide over these patches of rock even if my engine suddenly quit.

Important Lesson Number Two: "Always stay within gliding distance of a safe landing area." Hugh had drummed into me that my little powerplant could quit at any time, so I should always be prepared to land.

I reached the town of Cayucos after about twenty minutes of flying. The beach had grown very large again, and the rocks had long since disappeared. There were a lot more people on the beach near the town, and my arm soon grew tired of the constant waving. Flying seemed to have its duties along with the privileges.

On the far side of the town was a gigantic fishing pier that reached hundreds of feet out into the ocean. It also marked the effective end of the beach. Beyond the pier, the ocean pounded against unbroken rocky headlands, with no good place to land. Hugh and I had earlier agreed that the pier would be a good place for me to turn around.

As I approached the pier, I spotted a lone tourist on the pier, directly in my path, waving and taking my picture. I waved back, then eased off the throttle and swung around to the left to start back. I was flying over the ocean, several hundred feet offshore, but I knew that I could easily reach the beach if my engine lost power.

But my faithful little engine showed no sign of any problem. It continued to spin at almost six thousand revolutions per minute, propelling me through the sky. God, but this was a wonderful machine!

I headed back down the coast. I was now flying downwind and making close to thirty miles per hour over the ground. Quite a difference from flying into the wind!

I maintained plenty of altitude as I flew downwind. In case the engine quit, I wanted to have plenty of time to get turned around to land into the wind. I certainly did not want to touch down at well over twenty miles per hour, even on soft sand! Not when my legs were the landing gear!

At my greatly increased speed it didn't take me long to get back to Moro Strand beach. As I flew past my takeoff point, I could see the wind streamer flapping in the wind, but there was no sign of Hugh. I decided to make a couple of low passes over the beach, and get ready to land. I'd been in the air almost forty minutes, and was getting a little cold and stiff. I wanted to land, stretch my muscles, and inhale a thermos of hot coffee that was waiting for me on the ground.

As I turned into the wind, low over the beach, I noticed that I was moving much more slowly than when I took off. Obviously the wind had picked up in speed. It was definitely a good time to land, even though I had enough fuel for another twenty or thirty minutes of flying.

I made a right turn to fly downwind to set up for my landing approach. That's when I discovered just how fast the wind was blowing. I went racing away from the beach, over the parking lot, and over the low hills and dunes that separated the beach from the highway. The sudden speed of my downwind dash caught me by surprise. For a few seconds I simply watched the ground race beneath me, faster than I had ever seen it move before. Then I looked up to see that

I was heading directly for a set of power lines, and I wasn't high enough to clear them! I quickly turned away and added power to gain some altitude. As I pulled away from that steel spider web, I was uncomfortably aware of how close I had come to getting snared in it.

In just a few seconds I was facing back into the wind, once more slowly crawling forward over the dunes and hills. Although I was never in any real danger from the power lines, my margin of safety had shrunk a little too much for my comfort. I realized that when the wind blows strongly, things happen very quickly, and a pilot must be constantly thinking several seconds (or more) ahead of the wing.

Important Lesson Number Three: "Pay attention to the flying, and think ahead! Aviation is spectacularly unforgiving!"

As I drifted toward the beach, I got ready to cut the engine. About fifty feet from the edge of the beach, I realized that I would have no trouble making it to the sand, so I pressed the kill switch. The sound of the engine ceased, leaving only the whistling of the wind around my helmeted head. I slowly drifted down toward the smooth sand. I was really looking forward to that hot coffee.

But the sky had other plans for me. Suddenly my rate of descent quickened. I was coming down faster than normal. Not enough to be dangerous, but enough to spoil my planned approach. I was still moving toward the beach, but not quickly enough to make it to the flat sand. I realized that I was going to land among the sand dunes!

Oh how I wished I still had my engine! I could have simply squeezed the throttle, arrested my descent, and easily made it to the beach. But the engine was off, and I did not have enough time to restart it before I would be on the ground. I pulled some brake to slow my rate of descent, in one last attempt to make it to the flat part of the beach.

It almost worked. I landed right on top of a little sand dune, about three feet high. It was the last obstacle between me and the flat sand, and I landed on it.

I landed very softly, and immediately started to spin around to control the wing and bring it down to the ground. Unfortunately my feet sank into the soft sand on the top of the dune, and I couldn't get turned around in time. I also forgot to release the brakes to keep the wing flying overhead. With my brakes still flared for maximum lift, the wing lifted me off my feet and I toppled down the back side of the sand dune. My cage and propeller dug into the sand, but since the engine was off, no harm was done.

I slid down the dune on my belly, being pulled by both gravity and the wing. The wing was now on the ground, still inflated, and was flapping wildly in the strong breeze. I was pulling in one of the brake lines as fast as I could, to collapse the wing, but that left the other side of the wing free to fly, and it was starting to drag me up the next sand dune. I had visions of tobogganing up and down the sand dunes all the way to the highway.

My fine flight had gone to Hell rather quickly.

Just then a very helpful spectator came running up to me. He was a man in his late fifties, or early sixties. He had the presence of mind to grab the wildly flapping wing by its wingtip and pull it down to the ground. Between the two of us we managed to get the wing under control. It had been a rather vivid demonstration of how fast the situation can change; especially during the landing.

Without the wing yanking me forward, I was able to get to my feet and thank my rescuer. Without his help I might have been dragged another twenty or thirty seconds before getting the wing under control. He helped me take off my engine, and I answered his questions about the strange craft I was flying.

I was still trying to figure out what had happened to Hugh, when he came walking up from the direction of the parking lot. He held up his camera and grinned. "I hopped in the car and followed you up the coast, all the way to Cayucos," he said. "Got some great shots!"

I learned that it had been Hugh, waving and taking my picture from the fishing pier! In fact, it had been Hugh waving at me at numerous locations all the way up and down the beach.

I told Hugh about my unorthodox landing. He explained that sometimes there was a little downdraft hovering just above the sand dunes behind the beach. It was caused by the onshore wind hitting the low dunes, and trying to flow over them; like rocks in a stream. Hugh suggested that on future flights I keep the engine on a little longer, until I was certain that I would make it to the flat portion of the beach.

Important Lesson Number Four: "Don't cut the power too soon. Better to have power, and not need it, than no power, and need it."

Hugh pointed out that it was sometimes desirable to land with the engine still running, both to maintain control and to maintain the ability to abort the landing and go around again, rather than always cutting the engine before landing.

Landing on the sand dune would have been okay if only I'd remembered to ease off the brakes to keep the wing flying overhead, and under control. If I had kept the wing overhead, I would have had plenty of time to turn around, or to simply run down the sand dune to level ground, and then bring the wing down. Once again I was reminded of the nicest feature about flying at the beach. If you fall down, it doesn't hurt!

The next morning, as I was waiting in my motel room, Hugh called to tell me that today was going to be a little different. He wanted me to take my equipment out to the beach, get set up, evaluate the conditions, and make a flight without his supervision. This would be like a student pilot's first solo flight without the instructor present. In a way, it was kind of like Graduation Day for me.

I drove out to the beach, dragged all of my equipment out to the flat takeoff area, and got set up. Two of Hugh's acquaintances and fellow flyers, Paul and Art, just happened to show up as I was preparing to fly. I had met both of them earlier in the week. Neither of them was a PPG pilot, but both were experienced paraglider pilots. I was happy to have them present while I made my first solo flight. Perhaps Hugh had sent them to the beach, to keep an eye on me, and to give me moral support? It didn't matter. I was glad they were there.

The wind was again blowing about seven miles per hour. It was perfect for a reverse inflation, and very shortly I was once again in the air. Since I had flown up the beach on my last flight, I decided to fly down the beach this time, toward Moro Rock. With a strong tailwind, it didn't take long before I reached that massive monolith, jutting up out of the ocean.

Just beyond the rock was an ocean inlet several hundred feet wide that opened into Moro Bay. I was tempted to fly past the Rock and over the inlet, but I knew there would be fierce turbulence behind Moro Rock as the wind was forced to flow around the monolith like a giant rock in a stream.

Just before reaching the rock, I turned back toward Moro Strand beach where Paul and Art were waiting. The trip back took several times as long, as my wing struggled to penetrate the headwind that seemed much stronger than when I took off.

As I made my way back up the coast, I noticed a radio-controlled model sailplane soaring about fifty feet below me. A little further on, a group of small children were busily building a fort out of driftwood. Again, lots of people waved, and I waved back. It was just plain fun.

When I arrived at Moro Strand beach, I had been flying for about thirty-five minutes. I knew that the wind was getting stronger and that I would have to land soon. However Hugh had told earlier me that he wanted me to make five landing approaches to the beach. "Just come down with your engine idling, like you're going to land, then at the last minute hit the throttle and go back up. I want you to get a good feel for what the terrain looks like when you come in for a landing. That's a very important skill to acquire."

I flew out over the dunes to set up my approach, released the throttle to let the engine idle, and drifted down toward the beach. At an altitude of about ten feet I squeezed the throttle and promptly went back up. There was no problem at all making an approach for landing. Of course the strong headwind made the approach easier by greatly reducing my forward speed.

On my sixth approach I killed the engine and drifted down for a landing. I had launched in a seven mile per hour wind, but was landing in a fourteen mile per hour wind. Not that I was worried. A wind actually makes landing easier. I drifted down like a snowflake, applied just enough brake to stop my forward progress, and stepped down onto the sand in a perfect landing.

And then I blew it. Instead of turning around and collapsing the wing, I just stood there and pulled the brake lines all the way down. I was immediately pulled over backwards as the wing caught the wind on its way down. I managed to get half turned around as I fell, and was glad that the engine was stopped as the cage and prop dug into the sand. Once again I got dragged a few feet on my belly before Paul and Art came to my rescue. Some gasoline leaked out of the overflow tube on top of the engine, and splashed onto my right shoulder, wetting my jacket with gasoline. Stupid!

Important Lesson Number Five: "The flight isn't over until the wing is safely collapsed on the ground! Continue to fly the wing even after you've landed."

I made two more powered flights before leaving California. On flight number five I waited too long to kill the engine, then could not take my eyes off the ground long enough to find the kill switch on my throttle. So I made my first power-on landing. I touched down in my usual fashion, spun around, collapsed the wing to the ground, then killed the engine. No problem.

I have mixed feelings about power-on landings. On the one hand it's very nice to have power all the way to the ground. It keeps all your options open. It's a handy way to avoid last-minute obstructions, like cars driving on the beach. On the other hand, any time you touch down with the engine running, you run the risk of striking the ground with your cage, possibly destroying your prop. At the moment, I have to say I prefer power-off landings. Perhaps when I have more flying experience, and feel like I'm less likely to make a mistake near the ground,

I'll switch to power-on landings.

On my sixth flight I flew back to Moro Rock. On my return, I made several landing approaches, just for the practice. I knew I was getting low on fuel, but I decided to make one more practice approach, then go around and land. Just a few feet above the sand, I hit the throttle to go back up. I had gained maybe thirty or forty feet of altitude above the breaking waves, when suddenly the engine sputtered and went dead. Out of gas. Immediately I turned to the right, to get away from the ocean, and landed on the beach. No big deal, but it made me resolve to get a little hand mirror so that I could keep an eye on my fuel level in flight.

Flight number seven never happened. I was scheduled to meet Hugh at the beach, but when I got there, a work party of half a dozen park rangers was erecting some kind of netting along certain portions of the beach. I later learned they were fencing off a bird sanctuary. I wasn't sure whether or not I should get the engine out and start setting it up. I knew that we had permission to fly paragliders at this beach, but I wasn't certain if that permission extended to powered paragliders, or not. I decided not to jeopardize Hugh's toehold on this excellent training beach, so I just sat tight.

When Hugh arrived at the beach, I pointed out the ranger activity and voiced my concern. We decided not to get in the way of the rangers, and instead traveled a couple of miles up the coastline to a stretch of beach that was privately owned by the Exxon oil company (and they did not care what we did on it).

Getting down to this beach was not as easy as at Moro Strand beach. We had to carry our gear through a hole in the fence, and then down a short slope. I eyed the new beach dubiously. This beach was much smaller to begin with, and was now even smaller because the tide was in. On one side was the water, and on the other side was a retaining wall made of huge timbers. In between, the flat sand was only about sixty feet wide. There was not a whole lot of room to maneuver. I probably would have been willing to launch, except that the wind had suddenly died away. It was no more than 1-2 miles per hour; not nearly enough for a reverse launch. I was tempted to do a forward launch, but decided against it. I had never done a forward launch with the motor; only reverse launches. I had done plenty of unpowered forward launches, and had no reason to think I couldn't do one with the engine, but I decided that a narrow stretch of beach, with water on one side and a high wall on the other, was not the place to make my first forward launch attempt. When I try something new, I like to have plenty of room for mistakes.

On March 20, I left San Luis Obispo. I had been there for two weeks. The first week had been spent learning to ground handle the wing. The second week had been spent making powered flights. I'd had six good flights. Most importantly, I was now a powered paraglider pilot. I knew I could fly this thing. Even more important, for the first time in my flying career I was going home with no damage to me or to my equipment! Hugh Murphy had certainly delivered everything he had promised, and then some. I was eminently satisfied with his instruction.

So satisfied, in fact, that I planned on coming back to San Luis Obispo in only eleven days, with my flying buddy, Mike. Mike was ready to learn to fly the engine, and I had told him that there was simply no better place to learn to fly than at Hugh Murphy's flying school. I figured that I could help Mike along with the learning process, while getting in some great beach flying for myself.

Also, I was eager to get home and re-invent the science of powered paragliding. Having gone through the learning process, I could see many areas for improvement. I simply couldn't believe some of the inconveniences that most PPG pilots were willing to put up with. I could see better ways to get the job done.

And so I went home. I had accomplished my mission. I was now a powered paraglider pilot. I was a man who could fly.

In Hindsight, What Would I have Done Differently?

Only two things. I'd have been more cautious about flying downwind. Flying upwind, you travel so slowly that it's easy to forget how fast you will suddenly start to move when you turn downwind. As a novice flyer, it would be easy to panic while flying downwind, hit the throttle to try to climb over a set of powerlines, and not make it.

Never take a chance when it comes to clearing an obstacle. If it isn't painfully obvious that you have enough altitude to safely clear the obstacle, turn away from it. If you're thinking, "I think I can make it," you're gambling with your life.

Second, I'd have paid more attention to my wing after I touched down. As a novice flyer, it's easy to forget about your wing once your feet are on the ground. But the flight isn't over yet. If you forget about your wing while it's still in the air, it may decide to take you on a ride where you don't want to go, in a manner you won't particularly care for.

If you had it to do over again, would you still have gotten your P2 rating before learning to fly the engine?

No. In perfect hindsight, I wished that I had simply packed up my engine and headed for Hugh Murphy's flight school. Or better still, bought the engine *and* the training from Hugh Murphy.

Having the prospective PPG pilot first earn his P2 rating, then learn to fly the motor, sounds very reasonable. Even Hugh had recommended that course of action to me. But having done it, I'm convinced that it's not the best way to go.

Certainly there's no question that the prospective PPG pilot must first learn to fly the wing before adding the engine. Not only must he learn how to ground handle the wing, but he needs to make about a dozen flights, either on a tow line or from a small training hill, before adding the engine.

But at that point, the PPG pilot goes one way, while the unpowered PG world, and its P2 rating, go a very different way. The unpowered PG pilot is ready to start making high flights from high mountains, and to start getting intensively involved in Parawaiting and Paradriving (driving hundreds of miles to a suitable mountain, then waiting all weekend for the wind to get right). In contrast, the PPG pilot is ready to put on his engine and start flying.

Also, the budding PPG pilot needs far more ground handling training than does an unpowered PG pilot. Launching a powered paraglider is a very delicate balancing act. Anything less than perfect, and you won't make it into the air. Worse yet, you may damage yourself or your equipment. (I managed to do both.) By contrast, an unpowered PG pilot has much more room for error.

Certainly it does no harm for the budding PPG pilot to get a P2 rating. He will mostly learn how to fly off high mountains without killing himself, and this can be very thrilling. (Having done so, I can vouch for it.) But it won't teach him much about launching or flying with a motor. Nor will getting the P2 rating give the PPG pilot the necessary ground handling training that is required in order to successfully fly the motor.

So I feel it's mostly a waste of time and money for the PPG pilot to get a P2 rating first. Instead, find a good PPG school that emphasizes ground handling (like Hugh Murphy), and that uses a towing rig or training hill to teach you how to fly the wing. Then strap on your engine and start to fly. Once you start flying the engine, you will rack up as much flying experience in two days, than you will in two weeks at an unpowered paragliding school.

Anyone interested in contacting Hugh Murphy can do so at http://bmac.net/paragliding/about.html. Or phone 805-772-8989. They just don't come any better than Hugh.

Chapter 13

Making The Whole Thing Easier

My trip to California had been a most educational experience. In addition to learning to fly my PPG, I had learned that carrying a PPG engine around on your back, while walking out to the flying field, really sucks. All of the weight hangs from your shoulders, and it gets really heavy, really fast. I'd also learned that trying to get up off the ground with a PPG engine on your back, really sucks. It saps your energy faster than anything. And finally, I had learned that it really sucks to have to assemble and disassemble your equipment every time you go flying.

So I had several sucky problems that I needed to solve in the eleven days before I returned to California. I wanted to be able to transport the engine, by car, fully assembled. I wanted an easy means to haul the engine out to the flying field. And finally, I wanted an easy means to get up off the ground after strapping the engine to my back.

The last two problems were by far the worst. Transporting the engine in pieces, in the trunk of the car, was a real pain, but it simply took extra time to deal with. However hauling the engine around on my back, and getting up off the ground while wearing the engine, were enormous drains of my energy. I wanted to solve those problems right away.

The problem of transporting heavy objects over the ground had been solved a number of years earlier. It was called a wheel. Somehow I had to equip my motor with wheels. Preferably with wheels that could be removed for flight.

I considered simply attaching a set of wheels to the bottom of the engine frame. But that would add weight and bulk, not to mention looking pretty silly in flight. Also, the engine was not tall enough to offer a convenient handle to grab, to tow it on the wheels.

The answer was a two-wheeled utility cart, like movers use to haul refrigerators. Just set the engine on the cart, grab the handles, tip the whole thing back on the wheels, and trundle it off to wherever you want to go. At the destination, simply remove the engine from the cart, and fly. The wheels and the cart stay on the ground. After flying, reverse the procedure to return the engine to the car.

Simple and inexpensive. A quick trip to the hardware store showed that utility carts came in many shapes and sizes. Since my engine only weighed about sixty pounds, the smallest cart would easily do the trick, and would only cost about $70. I decided to get one with big balloon tires for easy hauling over loose beach sand. The cart fit very nicely in either the back seat or the trunk of the car.

As soon as I tried to set the engine on the cart, I discovered the first problem. The little platform at the bottom of the cart was too narrow to hold the engine. No problem. I simply cut a piece of plywood about twenty inches wide, and a foot long, and bolted it to the base of the cart. Now I had a platform big enough to carry the engine. I set the engine on the platform, used a bungee cord to fasten the top of the engine frame to the top of the cart, and *voila!* My engine now had wheels and a convenient handle to grab for steering and hauling. I opened the garage door and rolled the assembly around the front yard. It worked perfectly. Now it wouldn't matter how far the flying field was from the car. I'd just wheel the engine wherever it needed to go. Problem solved.

Now for the second problem. It was still very exhausting to sit down on the ground, strap the engine to my body, and then try to get to my feet with the engine on my back. The mechanics of this were truly horrendous. I wanted to save my precious energy for running with the engine.

Obviously the answer was not to get up off the ground while wearing the engine. Instead, pick the engine up and set it on some sort of platform that was high enough to put the shoulder straps level with my shoulders. Then I could just back up to the engine, slip my arms through the shoulder straps, and walk away with the engine on my back. Fasten the leg straps and the chest strap, and I'm ready to fly. Yes! That was the obvious answer.

I went back to the hardware store, looking for just such a platform. There were lots of small stools and ladders that would do the trick, and they all folded up flat for easy transport, but I would have to drag the cart and the platform out to the flying field. Time to simplify.

The answer was to make the utility cart do double duty. I wanted to use the cart to haul the engine around, and then use the cart as an elevated platform to help me don the engine. Certainly I could install another plywood platform near the top of the cart, about three feet above the ground. That would make an ideal support platform on which to rest the engine. But with the elevated platform in place, I wouldn't be able to transport the engine on the cart. It seemed I could have either a transporting platform, or a launching platform, but not both.

A couple of nights later, in a neighbor's basement, I noticed a flap of plywood being held in place by a dowel rod while some glue was drying. Suddenly I had the answer. The elevated platform would actually be a hinged flap! That would permit the platform to fold down flat, allowing the engine to be carried on the cart. Once out on the field, I could remove the engine from the cart, raise the upper platform on its hinges, and hold it in place with a long dowel rod. Then I would simply pick up the engine, set it on the elevated platform, and put the engine on while standing up. Perfect!

It didn't take me long to fabricate and install the hinged flap. With a dowel rod supporting the flap, the engine balanced very nicely on the elevated platform. With the engine resting on the platform, I turned around and backed up to the engine and slipped my arms through the shoulder straps. Then I simply walked away from the cart, carrying the engine on my back.

Eureka! Problem solved. No more struggling to get up off the ground with sixty pounds of engine on my back. Now the process was virtually effortless. With the engine on my back, it took just a few seconds to bend over and fasten my leg straps, and I was ready to fly. And it only took a fraction of the energy required to do it the old-fashioned way. Yes!

But one challenge still remained; how to transport the engine, by car, to the flying field, without having to disassemble the engine each time. The PPG videos always showed the happy pilot disassembling his engine and loading the pieces into the trunk of his car while his beautiful, adoring girlfriend looked on with approval. Believe me, it's much more fun to haul the engine around in one piece!

I knew I could carry the engine in one piece with a trailer, van, station wagon, or truck. But I didn't want to have to pull a trailer, and I couldn't afford to buy a new vehicle, so I needed to find a way to haul the engine on the outside of my existing car. My first thought was a car top carrier, but they had two problems. They were expensive (up to $1,000), and none of them were quite big enough to handle my assembled engine with its bulky cage and prop. Also I realized that heaving the engine up into a car top carrier would be quite a feat of strength. And no fuel could be left in the fuel tank, or it would leak out through the overflow tube when the engine was laid flat inside the carrier.

I considered putting the engine in some sort of protective bag, and then tying it to a standard car top luggage rack, but this had all the drawbacks of a regular car top carrier, and none of the benefits (no protection from vandals or the elements). Also, how do you tie ropes to the engine if it's sealed inside a waterproof bag? A luggage rack on the trunk would be a little easier to use, but still had many drawbacks, including blocking the driver's rear vision.

Eventually I realized that the only thing that made much sense was some sort of bumper carrier. This was a carrying rack that could either attach to the bumper, or could plug into a trailer hitch receiver mounted just beneath the bumper. The bumper carrier was a very popular way to carry bicycles, and I could see no reason why such a carrier couldn't be used to carry a PPG engine as well.

There were many sizes and styles of bumper carriers available. Most of them required a trailer hitch to be installed on the car, and some of them were pretty pricey. None was exactly the right size or shape. I finally decided that the only way to get what I really needed, was to build one myself.

My final design was a simple steel frame that slid into a trailer hitch receiver, with a small plywood platform mounted on top of the frame. The platform would be level with the bumper, and only about twenty inches square, but that would be big enough to support the base of the engine. I cut two slots on either side of the platform for a nylon tie-down strap. The strap would go over the footbars of the engine, then down through the slots in the platform and under the steel frame beneath. That would firmly anchor the base of the engine to the platform.

But I soon realized that the platform wasn't enough. With the cage and prop in place, the engine stood almost five feet tall. About half of the engine stuck up above the trunk, into the slipstream. Going down the freeway at seventy miles per hour, there would be a lot of air resistance on the engine and the prop cage. It would put a great deal of strain on that nylon tiedown strap, and on the aluminum footbars of the engine. And if that strap ever gave way, there would be PPG engine all over the freeway. Not good! It was obvious that I also needed some sort of mast to serve as a strong anchor point for the top of the engine.

I made a strong mast out of some square steel tubing. The mast fitted securely into a socket on the steel frame of the bumper carrier, and extended just above the level of the trunk. Rather than simply tie the engine to the top of the mast, I added a U-shaped hook to the top end of the mast. When it was time to load the engine, I simply set the engine on the plywood platform, then inserted the mast into its socket. As the mast slid into its socket, the U-shaped hook on the top of the mast dropped down over the top crossbar of the engine, locking the engine securely in place. Then I used the nylon tiedown strap to secure the footbars of the engine to the plywood platform. At the field, I would simply remove the mast, unstrap the footbars of the engine, set the engine on the utility cart, and wheel it out to the launching point.

And they all lived happily every after.

With the mast in place, and the nylon tiedown strap pulled tight, the engine rode very nicely on its little plywood platform. With the cage and prop in place, the engine resembled an oversized spare tire on the bumper. Now all I needed was a rain cover for the engine. I didn't want to pay to have a custom cover made, so I started searching for a cheap, ready-made cover. I finally located a big barbecue grill cover at Sears that was just about the right size. I had an upholstery shop install a drawstring at the bottom of the rain cover so I could snug it up tight around the base of the engine.

With the rain cover in place, it looked like the engine was ready to travel to California. But I was worried about the wind resistance on the cover, and the pressure it would put on the engine's aluminum prop cage. Would the cage take the pressure? Or would it fold up and collapse like tinfoil? There was only one way to find out.

With everything in place, I went for a drive. Cautiously I eased up to forty miles per hour. Then I stopped the car, removed the rain cover, and carefully inspected the engine. It was hard to tell for certain, but it looked like the cage might have started to buckle a bit under the strain. The cage was solidly anchored to the motor frame at the top and bottom, but was completely unsupported on the sides. I decided to fabricate a couple of removable wooden braces, for the sides of the cage, to give the cage some extra support while the engine was riding on the bumper.

With the wooden braces in place, I put the rain cover back on the engine and took it for a drive on the freeway. At seventy miles per hour, the cage seemed to be taking the wind resistance load just fine. I returned home, removed the cover, and inspected the cage for any signs of deformation. There appeared to be none. Problem Number Three appeared to be solved. Now I could transport my engine on the car, without taking it apart every time I wanted to fly. Nice!

But would my auto insurance cover the engine against damage? I learned that

I was fully covered if some idiot plowed into me from behind, but if I backed into a tree, I was on my own. Okay, that just meant I needed to be very careful while backing up.

It had been eleven days since my return from California. During that time I'd managed to solve the vexing problems of hauling a bulky, heavy engine around in the car, and on my back. The bumper carrier was ready to haul the engine back to California, while the utility cart was ready to haul it out to the beach. My wing and luggage rode in the back seat. It added up to quite a load, but a little more air in the air shocks took care of that.

On May 3, I left once again for California.

In Hindsight, What Would I have Done Differently?

I would have tried very hard to dig up the money to buy a van. Yes, you can haul a PPG engine on the outside of your car on a bumper carrier. It sure beats taking the engine apart every time you want to fly. But nothing beats the ease, comfort, and security of hauling your assembled PPG engine inside a van. Plus you have plenty of room for all the rest of your flying gear. When the engine is inside the van, it's out of the elements and safe from curious hands. You can stop at a restaurant and go inside without constantly worrying about the engine being exposed to vandals. Strapping your PPG engine to the bumper is sort of like strapping your kid or your wife to the bumper. It works, but you can never really relax.

Chapter 14

The Demon Behind The Rock

My second trip to California was much the same as the first, but with one important difference. This time, instead of having the engine packed away in the trunk, it was riding outside on the rear bumper, on the new carrier that I'd just finished building.

In addition to the engine, I also had both paragliding wings with me. Hugh Murphy had recommended that my flying buddy, Mike, buy his own wing, since Mike weighed too little to safely fly my wing. So now Mike had his own Pro Design Compact wing which was slightly smaller than mine. The plan was to each fly our own wing, but to share the engine.

The first couple of hundred miles of the trip were the worst. Every time I speeded up to sixty or seventy miles per hour, I worried about the wind pressure on the engine cover causing the cage to collapse. At every rest stop I checked the cage very carefully; like a mother checking on her newborn every five minutes. The cage always looked fine. Either that cage was a lot stronger than it looked, or else the extra wooden bracing was making a difference. Maybe both. The only thing I didn't like about the new bumper carrier was that the top half of the cage stuck up above the trunk. Wearing its rain cover, the cage effectively blocked my rearview mirror. If someone was directly behind me, it was almost impossible for me to see them.

When I stopped for the night, I simply unfastened the engine from the carrier and took it into the motel room with me. As I result, I slept much better at night since I wasn't waking up every hour or so to look out the window to see if anyone had broken into the trunk to steal my precious engine.

When I arrived in San Luis Obispo the rain was pouring so hard that I could barely see the road. As I was unloading the engine at the Howard Johnson motel, my flying buddy, Mike, arrived in a cab from the airport. He had been able to fly into San Luis Obispo (the lucky stiff).

The next day dawned clear. Hugh met us at the motel, and was introduced to Mike. Then we slung on our gear and headed out for Moro Strand Beach for some kiting practice for Mike. I was really worn out after my long drive to California, so I just sat on the beach, took it easy, and occasionally gave Mike some assistance. It was fun to sit back like an old pro and watch a newcomer go though the training program. Having just finished the training myself, I was in an excellent position to know exactly what Mike was experiencing. I was able to give him some good pointers. (There's just nothing like a newly-minted expert to give tons of helpful advice.)

The next day we returned to Moro Strand Beach for more kiting practice for Mike. While Mike worked on his ground handling, I decided to take the engine up for a spin. I was also eager to give my utility cart its first real test. I removed the engine from the bumper carrier, then opened the trunk and lifted out the utility cart. I strapped the engine to the cart, slung the wing on my back, and headed for the beach.

What a difference! Instead of staggering over the soft sand with sixty pounds of engine on my back, the cart rolled along almost effortlessly on its big balloon tires. Now THIS was the way to transport a PPG engine!

I rolled the cart out to my selected takeoff spot on the beach and started setting up. The utility cart stood up on the sand very nicely. I removed the engine from the cart, raised the table flap, and propped the flap into place with the dowel rod. I started the engine and warmed it up for a few minutes, then killed the engine, picked it up, and set it on the table flap. I slipped on my flight gear and hooked the wing risers to the engine. Then I turned around, backed up to the engine, and slipped my arms through the shoulder straps. I leaned forward to pick up the engine slightly, then stepped away from the cart. What a difference! It was almost effortless. No more struggling to get to my feet with sixty pounds of engine on my back.

Hugh wheeled the cart out of the way while I bent over to fasten my leg and chest straps. I had ordered the vest extension that Hugh had suggested, and now my vest fitted much more comfortably around my big barrel chest. When everything was ready, I pressed the starter button and the engine roared into life again.

A few quick tugs on the front risers, and I'd built a fine wall with the wing. Another sharp tug on the front risers, and the wing shot up into the sky. It had been two and a half weeks since my last flight, but I didn't seem to have forgotten anything. The wind was blowing a perfect six miles per hour, and the wing flew very nicely in the smooth sea breeze. I spun around, hit the throttle, and started running. I was off the ground in just a few steps. This was the first time Mike had seen me fly. In fact, this was the first time Mike had ever seen a PPG actually fly (except on video).

What a difference the vest extension made! Now I could breathe while hanging in the leg straps. No more frantic efforts to get the footbar dropped so that I could kick back into the seat and start breathing again. Now I could take my time.

It was a really wonderful feeling to have mastered a new skill. Everything worked like it should, and I finally felt like I was in complete control.

Having flown the beach numerous times, I was ready for a change of scenery. About a mile behind the beach was a range of low, grass-covered hills. They were quite scenic, and I decided to fly over them. Before leaving the safety of the beach, I gained plenty of altitude. When I was about eight hundred feet up, I turned away from the beach and headed for the hills.

The view from up here was simply outstanding. It was half ocean, half land, and all sky. I was warm and comfortable, and the air was smooth as silk. I crossed over the coastal highway and drifted over the Exxon tank farm that sat atop one of the hills. It was so wonderful just to sit up here in the sky and to be able to see everything.

The wind was still blowing in off the ocean, so I crabbed the wing a little to the left to permit it to fly parallel to the range of hills. I slowly drifted over the wide valley that separated the tank farm from Cayucos Peak. I flew past the peak, only a couple of hundred feet above the summit. It was really cool to look down on the peak that I had launched from just a few weeks earlier.

Beyond Cayucos Peak was Whale Rock Reservoir. I didn't want to fly over the reservoir, so I started to make a gentle left turn to fly over the town of Cayucos. A small cloud drifted beneath me. Suddenly, two things hit me. The first was my realization of just how high I was. I was almost one thousand feet in the air, and felt very small and vulnerable. The world below looked absolutely enormous, and I actually felt a slight fear of falling. This was as high as I'd ever been with my PPG (although I'd been higher on unpowered PG flights). I felt like I might be getting just a touch of acrophobia. No problem. I would just descend a little.

The second thing that hit me was a slight bump in the air. The wing gently rocked for a couple of seconds, then returned to smooth flight. No danger, but it was enough to give me a scare. This was the first time I'd encountered any real turbulence, and I decided that I didn't much care for it. No problem. I would just head back to the beach where the air was always smooth.

I looked up at my trusty wing. Only now it didn't feel quite so trusty. I had just learned that it was not a rock-solid platform. It was a wing, flying through the air. If it hit a bump in the air, it would shake and I would feel it. Suddenly I got the same feeling that I'd experienced during my last high flight off Saddle Mountain. I realized that I was very high in the sky, and if anything managed to cause my wing to collapse and it didn't recover, I would plummet to the ground. It made me feel very vulnerable. I started thinking about flying with the reserve parachute I had bought while learning to fly unpowered paragliders. Even if I never had to use it, the reserve would probably give me great peace of mind.

But for now, the air had returned to smooth sailing. I drifted back over the beach and followed the coastline down to Moro Strand Beach. Below, on the beach, I saw Mike practicing his kiting on the sand. I had flown for nearly forty minutes and was thinking about soft landings and hot coffee.

In spite of the aerial bump, it had been a wonderful flight. However I was starting to notice a new problem. After about twenty minutes of flying, my arms started to get horribly tired. The problem was that I had to hold my arms over-head while flying, because that's where the steering line handles were located. I had never noticed this problem during unpowered paragliding flights. Of course my longest unpowered flight was only eight minutes, not really long enough for anything to become much of a problem. Also, the harness attachment points for the wing were about ten inches higher on my PPG harness than on my unpowered paragliding harness. That meant that my hands were being held about a foot higher while motoring. It made a tremendous difference. Obviously my wing had not been designed with powered paragliding in mind.

I finally let go of the steering lines, and rested my aching arms in my lap. What a relief! But I couldn't leave my hands in my lap for too long. With my hands in my lap, I wasn't holding onto the steering lines. That made me a pas-senger along for the ride, rather than the Pilot In Command. It was like taking my hands off the steering wheel in a moving car. Even if the road were very smooth and straight, I wouldn't want to keep my hands off that steering wheel for very long. I liked to keep my hands on the steering lines so that I would al-ways be in control of the wing. But flying around with my arms constantly held high was like being crucified. Obviously I was going to have to find an answer to this problem.

I made a fine landing on the beach and was soon relaxing in my beach chair, sipping hot coffee and watching Mike and Hugh work on kiting the wing. This was the life! I stared over at that little pile of cloth lying next to the engine. I still couldn't believe that thing actually flew! I still couldn't believe that it could pick me up into the air and carry me over mountains and valleys and oceans. An aircraft that I could put in the trunk of my car (or at least on the bumper). Unbelievable!

In spite of the aerial bump, and sore arms, I felt really good about this last flight. I felt a real sense of accomplishment. I had taken off, plotted a course over hills and valleys, and then steered back to my departure point. Of course having the ocean for a reference point, helped. I did everything that I was supposed to do, and I did it right. I felt about ten feet tall and covered with hair.

Little did I know what was heading my way. I was about to encounter the Demon Behind The Rock. But first it was time to pull another Really Dumb Stunt.

The next day it was off to Montana Del Oro Beach for some bunny hill flights for Mike off the sand dunes. I watched Hugh do a reverse inflation with Mike's wing, run it up the side of the dune, then turn and fly off the top. Three weeks earlier, when I watched Hugh do it for the first time, I'd been impressed. But now it looked easy. I decided to give it a try. (There's just nothing that a newly-minted expert can't do!)

As I inflated my wing, Hugh reminded me that the wind speed would steadily increase as I went up the dune. No problem. I was a bona-fide expert now. I went running up the dune, steering the wing as I ran. Near the top, I spun around to fly off the dune. But I didn't go anywhere. At this altitude, the wind speed was greater than the forward speed of my wing. I ended up going backwards, and getting dragged up the dune.

Oh dear! The only thing I could do now was collapse the wing. I did so, but I was facing forward, and I couldn't see the wing behind me. And the wing still had plenty of fight left in it. It proceeded to drag me across the face of the dune before I could finally get it completely collapsed. In the process I strained my back, resulting in a lot of lower back pain for the next several days, and no flying.

Important Lesson Number Five: "Just when you think you know everything, watch out!"

The next day, my lower back really hurt. I decided that I would just rest, and take it easy on the beach, rather than stay in the motel room and be bored. We returned to Montana Del Oro Beach for some more bunny hill flying for Mike. I decided to sit and watch from my beach chair at the bottom of the sand dune. When Hugh finally showed up to start Mike's lesson, I was sitting in my beach chair, drinking coffee, comfortably ensconced under a shelter made of driftwood and plastic ponchos.

I nodded at Hugh over my cup of coffee. "Like my beach shack?"

Hugh shook his head in disgust. "No hammock?"

"Working on it."

The next day I was back in my beach shack, watching Mike make some more bunny hill flights. Mike's ground handling skills were much improved, and so was my back, but it was still too sore for me to do any flying.

The following day, my back was even better. I made the mistake of mentioning this to Mike, and he suggested that if I would carry his wing to the top of the dune after each of his flights, he would have much more energy and could get in more flights. For some reason, I was willing to go along with this nonsense. With me packing his wing up the dune after each flight, Mike managed to get in seven practice flights that day. In spite of trudging up the loose sand, I was becoming a firm believer in using sand dunes for training hills. The student could concentrate on the flying and not worry about getting hurt if he fell down. Even a grassy hill was not nearly as forgiving as soft sand.

After three days of bunny hill flying at Montana Del Oro Beach, Hugh had us back at Moro Strand Beach. There was more ground handling training for Mike. My back was feeling pretty good by now, so I decided to go for another motor flight. I was planning to follow the beach past Moro Rock, and then continue on to Montana Del Oro Beach at the far end of the bay. It was a round trip of about twelve miles, and would take about forty minutes. Hugh warned me again about the lee-side turbulence that could be found behind Moro Rock, between the Rock and the shore, so stay out of it! He cautioned me to cross behind the Rock at least one hundred feet higher than the summit, in order to avoid the turbulence.

The wind was blowing about seven miles per hour as I took off. I stayed oriented into the wind until I'd gained a few hundred feet of altitude, then turned downwind toward the Rock. I kept the throttle at full power since I was going to have to go up to six or seven hundred feet to clear the Rock and its associated turbulence.

The ride down the beach was enjoyable, as always. As I approached the Rock, I saw that I was at least one hundred feet higher than the summit. I maintained my course and heading as I crossed behind the Rock and flew over the inlet to Moro Bay. In less than a minute I was clear of the Rock and across the inlet. I eased off the throttle and slowly descended as I continued to fly downwind along the beach.

When I was at two hundred feet of altitude I started to notice large numbers of birds flying beneath me. *Big* birds. Buzzards, in fact. Big, ugly buzzards. Huge flocks of them. They didn't seem to care much for the sound of my engine, but they made no move to approach me. That suited me just fine.

This area of the beach was largely deserted. It was easy to understand why. It was essentially a long spit of land, wrapping around the far side of Moro Bay, and it was a long walk to reach the end of it. And once you had reached the end, the only thing to do was to turn around and walk all the way back. I only spotted one elderly couple on the beach below me. They waved, and I waved back. I later learned that this part of Moro Bay was a nature refuge. Good thing I didn't try to land. I probably would have gotten a heavy fine.

After about fifteen minutes of flying I finally reached the end of the beach. Rocky headlands lay beyond, with no good place to land in case of engine failure. But I had reached my destination. Directly below me was Montana Del Oro Beach. There was the big sand dune where Mike and I had made so many training flights, and I could even see the remains of my beach shack at the base of the dune.

I circled the beach a few times and then started home on the return leg. Now I was flying into the wind, and my progress was much slower. It was a little chillier today, and I was not dressed quite warmly enough. I hunkered down in my harness, turned up my collar, and slowly worked my way back up the empty beach toward Moro Rock.

About halfway back to Moro Rock I saw what must have been a high school or college biology class, out to the beach for a little field work. The students were standing around while the instructor lectured them. I waved as I flew by, but nobody waved back. Strange. When did education become that interesting? Maybe the Professor had threatened to flunk anyone who looked up?

After several more minutes I was approaching Moro Rock. I realized that I was going to need more altitude to clear the summit safely, so I squeezed the throttle and started to climb. It quickly became a race to see if I would gain enough altitude before I reached the Rock.

I reached the shore of the inlet, close to the edge of the Rock, and it was decision time. Did I have enough altitude? I was plenty high enough to safely cross the inlet, but was I high enough to fly safely behind the Rock? I looked out at the nearby summit of the Rock. I was just about even with the top of it. Maybe a little higher. However I was not as high as I'd been when I crossed behind the Rock on the downwind leg of my flight. And I certainly did not have the one hundred feet of clearance that Hugh had recommended.

Was I high enough to avoid the lee-side turbulence behind the Rock? I wasn't certain. A huge rock, sitting in the flow of moving air, was just like a big rock sitting in the middle of a stream of water. Upstream of the rock, the water is smooth and undisturbed. However downstream of the rock, the water is rough and turbulent. Since I was passing "downstream" of the rock, I needed to be certain that I was high enough to avoid the turbulence behind the rock.

I knew that I could circle to gain more altitude before attempting to cross the Rock. But I'd been flying for half an hour and I'd already gained and lost a lot of altitude. It took extra fuel to gain altitude, and I'd burned up a lot of fuel to get above the Rock in the first place. Now I was proposing to burn up still more fuel to gain some additional altitude. If I stopped to gain more altitude, I might run short of fuel on the trip back. Although that would not be dangerous, it could be damned inconvenient. Unless there was a parking lot nearby, I might end up having to haul my rig quite a distance down the beach, on foot. Even with the utility cart, it would be inconvenient.

Unfortunately I could not check my fuel supply. I could not see the fuel tank, sitting directly behind my back, and I still had not acquired a hand mirror to enable me to see the fuel tank while in flight. And I was getting cold. I just wanted to finish this flight and relax in my beach chair with a cup of hot coffee.

The hot coffee won out. I decided to keep on going. I was level with the summit of the Rock. That should be enough to get me above the turbulence.

I was about hallway across the Moro Bay inlet, directly above the water, when it happened. One second I was flying along through smooth, steady air. The next instant I was being tossed around like a mouse at a cat convention.

I felt a violent jerk on my harness; harder than anything I'd ever felt before. I looked up in terror to see my wing thrashing around like a rattlesnake with a broken back. The wing was violently surging back and forth, and rocking from side to side. I watched in horror as the wing suddenly bent in the middle; the two wingtips swinging toward each other. I had run smack into the teeth of the Demon that lived behind the Rock.

I remembered what I'd been told about keeping the wing overhead, in turbulence. I tried to damp out the wing surges by applying some brake as the wing shot forward, and releasing the brakes when the wing rocked backward. I had no idea if I was doing any good (or even making the situation worse). Any second I expected the wing to collapse like a punctured balloon. I caught a glimpse of the cold waters of Moro Bay, directly below. If the wing collapsed and failed to recover, I might survive a water landing, but I didn't think much of my chances of getting out of the harness and floating to the surface without getting tangled in the chute and the lines. I had no flotation equipment.

Strangely enough, I didn't panic. I was a pilot, dammit! I was going to fly this thing until I either hit the water or reached safety. But which way should I fly? Straight ahead, or try to turn around? The way the wing was thrashing about, I wasn't even certain that I *could* turn around. Suddenly I remembered a piece of advice that Hugh had given me shortly after I started flying the engine. He said, "If you find yourself in trouble, that throttle is your Guardian Angel." Instantly I squeezed the throttle to full power. The wing continued to thrash and shake, but now I was climbing.

Suddenly, just as quickly as it had started, the turbulence vanished. I was climbing above the summit of Moro Rock, and I was out of the turbulent zone and back into smooth air. I had escaped from the Demon Behind The Rock. *Whew!*

It turned out that hitting the throttle was exactly the right thing to do. I was right on the edge of the turbulent zone, and by gaining just a bit of altitude, I lifted myself out of the turbulence. If I had not hit the throttle, but just plowed ahead through the turbulence, who knows what might have happened? Either way, I was very, very happy to have been flying that rock-solid, Pro Compact Design wing. It came through like a trouper. It shook and rocked and rolled and flexed, but it never collapsed. It kept flying, and brought me home safely. Good wing!

The rest of the trip back to Moro Strand beach was quite uneventful. However I didn't notice the scenery much. I was too busy thanking my lucky stars for letting me get out of that turbulence alive. I'd been lucky. I had let myself fly into lee-side turbulence. Stupid! I swore I would never make that mistake again. Turbulence is invisible, and you're bound to run into some from time to time, but at least you can avoid lee-side turbulence, because you always know where it is.

Important Lesson Number Six: "Stay out of lee-side turbulence!"

After I landed safely back at the beach, I got out of my flight gear and poured myself a cup of coffee. Then I let myself get the shakes. I described my experience to Hugh, and thanked him again for his good advice that pulled me out of the soup. Later that night I talked to Mike about it. He agreed that it's always good procedure to save the panic attack until after the emergency is over. Then you can wallow in it.

Once again I was reminded that there is a fine line between the thrill of flying, and disaster. Danger was always lurking just a short distance away. This was aviation. It could kill.

Two days later, after a day of rain, we were back at Montana Del Oro Beach. Mike practiced his reverse inflations and made a few more flights down the dune. I was still a little shaken after my encounter with the Demon of Moro Rock, so I just watched.

On March 14, Hugh announced that it was time for Mike's first motor flight. Mike had had done very well in his eight days of training, and had decided to make his first powered takeoff attempt without doing any practice kiting with the engine on his back. I couldn't blame him. Mike was smaller and lighter than me, and the sixty pound engine was a heavy load for him to carry. Also, Mike did not have the memory of a shattered prop to contend with, so he was very eager to fly. By contrast, I wanted to rehearse everything before I actually tried to fly with the engine.

As Mike got ready to launch, I was standing about a hundred feet away, operating the video camera. I'd discovered that the camera was a great way to critique a pilot's performance, and to spot errors. Mike had the engine on, and running. He was standing facing the wing with the steering lines in one hand and the front risers in the other. Hugh was giving him some last-minute instructions. Finally I saw Hugh clap Mike on the shoulder and move away. Mike started to tug on the risers to build his wing into a wall. The wind was blowing about seven miles per hour. The flying conditions were perfect. Although the day was quite cool, I was sweating blood. The only thing more nerve-racking than making your own first flight, is watching your best friend make *his* first flight.

Mike pulled on the front risers, and the wing shot up into the air. Mike took a step or two backwards, steering gently with the brake lines as the wing flew overhead. It was looking good. *Turn around and go!* I shouted to myself.

And that's exactly what Mike did. He spun around one hundred and eighty degrees, squeezed the throttle, and started running.

And promptly made his first mistake. Mike should have been off the ground in just a few steps, but he failed to look up at his wing while running forward. Almost immediately Mike ended up running one way, while his wing was going in a different direction. It prevented him from developing enough speed for liftoff. I held my breath. I was certain that the wing was about to become unrecoverable, and the launch would have to be aborted.

Suddenly Mike changed course about ninety degrees in the opposite direction. In only a moment he was back under the wing. Yay! But he quickly ended up going out of control in the opposite direction! Argh! Once again, the wing was about to become unrecoverable. I groaned. There was just no way Mike was going to get that wing off the ground. He and the wing were going to zigzag down the beach until they ran out of beach.

But today the Wind God was feeling merciful. In spite of his zigzag path, Mike had managed to build up a good bit of speed. He didn't weigh as much as I did, and that one hundred pounds of thrust on his back was really pushing him forward. As Mike reached one side of his zigzag path, he was suddenly yanked off the ground by the wing. Mike, the wing, and the engine, soared into the sky. He was up! He was flying!

I watched as the wing rocked from side to side, slowly dissipating the pendulum momentum that Mike's zigzag running had imparted to it. But then the wing quickly settled down and began to fly normally. I watched as Mike worked the steering lines to fly parallel to the beach, and climbed into the sky like a rocket. I started breathing again.

I walked over and shook hands with Hugh. I congratulated him on another successful student launch. Other than not looking up at the wing, and not staying centered under the wing, Mike did okay for his first powered flight. Fortunately the rig he was flying had enough power to overcome his less-than-perfect launching technique. If I had done likewise, I'd never have gotten off the ground. For me, there was barely enough power to fly, so I had to do everything right.

I watched as Mike slid back into his seat with no problem. Already he was doing much better than I had done on my first flight. For the next half hour Hugh and I watched as Mike flew around the beach, practicing his landing approaches. I noticed that the wind was steadily increasing. It was up to ten miles per hour. I didn't think Mike had ever landed in so much wind. Would he remember to use less brake? I found myself wishing that I could talk to him as he flew. But Hugh did not use radios in his instruction.

Finally Mike signaled that he was ready to land. I put down the video camera and watched as he came in much too low on his landing approach. However with engine power, it wasn't a serious problem. Mike kept the engine on until he had cleared the fence around the bird sanctuary. Then he realized that he was too close to the ground to take his eyes off the ground long enough to locate the kill switch on the throttle. I had made exactly the same mistake on one of my early engine flights. Either he must land with the engine running, or else abort the landing and go around. I was certain that he would abort.

But Mike was afraid that he might be nearing fuel exhaustion, so he elected to make a power-on landing. He actually touched down quite nicely, but then flared too hard with the brakes. Instead of collapsing, the canopy surged upward and backward, pulling Mike off his feet. Mike was about halfway turned around as he started to topple, *and the engine was still running!* If the spinning prop hit the sand, it would surely be destroyed. All I could do was run toward Mike, screaming futilely, "Kill the engine! Kill the engine!"

Mike fell down on his side, and I watched in horror as the cage and prop dug into the sand. But amazingly enough, neither was damaged. I later learned that Mike had managed to hit the kill switch as he was falling! He literally stopped the engine at the last possible second. The engine, cage, and prop, were undamaged. *Whew!*

Since the wind was now blowing too fast for a second flight, we all went to a nearby restaurant for lunch, and to discuss Mike's first flight. Needless to say, it was a very happy occasion.

The next day we returned to Moro Strand Beach for Mike's second flight. Unlike the previous day, this day was a complete disaster. The wind was blowing 10-12 miles per hour, and it turned out to be too much wind for Mike to handle, especially with the engine on his back. The wing thrashed like a tiger caught in a leg-hold trap. It was all Mike could do to remain on his feet. I kept hoping that Mike would decide to cancel his flying for today, but he very badly wanted to make that second flight. Nevertheless, I felt that conditions were marginal for a novice pilot. Mike could get the wing overhead, turn around, and start running, but the wing always ended up going sideways and collapsing. Once or twice Mike almost made it into the air. He worked very hard, but he simply couldn't get airborne.

If a PPG pilot can't launch, there are only two reasons why. Either he doesn't have enough training yet, or else the conditions are too strong for him to fly. I was convinced that I was seeing a little of both situations here. The wind was very strong for a novice pilot. I felt that Mike needed to practice kiting and launching the wing with the motor on his back; something he had never practiced. That was my newly-minted Expert Opinion, anyway. But I was not the instructor, and I was not confident enough in my diagnosis to push the point. Hugh thought that Mike just needed a little time to think about what he was doing, so we kept quiet while Mike sat on the ground, wearing the engine, going over his takeoff procedure in his own mind. Privately I suggested to Hugh that Mike take the prop and cage off the motor, and practice kiting with just the wing and motor. But Hugh didn't want to risk damaging Mike's self-confidence. Unfortunately, Mike was already starting to lose it.

It was a judgment call. Sometimes a student really does need to fall back for some additional training, and sometimes all he needs is a little push to get over the hump.

To his credit, Mike tried again and again to get airborne. But nothing seemed to work. At one point Mike managed to collapse the wing, causing the lines to fall down onto the prop cage with the engine still running. Mike killed the engine in time, but it was a *very* close call. He came within a hairsbreadth of duplicating my prop accident of the previous August. I decided that the prop cage needed to be covered with some fish netting to protect the lines from being sucked into the prop. The existing netting simply didn't get the job done. The gaps between the netting lines were too big.

After eight launching attempts, Mike decided to call it quits for the day. I really couldn't figure out exactly what he was doing wrong, and Hugh seemed to be uncertain as well. Maybe the wind was just too high for a beginner. Perhaps tomorrow Mike would have better luck.

The next day we returned to Moro Strand Beach, but the wind never fell below fifteen miles per hour. Too much wind for Mike *or* me to fly. Mike and I decided to return to the beach at sunset, in the hope that the wind would have died down. Hugh thought that was a good idea, even though he would not be able to join us.

About six hours later we were back at the beach. The wind had died down considerably. In fact, now it was almost too little wind. The wind was only blowing 4-5 miles per hour, and was fading. That was barely enough for a reverse launching, which was all Mike had been trained to do.

We hurried to lay out Mike's wing, and to get the engine warmed up before the wind fell too low for Mike to fly. Mike got into his flight gear, strapped into the engine, started the engine, and pulled the wing up into the air. It was a perfect launch. All he had to do was spin around and go.

But he didn't. Mike stood there for several seconds, steering the wing, until it started to collapse due to insufficient airspeed. Mike instantly killed the engine. When I asked him why he hadn't launched, he said that it "just didn't feel right" when he pulled the wing up. I commended him for his caution. Any time the pilot feels that something "just doesn't feel right," he should abort his launch.

I told Mike that his pull-up had looked perfect to me, and that all he had to do was turn around and fly. He decided to try again. In just a few minutes we had his wing repositioned for launch. Mike had the engine on his back, and was ready to pull the wing into the air. The wind was holding at a steady five miles per hour, and the sun was just above the horizon. This time I was convinced that Mike would get into the air, especially since there was no high wind to give him grief.

But this time our grief was man-made. Before Mike could launch, a park ranger's truck suddenly appeared on the beach, heading straight for us. The ranger stopped next to us and got out. He had a big NO written all over his face. Mike reluctantly killed the engine while I considered killing the ranger. Argh!

The park ranger was elderly (i.e., older than me), and kindly-looking. He was very apologetic, but very firm. He told us that he had to shut us down. He told us that paragliding wasn't permitted on California beaches. I told the ranger that I had talked to some of the local pilots, and they had said it was okay to fly on this beach. The ranger told me that I should have checked with the Park Service, because it was against the law.

At this point I wasn't certain what to say. Hugh had assured me earlier that he had a variance with the Park Service to fly paragliders on this beach, but even he wasn't absolutely certain if that included *powered* paragliding. That was a gray area that he was planning to discuss, one day, with the Head Ranger. In the meantime, this ranger was determined to do his sacred duty. At least he wasn't fining us, or writing us a ticket. He just wanted us to pack up and leave. Actually he was being a pretty good guy.

I decided to keep quiet, and not risk jeopardizing Hugh's toehold on this beach. I decided to let the ranger think that we were just a couple of out-of-town idiots who didn't know any better.

The next morning I told Hugh what had happened to us the previous evening. Hugh assured me again that he had a variance to fly that section of the beach. But he also told me that it might be best to wait until he'd had a chance to talk to the Head Ranger, the next day, and make certain that powered paragliding was okay. In the meantime he suggested that we go up the coast and fly at the Exxon beach.

Mike and I talked it over, and we decided that it was time to go home. We'd been in San Luis Obispo for thirteen days now, and we were scheduled to go home the day after tomorrow. I pointed out to Mike that we had accomplished what we had come here for. Mike had gotten the necessary training to fly a powered paraglider. All we needed now was a good place to continue flying, and we had plenty of those back home. And Mike and I were both getting tired of living in a motel room. We had accomplished what we had come to California to do. It had been a wonderful trip, but it was time to go home.

In Hindsight, What Would I have Done Differently?

Stayed out of the lee-side turbulence behind Moro Rock!
Stayed out of the lee-side turbulence behind Moro Rock!
Stayed out of the lee-side turbulence behind Moro Rock!

I wish Hugh had slapped me in the face while he was telling me to stay out of the lee-side turbulence behind Moro Rock. Flying into that turbulence was a dangerous and stupid thing for me to do. And to do it over water, with no flotation gear, was stupidity squared. I had been very lucky.

If I had it to do over again, I would also insist on doing all of my flight training with a radio. There are times when it can be an enormous help to be able to talk to the student in flight. For example, when Mike was making his first motor flight, and the wind suddenly picked up, we could have warned Mike, and then helped talk him down safely. Instead, Mike flared too strongly, fell down, and barely managed to kill the engine in time. He was very lucky. An instant later, and the prop and cage could easily have been damaged.

As long as a student pilot is being supervised by an instructor, he should carry a radio. It need not be two-way. It's quite enough for the instructor to simply be able to speak to the student in the air. With radios as cheap as they are, there's really no longer any excuse not to have one. For a student, it's a vital piece of safety equipment.

Chapter 15

Cops And Wings, And Things With Wings

After returning home from California, Mike and I were eager to continue flying. Mike was especially eager, since he had managed to get only one motor flight while in California. We decided that the smooth air and soft sand at the beach provided just the sort of conditions a couple of novice pilots like us needed.

The town of Ocean Shores, in the State of Washington, was a popular tourist attraction, but it appealed to us because we could drive a car right out onto the beach. In fact, you could drive a car for miles up and down the beach. The beach was actually designated as an official state highway! Could there be a more perfect setup for PPG flying?

Mike and I arrived in Ocean Shores in early evening and drove out to the beach. The day was overcast, windy, and somewhat cold for a day in June. But what a beach! If the beach at San Luis Obispo had been big, the beach at Ocean Shores was enormous. No worry here about running into the ocean!

The wind was blowing about five miles per hour, and Mike was eager to make his second motor flight. As he laid out his wing and got into his flight gear, I warmed up the engine. Very shortly Mike was standing in front of his wing, his engine idling, and he was ready to launch. But just as he took the steering lines and risers in his hands, preparing to pull the wing up, the wind abruptly died. As if someone had thrown a switch, the wind speed suddenly plummeted to zero.

I asked Mike if he wanted to try a forward, no-wind launch, but he said no. He'd had no experience or practice doing a forward launch, and he didn't feel he was ready to attempt one. I agreed.

But until Mike learned to do forward launches, he was at the mercy of the wind. To do a good reverse launch, the wind had to be blowing at a speed of at least five miles per hour, and right now it was absolutely calm. It was almost spooky. I'd *never* seen an ocean beach with a total absence of wind.

I'd done forward, no-wind launches from hills, but never with the motor, and never from level ground. Maybe it was time to try an inflation run in the calm air on the level beach, but without the motor. I got out my training harness, laid out my wing, and clipped in. I faced forward, took the steering lines and risers in my hands, and started running. The wing popped up overhead without difficulty. I ran forward, keeping the wing centered overhead. It flew fine. Heck, it was easy! I brought the wing down and tried it again. Again the wing launched with no problem and flew just fine.

I decided to try a forward, no-wind launch with the engine. I got into my flight gear, put the engine on, and got it started. But then, just as I was about to pick up my steering lines and risers, the wind started blowing again! In less than a minute, the wind speed meter was registering six miles per hour. Conditions were now perfect for a reverse launch. In fact, there was now too much wind for a forward launch! Mike suggested that I go ahead and do a reverse launch, and go for a flight, but I disagreed. The main purpose of this trip was to get Mike a second motor flight. After his first motor flight, the poor guy had tried *ten times* to get into the air again! Eight times he was frustrated by high winds and bad technique; the ninth time a park ranger chased us off the beach, and the tenth time the wind had suddenly died. I insisted on unhooking and getting Mike ready to fly.

Once again Mike went through the process of getting into his flight gear and strapping on the engine. He faced the wing, started the engine, and got the steering lines and risers in his hands. He got ready to pull the wing into the air.

And the goddamned wind promptly died again! I couldn't believe it! It was like some sadistic bastard was playing with the wind switch. At that point Mike said to hell with it, and started getting out of his flight gear. He announced that he would not fly again today, no matter what the wind decided to do! Mike started to unfasten his wing from his harness, then decided to take the engine off first.

I decided to go ahead with my original plan to do a forward inflation. Mike finished taking off the engine, then hurried over to help me lay out my own wing. Then he returned to his own rig to finish disconnecting the engine from his wing, and bring it over to me. A few moments later he was back. He had a funny look on his face. "What's wrong?" I asked.

Mike motioned for me to follow him. We walked over to where the engine sat on the sand. Mike's wing was still attached to the engine. He pointed to the left carabiner. I looked, and blanched.

The wing riser was only half connected to the carabiner! The riser strap had only been shoved about halfway inside the carabiner. The nylon strap was poised on the open shank of the carabiner; half in, half out. If Mike had succeeded in taking off, the riser might have stayed snagged on the point of the shank, or it might have slipped off and completely disconnected from Mike's harness. If the latter had happened, the entire left side of Mike's wing would have been disconnected from his harness, and would have collapsed. Even though the right side of the wing would have remained inflated, I doubt that Mike could have kept the wing under any sort of control. He could easily have been killed in the resulting crash.

And it would have been my fault, because I was the one who had originally hooked Mike's wing to his harness. I stared at the half-open carabiner in disbelief. How in the hell could I have only pushed the strap halfway inside the carabiner? I always pushed the strap all the way in, then made certain that the carabiner gate had clicked closed behind the strap. Then I always wriggled the strap to make absolutely certain that the nylon riser was securely locked inside the carabiner. How could I have failed to notice that the riser was only halfway inside the carabiner? That's like failing to notice that one of your legs isn't inside the car before you drive away.

But the evidence, no matter how impossible it might seem, was sitting right in front of my face. Something must have distracted me as I was hooking the left wing riser to the engine harness. I vowed that it would never happen again. Mike suggested that we should use a written checklist in the future, to avoid similar mistakes. I heartily agreed.

What do you say to your best friend after your negligence has just put his life in danger? "I'm sorry," just didn't seem to cut it.

Mike pointed out that it was an accident that could have happened to anyone. It could just as easily have happened the other way. He could have been the one who screwed up. So both of us had just learned a valuable lesson. This was aviation. It was spectacularly unforgiving of errors. Safety first! Live to fly another day.

Mike pointed out that it was also possible that he himself had partially disconnected the riser from his harness after deciding to cancel his flight. In fact, he specifically remembered starting to disconnect the riser from the carabiner, but then he changed his mind and decided to take off the engine first.

Mike's words made me feel a little better. It could have been that Mike partially disconnected the riser before he came over to help me. Maybe I hadn't really screwed up. Maybe Mike's flight would have been fine. We'll never know. But if we'd had a proper checklist, and had followed it religiously, there would have been no problem.

In the meantime the wind was still blowing a steady, four miles per hour. I decided to try a reverse inflation and launch. I'd never done a reverse inflation with the wind this low. Before I took off, I triple checked my wing risers. Mike then double-checked them. Then I started the engine, pulled the wing into the air, and started walking backwards as I steered it overhead.

As long as I continued to walk backwards, the wing flew just fine. If I slowed down, it threatened to collapse. Quickly I spun around, hit the throttle, and started running. About a dozen steps, and I was airborne. Yeehaa!

Damn but it felt good to be in the air again! I quickly kicked back in my seat and headed up the beach. I climbed to several hundred feet of altitude and started to enjoy the magnificent view. The whole town of Ocean Shores was spread out on one side, and the Pacific Ocean was spread out on the other. It was gloomy and overcast, but who cared? I was flying!

I flew up the beach for about ten minutes, then turned around to fly back to my takeoff point. As I passed over my takeoff point, I looked down to see a cop car parked nearby, and a couple of cops standing next to Mike. Uh-oh! This did not look good! I waved as I passed overhead, but nobody waved back. Definitely not looking good! (On the plus side, nobody shot at me.)

Being a brave man who never runs away from danger, I decided to let Mike handle the situation. I flew on down the beach, away from the cops, and circled over some people building a beach fire. I figured the cops couldn't touch me as long as I was up here. Eventually, of course, I was going to run out of gas, but by then I was hoping that the cops would have gone off to look for a donut shop.

After about twenty-five minutes of flying, I passed over Mike's location again. The cops were gone. Bursting with curiosity, I decided to land. It was starting to get dark anyway, and we still needed to find a place to stay for the night.

I made a fine landing in a gentle wind, and Mike wheeled the utility cart over the sand to pick up the motor. Mike waited until I removed my ear plugs, then told me what I'd already suspected. The cops said we couldn't fly here. It seemed that the beach was officially part of the State Highway System, and State Law prohibited aircraft from flying off a State Highway. Yeah, right. I looked around at the people building beach fires, and flying kites on the beach. Apparently it was okay to do *that* on a State Highway. Mike and I decided to find another place to fly; one with less chickenshit.

We found a motel room for the night. The next morning, Mike called the State Department of Transportation to get the straight dope. Cops frequently bend the law to suit their own prejudices, and we were determined to find out what State Law actually had to say about aircraft operating from ocean beaches in Washington State. I knew that I'd seen single-engine aircraft sitting on the sand, on these beaches, in years gone by. In fact, it had always been my understanding that aircraft were allowed to operate from the beaches.

Unfortunately, in this case, it turned out that the cops were right. According to State Law, aircraft were specifically prohibited from operating from State Highways, and the ocean beaches were classified as State Highways (so the tourists could legally drive on them). Damn!

But what about the aircraft that I'd seen operating from the ocean beaches? It turned out that one of the beaches to the north, Copalis Beach, was designated as an Official State Airport. It was perfectly legal to fly from there. Obviously that's where I'd seen the aircraft before.

But the helpful gentleman from the Department of Transportation also advised us that we might have a problem flying from Copalis Beach. It seemed that there were no roads going to Copalis Beach. Who needs roads when you've got an airplane, right? To get to Copalis Beach, we would have to walk for several miles, carrying our gear. Could we drive on the regular beach, to Copalis Beach? No, there was a nature preserve (which was neither driveable nor flyable) between the public beach (which was driveable, but not flyable) and Copalis Beach (which was flyable, but not driveable). Arrrggghh!

Welcome to the wonderful world of government.

We decided to pack up and drive toward Copalis Beach. Maybe we could find a way in. We knew that we could legally fly at Copalis Beach, and the cops couldn't touch us. All we had to do was find a way to get there.

Ya gotta be dedicated to be a powered paraglider pilot.

After a couple of hours of driving up and down the coast and asking questions of the local Gentry, we were forced to conclude that Copalis Beach was like the Hoboken Post Office. You Can't Get There From Here. So here we were, ready to fly, and no place to launch our fabulous flying machine. All dressed up, and no place to go.

But this part of the State was wild and lonely. There were many, many miles of ocean beaches, and very few cops to patrol them. We decided to head north, find a deserted stretch of beach, and fly anyway. It was time to become airborne criminals.

Important Lesson Number Seven: "Sometimes it's easier to ask for forgiveness than to ask for permission."

About fifteen miles north of Ocean Shores, and Copalis Beach, we passed a small sign on the road that pointed to "Roosevelt Beach." We decided to check it out, and turned onto a small side road. The side road ended in only about a hundred yards at an enormous, deserted beach. Paydirt! The beach was very wide, miles long, and there were no humans in sight. Perfect! We drove onto the hard-packed sand and drove about a mile down the beach. It looked like our luck had finally changed.

The morning fog had burned off, and the sun was starting to come out. The tide was out, and the beach was wide and dry. The wind was about six miles per hour. I told Mike to get his flight gear on while I mixed the fuel and warmed up the engine.

For Mike, attempt number twelve proved to be the magic number. He pulled the wing up into the air, turned around, and squeezed the throttle. Once again Mike failed to stay centered under the wing, and ran a zigzag path back and forth from one end of the wing to the other. But this time luck was with him. After a short run, the wing jerked him into the air. Mike oscillated back and forth a bit, but the wing quickly settled down for a fine flight. The important thing was that Mike was airborne again. He was away on his second flight. Now he knew that his first flight wasn't just a lucky accident (but we still gotta work on those take-offs!).

Mike flew up and down the beach for about forty minutes. He made several practice approaches before he finally killed the engine and drifted down for a landing. At touchdown he was not facing directly into the wind. This caused him to get blown sideways and to fall down. Luckily there was no damage to the engine or the pilot.

Mike was very, very happy. He had finally gotten his second flight. Now he was starting to feel like a real PPG pilot!

I asked Mike if he wanted another flight while the weather conditions were still good, but he declined. This last flight had taken a lot out of him. I knew exactly what he was talking about. The first few flights were always full of adrenaline rushes, and it was very exhausting. It made you feel like you'd done a full day's work in less than an hour.

While Mike rested, I decided to go for a flight. The wind was still blowing about four miles per hour, so I set up and did a reverse launch, followed by a perfect takeoff. I flew up and down the beach, enjoying the warm sunshine and magnificent view. About half a mile up the beach was the carcass of a dead whale. It was at least 15-20 feet long, and judging from the downwind stench, it had been dead for a long time.

I flew for about half an hour and then landed because my too-small harness started to get uncomfortable. I really needed to find a solution to my harness problem. The vest extension was nice, but there was still a problem with the height.

I finally landed next to a giant tree root snag that had washed up onto the beach. With miles of open beach to land on, I seemed irresistibly drawn to the only major obstacle on the beach (the snag). My landing was fine, but the wing fell on the tree root and became hopelessly entangled in the root system. It took us about forty minutes to free the wing from the snag, but fortunately there was no damage to the wing. Next time use some common sense.

By now it was the middle of the afternoon, so we decided to drive to the nearby town of Pacific beach for a late lunch.

Pacific Beach turned out to be a pleasant little place. It was only a fraction of the size of Ocean Shores, with just a couple of restaurants and gas stations, but it wasn't thick with tourists either. The Navy used to have a large warehouse facility in the town, but it had been closed for years. Pacific Beach was a quiet, peaceful little town.

After a tasty lunch of fish and chips, Mike and I returned to Roosevelt Beach. By now it was about 5:30 p.m., and a high overcast was starting to move in. There was a possibility of rain later that night.

Mike decided that he was still too tired to fly, so I decided to fly again. The wind had increased to about seven miles per hour, so I did a reverse inflation and launch. By the time I got into the air, it was six o'clock in the evening and fully overcast. The warm sun had disappeared.

Since I had flown up the beach the last time, I decided to fly down the beach this time. I knew that Copalis Beach was just a few miles down the coast, and I was eager to take a look at Washington State's answer to Shangri-La.

Flying downwind, I made excellent time. About a mile down the beach I flew along a high bluff that reached nearly two hundred feet above the beach. Atop the bluff were several expensive beach homes. One elderly gentleman was walking out onto his expensive deck to enjoy his magnificent ocean view, when he suddenly caught sight of me, whipping past at nearly thirty miles per hour, level with his deck, and only about a hundred feet away. I thought he was going to drop his drink. I don't think he had any idea what he was seeing. I wonder if anyone ever believed his story?

Another mile beyond the beach homes, and I was rapidly running out of beach. The enormous beach had dwindled away to a mere, wave-washed shelf below the high bluff. Obviously I was rounding a headland. No doubt the beach would soon reappear, but for the next few minutes I would need to make certain to keep plenty of altitude so that I could glide to safety if my engine quit.

I was now out over the ocean, about two hundred feet above the water. On my right was the vast expanse of the Pacific, looking very cold and unfriendly. On my left was the bluff. But there were no houses here; just tall, stately firs.

Suddenly I spotted one dead tree, taller than all the rest, with a very large nest at the top. Uh-oh! That nest was big enough to hold me. There was only one bird that built a nest that big. I looked to see if anyone was home. At that moment, Mamma Bald Eagle spread her wings and lifted off the nest. I didn't know how many little eaglets were in that nest, but it was quite obvious that Mama Eagle did not consider me to be a welcome visitor. She circled her nest several times before heading straight toward me. I wondered how long it would take her razor-sharp claws to shred my wing and send me plummeting into the cold waters of the Pacific? I suddenly realized how utterly vulnerable I was. I felt like an old, lumbering, World War II bomber being attacked by an agile German fighter.

Instead of continuing to follow the shoreline, I turned to the right, about thirty degrees. This took me further out over the ocean, but it also took me away from the eagle nest. I could only hope that my departure was fast enough to suit the eagle. I found myself wishing that I could get out and push.

I kept nervously glancing behind me. I was relieved to see that the eagle had broken off the chase. She still flew around in the vicinity of the bluff, but seemed to be making no further effort to chase me. After about a minute, she returned to her nest. *Whew!* In the future I would make a strenuous effort to avoid eagle nests.

Important Lesson Number Eight: "Avoid big birds with big sharp claws!"

As I expected, the beach opened up again beyond the headland. In the distance I could see the town of Copalis. That meant the long stretch of sand, just ahead of me, must be Copalis Beach. This was where aircraft were permitted to land and take off. Only there were no aircraft around; just a few lonely hikers trudging along the shore. I reduced engine power and drifted down over the beach.

The beach was actually a very large peninsula, formed by a small river that flowed into the sea. Only now the tide was in, and the small river had become a rather large inlet, several hundred feet wide at the mouth. I crossed the inlet safely, but I wasn't too comfortable as I flew over it. Without any flotation gear, I doubted that I'd survive a water landing.

I dropped down low over Copalis Beach. It was definitely big enough for small aircraft to land and take off, but the DOT man had been right. There simply were no roads going to Copalis Beach. Apparently the only way to get here was to walk up the beach from the town of Copalis. It was at least a two-mile walk. Even with my utility cart, it wasn't a trip that I'd care to make. Besides, who needed Copalis Beach when we had Roosevelt Beach? (At least until the cops caught us.)

It was getting darker, and I decided that it was time to start back. I turned the wing around and headed back up the coast. Flying into the wind, I barely seemed to be moving. Obviously it was going to take a lot longer to get back than it took to get here. And I was starting to get chilly. Without the sun, it was getting pretty cold up here.

But the cold quickly became the least of my worries. The wind was blowing at seven miles per hour when I took off, and it seemed to have gotten a little stronger. As I started to cross the inlet that formed the Copalis Beach peninsula, I noticed how slow my ground speed had become. Obviously it was going to take much longer to get back across the inlet. It was one thing to be over water for just a few seconds; it was quite another to be suspended above the water for several minutes. And if that wasn't enough, the wing suddenly started to rock and bump a bit in some turbulence. The ocean air, which was normally smooth as silk, seemed to have found some turbulence somewhere, solely for my benefit. Once again I was aware that without a reserve parachute, I was utterly dependent on that fabric wing stretched out overhead.

I was starting to think that I might be getting into a bad situation. If this turbulence got any worse, I might have to turn around and land back on Copalis Beach. I couldn't risk crossing a stretch of water if there was any chance that I might take a wing collapse. If I went into that water, I'd probably die of hypothermia, even if I didn't drown first.

But the turbulence stayed light as I slowly made my way across the inlet. It was amazing how something that looked so harmless, just ten minutes earlier, now looked so threatening. Fortunately the turbulence didn't get any worse, and a few minutes later I was safe on the other side of the inlet.

Well, not completely safe. I wasn't home yet. I still had to pass the eagle's nest to get home. Fortunately it was late enough in the evening that the eagle had probably settled down for the night. (Did eagles fly at night?) I didn't think she'd bother me. Nevertheless, I decided to give her nest as wide a berth as possible, even though it meant flying out over the ocean.

It was at that moment, flying several hundred feet above the cold, crashing waves, a couple of hundred feet offshore, with no place to land in case of emergency, that I realized that I hadn't exercised the best judgment in the world. It was almost dark, and I was flying a very frail craft over some of the most rugged territory imaginable. If I crashed, even if I managed to reach land, it could take days for the searchers to find me. This was very wild, rugged country, and it only took a single misstep to get yourself into deep trouble. In hindsight, I realized that I should have skipped this last flight. True, there had been enough time to make the flight, *but only if everything went right.* If any single thing was to go wrong, I could be looking at disaster. At the very least, I could find myself down on a strange beach, at night, in the cold rain, with no shelter, miles from the car, with Mike having no idea where I was.

Important Lesson Number Nine: "Never try to cut it too close. Always give yourself plenty of safety margin. You may need it."

But tonight my luck held. I rounded the headland with no sign of the eagle. Roosevelt Beach quickly regained its former size, and in only a couple of minutes I was back over safe territory. If something was to go wrong now, the worst that could happen was that I would have to walk a couple of miles to reach the car. Inconvenient and uncomfortable, but not life-threatening. I even felt a little warmer.

Forty minutes after taking off, I spotted the car in the distance. Mike had even turned on the headlights to help guide me in. It was a very welcome sight. I landed with no problem. And the hot coffee in my thermos was pure ambrosia.

We packed up the equipment and headed back to the town of Pacific Beach. There was a nice little motel a few blocks from the beach. Since it was the middle of the week, the manager gave us a multi-room suite for only sixty dollars. The room came with a completely equipped kitchen with a dining area, a living room with a sofa, and two separate bedrooms. Nice! We had paid a lot more, for a lot less, the previous night in Ocean Shores.

The motel manager noticed the engine, riding on the bumper, and asked what it was. Mike explained how it worked, and showed him some pictures. The manager seemed very impressed. He gave us a ground-floor suite, which meant that I didn't have to carry the engine up a flight of stairs (much appreciated!). We told the manager about our experiences with the Ocean Shores police, and how we happened to end up in the town of Pacific Beach. The manager assured us that we were quite welcome to fly our PPG from the local beaches, and that the local police wouldn't bother us up here in God's Country. What a wonderful place! Good food, inexpensive accommodations, and a constabulary that welcomed us rather than chasing us away. I was beginning to like this town!

The next day, we went back out to Roosevelt beach. It was overcast, windy, and the sky was spitting a little drizzle. Mike and I were both feeling cold and tired, so we decided to go home. But we both agreed that it had been a very worthwhile trip. We had found a great place to fly, and a nice place to stay, and Mike had made that all-important second flight. Now he knew that he could fly a powered paraglider. His basic training had been completed.

Both of us were now powered paraglider pilots.

In Hindsight, What Would I have Done Differently?

Stayed away from eagle nests.

Stayed away from giant tree snags.

Skipped my last flight of the day.

I really can't emphasize this last one enough. Don't go flying over rough, in-hospitable territory when it's almost dark. If anything goes wrong, and you have to make an emergency landing, you could have a very tough time of it.

I now carry one of those little Space Rescue Blankets in my pocket whenever I fly. In case I go down, and have to spend the night somewhere, at least I'll have something to keep the wind and rain off.

I also always carry a cell phone when I fly. Excellent for calling for help (providing you have coverage).

And finally, I also carry an Emergency Locator Transmitter (ELT). It's an electronic beacon about the size of a pack of cigarettes. If I crash, all I have to do is turn it on, and the searchers will know where to look.

It's tough enough to find a small *airplane* that has gone down in rugged country. A crashed PPG could easily prove to be impossible to find. A cell phone and/or ELT can be your electronic Guardian Angel if you regularly fly over inhospitable territory.

Chapter 16

Win A Few; Lose A Few

During my last flight I had encountered a bad-tempered eagle and some mild turbulence. I'm not sure which was more scary. I'd also been reading a lot of reports of wing collapses and other sorts of paragliding accidents. These were all in the unpowered paragliding world, but since they flew the same wings that I did, there seemed to be a certain relevancy. I felt that I might be taking unknown risks. I was especially worried about having a wing collapse close to the ground. I knew it wouldn't take much of an impact to really damage my landing gear, or even worse.

My limited flying experience brought up a lot of questions. How often did PPG pilots suffer wing collapses? What was their accident rate? Their mortality rate? Just how safe WAS this sport? I felt like I was moving into unknown territory, and was trying to "wing it" without adequate knowledge.

The chief problem was that powered paragliding was so new that there wasn't much of a supporting infrastructure in place yet. If you wanted to learn to fly an airplane, a fixed-wing ultralight, or even skydive, there were plenty of good books and other resources on the subject. There were books on unpowered paragliding, but they didn't address the safety issues from the point of view of powered paragliding. I knew there were dragons in the sky, waiting to bite me, but where were they? I had already run into one dragon, behind Moro Rock, and I had no desire to meet his relatives that lived elsewhere in the sky.

Even though I could now qualify for a P2 rating, I also knew that a pilot could earn a P2 rating without ever learning how to deal with the dragons. I knew there were training courses in advanced wing control, but it was also generally agreed that a pilot should have forty or fifty hours of flight time before taking such a course, in order to get maximum benefit from it. On the one hand, everyone agreed that the advanced wing control courses were well worth the money. On the other hand, most pilots didn't bother with them. Me, I just wanted the reassurance that no matter what happened to my wing, in flight, I would be prepared to handle it. And I did not feel that I was prepared. Far from it! I knew that I was still ignorant about many aspects of this sport.

I guess what I really wanted was a bona-fide expert to tell me what I needed to know, and what I needed to do, in order to fly safely. I did not want to continue to figure it out as I went along. Or to play Test Pilot. The School Of Hard Knocks is a very effective teacher, but the tuition tends to be outrageously expensive and painful.

We also needed to find some local fields to fly from. It was a long drive to the ocean beaches, and it was expensive to stay overnight in a motel. I also wanted to learn to do forward launches with the motor so I could launch in winds of less than four miles per hour. Forward launches had always hurt the muscles in my arms. I had heard that you could actually tear your arm muscles by pulling the wrong way. I wanted to learn the right way.

I figured that if I wanted to know where the local flying fields were, then ask the local fliers. I had met a local PPG flyer named Tyson Russel a few months earlier. I called him to see if he knew of any good spots nearby.

Tyson was pleased that I had remembered him after so many months. He told me that he mainly flew from local high school playing fields. They offered smooth, level, grassy surfaces, and they were frequently open to the public. I also learned that Tyson had recently become a PG/PPG flight instructor, and was starting his own business. I explained to Tyson that I thought I needed some follow-up instruction. He offered to give me five lessons for a reasonable price.

For my first lesson Tyson suggested that we fly from a large playing field at one of the local high schools. I drove down to the school and checked it out. It was a nice field, but it was surrounded by tall trees, shopping centers, and busy highways; a little too congested for my taste. It would be a fine place to fly as long as nothing went wrong, but I was uncomfortable with the setup. I wanted a wide open place to fly, surrounded by wide open fields.

So Mike and I went looking for such a place. We found one good possibility; a glider port nestled in the foothills of the mountains. It was wide open and grassy but was surrounded by tall trees. When the wind blew, I knew those trees would generate rotors. The rotors wouldn't bother a rigid-wing glider but could be deadly to a ram-air wing.

By chance we happened to drive by one of the overflow parking areas for the County Fair. It was outside of town, surrounded by open pastures, and was empty pastureland for fifty weeks out of the year. Perfect!

For my first lesson Tyson suggested that we meet on the playing field of another public school that he had recently discovered. He said it was better than the first one he had told me about. Plenty of wide-open areas around it. Plenty of room for mistakes. It sounded good to me.

Several days later, at the appointed time, I met Tyson at the school. It was everything he had claimed it to be. Yay! Unfortunately it was also swarming with kids who were playing Little League baseball. Yuck! Legally we had as much right to be there as the kids. However I did not want to fly a powered paraglider with hundreds of small children only a short distance away. I had visions of the propeller chopping a wide swath through a sea of children. I suggested that we retire to the parking lot at the County Fairground, which happened to be nearby, and Tyson agreed.

Unlike the school, the fairground parking lot was blessedly deserted. I spent the first hour of my lesson just talking to Tyson. It was so wonderful to have someone who could answer my questions and who could explain the principles behind safe PPG flying. I asked Tyson about the frequency of wing collapses, and he said that in his two years of PPG flying he had never had any sort of wing collapse; not even a tip fold. That was very reassuring to hear!

I asked Tyson why a PPG pilot was supposed to avoid flying in the middle of the day, when the thermals were at their strongest, while unpowered paraglider pilots deliberately sought out thermals for the lift they provided. Tyson explained that an unpowered paraglider pilot was much more aware of what his wing was doing. The unpowered paraglider pilot could hear every sound his wing made, and could feel every twist and tug. This was not the case with the PPG pilot. The roar and vibration of the engine completely masked many of the all-important clues that the wing provided. Thus it generally took the PPG pilot much longer to realize that trouble was brewing, and correspondingly longer to start taking corrective action. This was why a PPG pilot normally restricted his flying to early morning or late afternoon, when the thermals were not so strong. However if a PPG pilot wanted to fly in the middle of the day, and was willing to get the extra training in order to fly safely, it was possible.

Tyson answered all of my questions and put a great many of my fears to rest. After talking to him, I felt much better. I felt like I now had an experienced guide for my safari, and was no longer trying to find my own way through the dangerous, unknown jungle.

I told Tyson that I was very comfortable doing reverse inflations, but that I wanted to learn to do forward inflations so that I could fly in calm conditions. Tyson agreed to teach me how to do a forward inflation. I learned that forward inflations on level ground were done in much the same fashion as launching from hills. The major difference was that the pilot did not have the extra gravity assist of running downhill, and could not afford to be sloppy in his launch technique. He must do everything right, or he would probably fail the launch.

The first thing Tyson taught me was to pull with my chest, rather than with my arms. Just like a plow horse, I found that I had far more pulling power in my chest. Tyson also showed me how to back up all the way to the edge of the wing before starting my takeoff run. Very important! When flying from hills, I had just backed up a step or two, and then started my run. That was good enough for a hill launch, but it would never do on flat land. It took a lot of energy to pull a big wing up into the air. The farther and faster that I ran before starting to pull on the wing, the more momentum I could build up to launch the wing into the air. So back up all the way to the edge of the wing before starting the takeoff run! Don't waste that energy!

Under Tyson's instruction, I was able to do several forward inflations in no wind without wearing the motor. All of that ground handling practice I had put in with Hugh Murphy was paying off. I learned that it was more important than ever to stay centered directly under the wing, and it was even more important to keep moving at all times. If I managed to pull the wing up overhead, I could not stop to admire it for even a split second, or else the wing would lose too much airspeed and collapse on top of me.

I practiced and practiced and practiced under Tyson's guidance. Between lessons I practiced some more. I knew that if I couldn't inflate the wing without the engine, I'd never be able to do it with the engine. That seemed to be only common sense, but I learned later that this was not necessarily true.

After doing several successful forward inflations without the engine, I tried a couple of inflations while wearing the engine, but with power off. To my amazement, both inflations were successful, and fairly easy. The wing popped overhead and I was even able to run it down the field. If I'd had power, I'd have easily flown. I found that by increasing my weight and mass, the engine actually made the launching process somewhat easier (more moving mass = more kinetic energy for the wing).

After the successful power-off forward inflations while wearing the engine, I tried it with the engine running. Unfortunately, my two launch attempts with the running engine, failed. The wing collapsed before I could get it overhead. I was nervous, and probably pulled too hard on the front risers during the take-off, collapsing the leading edge of the wing. The video seemed to confirm that.

Mike and I took turns recording each other with the video camera. I quickly became a firm believer in videotaping every launch. You can't argue with a video camera, and you don't have to try to remember exactly what you did wrong.

The problem was that sometimes my forward launch technique worked just fine, and sometimes it didn't work at all. Sometimes the wing shot up overhead like a rocket, and I was able to easily run down the field with the wing flying overhead like a big, beautiful kite. Other times I could only pull the wing about halfway up off the ground before it would collapse back to earth like a dead bird.

And that simply drove me nuts! I hated uncertainty! I wanted things to be-have in a rational, orderly, and predictable manner. That damned wing seemed to have a mind of its own. It only flew when it felt like it.

It took awhile, but I finally tracked down the culprit that was responsible for my variable launching success. It was the evening dew! As soon as the dew started to form, the wing started to get wet. And when the wing got wet, it got heavier. And when it got heavier, it became much more difficult to launch.

Bit by bit I was slowly getting better at launching the wing in no wind. In-stead of pulling with my arms, I was now pulling with my chest. I used my arms as "feeler gauges" to follow the movement of the risers as they rose up behind me. That way I knew what the wing was doing from moment to moment. If it was not coming up perfectly straight and level, I could start to take corrective action before I could even see the wing overhead.

On my reverse launches in California, I had difficulty in gripping both front risers in my right hand while also holding the plastic throttle in my right hand. It was hard to keep the risers from slipping out of my hand when I pulled the wing up. I decided that what the front risers needed, were handles. Instead of trying to grasp a slippery nylon strap in my hand, I would simply hook my fin-gers through a handle.

I bought an extra pair of steering line handles and attached them to the metal links at the top of each front riser. The riser handles turned out to be wonderful for reverse launches. While grasping the throttle in my right hand, I simply hooked both riser handles over the bottom three fingers of my right hand, and then pulled when ready. No strain. No slippage. The handles gave me perfect, total control over the launching sequence.

I figured that if the riser handles worked so well for reverse inflations, they might work equally well for forward inflations. So I hooked a riser handle over each thumb, started a forward launch, and as the wing started to rise into the sky, pulled forward with both thumbs to move the wing overhead.

Unfortunately, the riser handles sometimes worked too well during forward inflations. I frequently pulled too hard on the handles and ended up causing the leading edge of the wing to collapse (my old nemesis). Or else I failed to pull hard enough, and the wing collapsed to the ground. The problem was that I couldn't see the wing during a forward inflation, and could not judge, solely from the pressure on my thumbs, what the wing was doing.

About then I remembered the "open-palm" technique that Marty had taught me back in Ellensburg. Instead of actively gripping the front risers during a forward inflation, he had taught me to simply hold my open palm against the front riser, and push lightly to help get the wing into the air. I figured that what had worked so well on the hill, might work just as well on the flatland, so I tried it.

To my surprise, it worked very well. I could simply use my open palms against the front risers to "push" the wing overhead. Lightly pushing on the front risers seemed to feed just the right amount of pressure to cause the wing to fly overhead. And the feedback on my open palms was excellent for telling me just what the wing was doing at any given instant.

Basically the secret for a successful forward inflation turned out to be judicious application of pressure to the front risers. The idea was to pull the wing up into the air using your chest, and to follow its progress by using your arms as feeler gauges. Then if the wing started to slow down before reaching its zenith, a little forward pressure on the front risers would cause the wing to finish moving overhead. Once the wing was flying overhead, I could simply squeeze the throttle and take off.

In other words, pressure on the front risers was only used to "tease" the wing to help get it overhead; not to drag it into the air as I sometimes tried to do. Sometimes I needed the extra pressure; sometimes not. The right amount of pressure on the front risers was simply an applied skill that had to be learned, but once it was learned, forward inflations became relatively easy.

If only I had stopped there! I had mastered the technique of the no-wind forward inflation. All I had to do was practice it a bit, and then put on the motor and fly. But as usual, I had to overdo it. I happened to ask Tyson about the typical success rate for no-wind forward inflations. He said that even the experts could only get them right, on the first attempt, about sixty or seventy percent of the time. The rest of the time it might take two or three attempts to do a successful forward launch in no wind.

Naturally that wasn't good enough for me. I wanted at least a 90% success rate for forward launches; preferably more. It took a lot of time and energy to get set up for a forward launch with a PPG engine. The wing had to be carefully laid out and lined up directly into the wind, the lines had to be checked, then the flight gear and the engine had to be donned. Then the pilot had to race forward with all possible speed. If I was going to do all of that on a hot summer day, I wanted that wing to fly the first time; not the second or third!

Assuming the wing was laid out properly, I realized that the difference between success and failure, on a forward launch, depended on the amount of pressure I exerted on the front risers. Too little, and the wing might fail to launch. Too much, and the wing might collapse. However just the right amount of pressure would cause the wing to leap into the sky like a well-trained horse. Then it was simply a matter of applying power and taking off.

It all hinged on those damned front risers! But requiring me, the pilot, to put the proper amount of pressure on the front risers, was too uncertain. Being human, I did it differently every time. I thought that if the pressure on the front risers could be standardized during takeoff, then virtually every forward launch would be successful.

That was the theory, anyway. I spent nearly a month trying develop a device that would always apply the correct amount of pressure to the front risers, and make forward launches automatic and successful every time. I came up with several different implementations. None of them worked well enough to be put into practice, but I mention them here, just in case someone else is thinking along similar lines. You might as well get the benefit of my blood and sweat. Maybe you can succeed where I failed.

First I tried mounting a bar across the top of my engine frame, just in front of the prop cage, with a prong at each end to hold the metal links of the front risers. The prongs pulled the front riser straps forward with a constant, steady pressure while the wing was being inflated. As soon as the wing was overhead, the front risers slipped off the prongs and the wing was ready to fly.

During unpowered ground tests, my riser bar system seemed to work just fine. I simply ran forward, and the wing promptly rose into the air. It made the launching process completely automatic.

I was convinced that I had a real winner. I was ready to turn on the motor and fly happily ever after. Perfect launches every time! But then I thought about it some more. What would happen if I needed to deploy my reserve parachute while flying? That riser bar stuck out on either side of my motor frame like a big metal claw, just waiting to snag my reserve. I decided it was too big a risk.

Oh well, it was a nice idea while it lasted.

So get rid of the bar, and substitute a pair of short ropes. Pulls just as well, and nothing to snag. I used a pair of short nylon cords to connect each riser strap to the straps of my harness, and thereby put just the right amount of pressure on the front risers. Then when the wing was overhead, I would release the cords from my harness and permit the wing to fly normally.

I tried it and it worked. The wing leaped into the sky every time. Once again I was convinced that I had reached Launching Nirvana. But there was just one little problem. The nylon cords maintained the perfect amount of pressure on the front risers, but they also required me to keep my hands in front of my shoulders, ready to release the cords as soon as the wing was overhead. Unfortunately, if my hands were busy in front of me, then they weren't behind me, monitoring the progress of the wing. If the wing was not coming up straight, or was drifting off to one side, I wouldn't know about it until it was too late to correct it. I hadn't realized just how important it was to keep my hands on the wing risers during the launch. Curses! Foiled again!

After spending all of this time trying to devise the perfect mechanical wing launching system, I decided to go back to the traditional method. I pulled with my chest, kept my hands behind me on the risers, and used my open palms on the front risers to help "tease" the wing into the sky.

And it worked! In fact, it worked every time I tried it. I tried launching six times, and every time the wing came up perfectly, under my complete control. And in no wind! I guess I just needed a little more practice, rather than a Rube Goldberg mechanical device.

I'm happy to report that my forward launching technique appears to be almost 100% reliable on the first attempt. I'm not really sure why other pilots have trouble with forward launches. Maybe Tyson was just being conservative with his 60-70% estimate. Or maybe I simply stumbled onto just the right combination of wing and technique.

Whatever it is, it seems to work every time. I'm very pleased.

In Hindsight, What Would I have Done Differently?

Remember the K.I.S.S. principle. Keep It Simple, Stupid!

The brake handles on the front risers, for easier reverse inflations, turned out to be an excellent idea. The many other ideas I tried in an attempt to automate the job of forward launching, were all too complicated. In the end, it was the absence of the extra devices that made me successful. Another important lesson to learn. Sometimes simpler is better.

Chapter 17

A Crisis Of Nerve

Almost two months went by while I trained with Tyson Russell and tried to invent the perfect forward launch technique. I wanted Mike to get some more flights, so I suggested we go back to the ocean beaches. At the beach, there would be enough wind for Mike to do some reverse launches. On August 8th, we went back to Roosevelt Beach.

We arrived at the beach in late afternoon and were greeted by winds that exceeded our ten mile per hour limit. In addition to the high wind, I was having a real crisis of nerve. I wasn't sure why. Maybe it was the turbulence I'd encountered during my last flight at Roosevelt Beach, or maybe it was all those depressing paragliding accident reports I'd been reading. Or maybe it was the videos that showed just how violently a paraglider wing could collapse. Whatever the reason, I found myself feeling very anxious at the prospect of flying. I felt like I was having a real anxiety attack.

I was also getting quite annoyed with the wind. Although I'd finally perfected my forward launch technique, I still had not actually done a forward motor launch in no-wind conditions. Now that I'd come to the beach, where I could expect to find enough wind for a reverse launch, the damned wind was blowing too hard!

Being limited to flying only when the wind was blowing between five and ten miles per hour was proving to be a real drag. I needed to expand my flight envelope. I had spent the last two months trying to figure out how to fly when the wind was less than five miles per hour. Now I was being denied flight because the wind was more than ten miles per hour. I was getting shafted from both ends.

I knew that a PPG could safely fly in winds up to fifteen miles per hour. I got

215

out the wind speed indicator and took a reading. The wind was blowing between thirteen and fourteen miles per hour. Since we couldn't fly with the engine, I decided to get out my training harness and do some high-wind kiting. The sooner I mastered handling the wing in these higher winds, the sooner I would be able to fly in such winds. And the beach was the perfect place to learn. If I fell down, at least the sand would be soft.

When the wind is zero, a paraglider wing is like a big kite that just won't stay in the air. You can get it airborne for a few seconds by running real fast, but you can't keep it there for long. When the wind is blowing at five miles per hour, a paraglider wing is like a faithful dog out for a walk on a fine spring day. It heeds your every command, and is a joy to handle. At ten miles per hour, the wing is like a spirited horse that needs to be controlled very carefully. But at fifteen miles per hour, the wing is like a berserk whale, and you are Captain Ahab. If you let it catch the wind, it will instantly turn into a giant drag chute and drag you, willy-nilly, across the ground. Under such conditions, the wing is far stronger than you are and cannot be beaten by brute strength. It must be kept under constant control. If your control lapses, even for a second, the wing will surge out of control and take you with it.

In light winds, the wing is controlled by holding the front risers in one hand and the steering/brake lines in the other. Pulling on the front risers permits the open cells to catch the wind, inflate, and rise into the air. Pulling on the brake lines keeps the wing on the ground. But in winds above ten miles per hour, the brakes are ineffective. To keep the wing under control, you must use the rear risers instead of the brakes. Only then can the wing be kept sufficiently collapsed to keep it on the ground.

The real problem with trying to launch in a high wind (10-15 miles per hour), is getting started. As soon as the wing is dumped out on the ground, some of the cells will immediately catch the wind, inflate, and try to fly. Usually the inflation occurs on only one side of the wing, causing control problems. If the inflation is sufficiently unbalanced, it can even cause the wing to turn upside down and smash into the earth with a mighty *whump!* The momentary overpressure from such an impact can actually cause the cells to burst open. I knew that if I could get the wing to inflate evenly, I could keep it under control, even in a high wind. But how to control the inflation?

I finally came up with the idea of holding down one end of the wing, using Mike as an anchor, and laying out the rest of the wing downwind. This prevented the wing from inflating, since the long axis of the wing was now parallel to the direction of the wind.

With Mike holding down the end of the wing, I secured the front risers in one hand and the rear risers in the other. Then, with my control firmly established, I slowly started to pivot the wing into the wind, using Mike as the pivot. Some of the cells started to inflate, but since the wing was still at an extreme angle to the wind, the cells did not fully inflate, and the wing stayed on the ground.

By slowly "introducing" the wing to the wind, I was able to gradually get all of the cells inflated while keeping the wing safely on the ground. Eventually I had the wing fully inflated and facing directly into the wind. Even with the rear risers firmly in hand, the wing was still very strong, and it was very tiring to exert the constant effort need to hold it on the ground. I told Mike to get out of the way, and as soon as he was clear, I released the rear risers.

Instantly the wing shot up into the sky. As the wing came up, I was exposed to the full force of its pull. I was dragged across the sand on my heels, like a water skier. But I only skidded for about ten feet, and once the wing was overhead it was quite easy to control. With the strong wind, the wing was generating so much lift that I was virtually weightless. Sometimes it was necessary for Mike to hold me down, and even then I slowly drifted down the beach, losing a few feet every time the wind gusted harder.

Eventually I decided to bring the wing down. I grasped both rear risers and pulled hard. The wing dropped to the ground. However the slightest release of tension on the rear risers would have allowed it to leap back into the sky. To prevent this, I quickly ran around to the side of the wing while Mike grabbed the upwind end of the wing. With the wing safely "weathervaned" once again, I could afford to relax a bit.

I was very pleased. For the first time in my flying career, I'd been able to launch a wing in high winds, control it, and then bring it back down without ever losing control. I spent the next several hours perfecting my new skill of handling a wing in high winds.

At sunset, the winds seemed to be getting even stronger. Although I'd made enormous progress in learning to handle my wing in strong winds, I still didn't feel confident enough to attempt a powered flight. So we packed up our gear, returned to our favorite motel in the town of Pacific Beach, and settled in for the night. Unfortunately there were no ground floor rooms available this time, but the kindly motel manager permitted us to store the engine in the motel office, so we didn't have to carry the engine up the stairs.

The next day we returned to Roosevelt Beach. The winds were still strong, blowing between fourteen and sixteen miles per hour. Mike got out his wing and did some kiting in the high winds, using my handling technique. He got pretty good at it, but didn't feel that he was quite ready to try a powered flight in such strong wings.

In spite of my good wing handling progress on the previous day, my crisis of nerve was becoming acute. I felt positively sick to my stomach. At one point I felt like walking away from the sport of powered paragliding, and never coming back. It just didn't seem to be worth the risk. What was I doing out here, challenging the sky in a contraption made of string and cloth? My emotions were telling me that I was foolishly risking my life. I could almost feel the presence of the unseen demons in the sky, just waiting to strike me down.

Intellectually, of course, I knew that these fears were largely overblown. Certainly there were risks in flying a powered paraglider. You could get killed if you took a bad collapse close to the ground. On the other hand, such things were very rare. Was it dangerous? Sure. But was it any more dangerous than hurtling down a highway, just missing oncoming masses of steel by only a few feet? Or knowing that a single drunken driver could suddenly cross the centerline and wipe you out? Yet I had no hesitation in driving a car. I had been doing it for years. Powered paragliding only seemed strange and dangerous because it was new and unfamiliar.

Nevertheless, I told Mike that I didn't feel that I was in the right frame of mind to push the high-wind envelope today. But my words came out more like a question than a declaration of fact. Instead of simply agreeing with me, Mike pointed out that while one should not ignore warning signals, sometimes you needed to push the envelope or you'd never get anywhere. His words rang true. My ground handling session on the previous day had gone extremely well, no question about it. I had proven that I could handle the wing in these high winds. So why not put on the motor, and fly? Mike let me stew in my indecision for several minutes, then told me that he would support whatever decision I made, but in his opinion I was ready to try a powered flight in strong wind.

I remembered an old saying. "Courage is when you go ahead and do it, even though you're scared to death." I also knew that sometimes the opinion of another man is better than your own, especially if he's in a better position to be objective.

I decided that the only way to conquer my fear, was to face it. I decided to fly. I got out the engine, fueled it, started it, and warmed it up. As I stood in the sand with my knee braced against the motor frame, with the engine idling at two thousand rpm, I started to feel more relaxed and confident. There was something reassuring about the roar of the motor. It matched the shriek of the winds, decibel for decibel.

With Mike holding the end of the wing, and the rest of the wing flapping freely in the wind, I connected the wing to the motor and slipped into the harness. I quickly fastened the buckles, adjusted my helmet strap, and grasped the front and rear risers.

Slowly I worked the wing around to face into the wind. Everything went according to the rehearsals I had done the previous day. I signaled Mike, and he released the end of the wing. Immediately I relaxed tension on the rear risers, and the wing shot up in the air. I steered the wing with the rear risers, keeping it pointed directly into the wind while I checked to make sure that the wing was properly inflated and ready to fly. Then I spun around, faced the wind, and went to full power.

I guess I was expecting to run forward as I had always done, being pushed along by the thrust of the engine. In hindsight, that was a perfectly ridiculous expectation. Since the wind was already blowing almost as fast as the wing could fly, there was no way that I was going to race forward at high speed. I should have expected to simply rise into the air like a helicopter as I went to full power.

Naturally I hadn't thought of any of this. Suddenly everything felt wrong. Not only was I completely unable to run forward, I felt like I was falling over backwards! I wasn't, of course. The engine was simply pushing me slightly ahead of the wing as it always did at full power. This thrust caused me to lean over backwards, somewhat, but there was no way I was going to fall on my ass. But I didn't realize that at the time.

If I had simply kept the throttle depressed, I would have tipped slightly backwards, then lifted off into the sky. But I thought something had gone horribly wrong and that the spinning propeller was going to smash into the ground. Naturally my first thought was to protect the prop, so I released the throttle and started to fumble for the kill switch. But before I could kill the engine, I felt the wing pulling me to one side. I looked up to see the wing way off to my left side. It was so far off-center that I was certain it had become unrecoverable.

But training is a wonderful thing. I found myself instinctively running to the left to get back under the wing. And it worked! Suddenly I found myself back under the wing, perfectly centered, and not falling over backwards. So I squeezed the throttle and instantly lifted off, just like a helicopter. I don't think I ran a single step forward. I just went straight up. Wow!

At fifty feet of altitude I entered a faster-moving layer of air and started to slowly drift backwards. This was certainly a new experience! I eased off the throttle and quickly descended to about thirty feet. Here the wind was weaker, and I slowly started to drift forward. But it was very slow progress. I could have walked faster.

With the wind nearly balancing my wing's forward speed, it took me nearly half an hour to go only one mile along the beach. But it was fun! I had to keep my altitude under fifty feet. Any higher and I would start moving backwards. Any lower and I risked bumping into the ground. A great deal of the time I just hung in space like a tethered balloon, unable to go forward or backward. I was constantly adjusting the throttle to adjust my altitude. I had been afraid of the high wind, but as soon I was up and flying in it, and just hanging in space, all of my fear vanished.

Eventually I reached the carcass of the dead whale. It smelled worse than ever. I flew a little further until I started to approach a small beach resort. Then I decided it was time to return to my takeoff point. I went to full power and shot straight up into the sky. It was fantastic! At an altitude of about seven hundred feet I turned around and started to fly downwind.

Flying downwind, my speed was tremendous. I suspect it was somewhere between forty and fifty miles per hour. In almost no time I had returned to my launch point. Mike waved as I zoomed overhead. I went about a quarter of a mile further down the beach, then turned around and slowly crept back to the launch point. I made several passes over Mike before landing. It was the softest landing I have ever made. I simply eased off the throttle and floated down onto the sand, light as a feather. I stepped down onto the sand, killed the engine, then spun around and brought the wing down to earth. Mike grabbed the upwind end of the wing, and I immediately ran around the wing to keep it from re-inflating.

The flight had been like a breath of fresh air. Afterwards I felt very good about the flight, and about myself. My crisis of nerve vanished, and never came back in so virulent a form.

What had caused my anxiety? I think I'd simply been too focused on the downside of paragliding. In my search for safety, I had steeped myself in accident reports, videos of terrible wing collapses, and had seen paragliding at its worst. The subconscious mind is like a sponge. It soaks up whatever you feed it, then spits out emotional reactions. Once again, I think I was simply scaring myself to death.

But the experience of a single good flight completely erased my fears. I remembered a phenomenon from my skydiving days that we used to call the "six jump slump." Basically, sometimes a skydiver would make his first six jumps with no problem, then suffer a crisis of nerve. ("What am I doing up here?") If he surrendered to his fear, then he never came back to jump again. On the other hand, if he forced himself to jump again, his fear vanished and he went on to enjoy the sport. I felt that I had just experienced something like that.

It's well to listen to those warning signs that you sometimes feel in the tips of your fingers. But sometimes you must ignore them and press ahead in order to win.

I had won. It felt good.

Chapter 18

The Great Ostrich Ping-Pong Ball Drop

Since returning from our training in California, Mike and I had been doing all of our flying on the beautiful ocean beaches of Washington State. The smooth ocean air was a wonderful place to fly, but there were a few drawbacks. It was a two-hour drive to the beach, the sand seemed to get in everything, and it was frequently too windy for either of us to fly. Also, there was some question as to just how legal our flying might be. Neither of us were hankering to get a whopping big fine from Ricky Ranger.

We had the use of the County Fairground parking lot, but sometimes the local farmer was harvesting hay out of it, and we couldn't use it. We decided it was time to find some more local fields.

We spent several days driving around, checking out small airports and fields. We quickly learned that many small airports in our area were mere slots hacked out of the tall forest. Unless the wind was blowing directly down the runway, rotors and turbulence off the treetops would make flying from such airports a dicey proposition. We also learned that farmers seldom let their fields lie fallow. Either the fields were being used for crops, or else they were being used to pasture livestock. Either way, the fields weren't very suitable for flying.

There was a huge grassy field just a short drive from my house. However when we checked it out, we discovered that a model airplane club had already claimed the field for their own, and they weren't too interested in sharing it with a powered paraglider. And since the owner of the field sided with model airplane club, that was the end of that.

We also checked out several of the local high school soccer fields. The surface of the fields was ideal (thick grass, cut short), but the fields were frequently surrounded by tall trees, power lines, or lighting towers. Also the fields were frequently full of kids playing soccer. Not the best place in the world for a couple of novice PPG pilots. Chopping up kids with your propeller tends to give the sport a bad name.

We paid another visit to the glider strip that we had found earlier, tucked away in the foothills of the mountains. For a small fee, the owner of the strip agreed to let us use it when the gliders weren't using it, which was most of the time. But the tall trees surrounding the strip could be a problem due to rotors and turbulence.

There was a really huge, open section of land at a nearby Army base. It would be perfect for powered paragliding. Unfortunately it would first be necessary for us to join the Army. We said no thanks.

There were a couple of small airports that welcomed us. Unfortunately they were rather busy, which meant we would have to carry radios. Also I wasn't crazy about flying in close proximity with fixed-wing aircraft. A powered paraglider can be difficult to see, and a collision with a fixed-wing aircraft can ruin your whole day.

We were starting to get discouraged. We had spent all this money on equipment and training, and now we couldn't seem to find a place to fly!

Since we weren't having much luck with a ground search, Mike suggested that we go up in the Cessna and scout from the air. While he piloted, I sat in the back seat, armed with maps and binoculars.

The Cessna made a fine aerial platform for our search. Although we quickly spotted several promising-looking parks and playing fields, our experience told us that getting permission to fly from these fields might prove extremely difficult. We also checked out several private country airstrips, but the owners were reluctant to share their fields with us.

And then, just when things looked very bleak, there it was! From the back seat of the Cessna I saw an area that simply looked too good to be true. It was acres and acres of beautifully manicured lawn, surrounded by flat farmland at the edge of a very scenic range of mountains. Mike circled the area while I checked it out with binoculars. There was some kind of picnic or carnival going on. Lots of food booths, game booths, and dozens of colorful tents. All kinds of ball games were being played. There were hundreds of cars in a grassy parking lot, with thousands of people crawling over the land. But right in the middle of the festivities was a giant, grassy polo field that was virtually deserted. It was at least a thousand feet long and nearly half as wide, without a single tree growing anywhere on it. Although it was surrounded by trees on all sides, the field appeared to be plenty big enough for PPG takeoffs.

I looked at Mike and he nodded approval. We had found THE PLACE! We headed for home.

The next day we drove out to the area, trying to locate THE PLACE. We stopped at a local tourist information booth and described what we had seen from the air. It turned out that THE PLACE was owned by a wealthy dentist who rented it out to large organizations for picnics. It was not open to the public, and in fact the owner was quite publicity-shy. Since this place does not crave publicity, we'll just call it "The Farm." Only a few weeks earlier, a *very* large corporation had been there for a company picnic. There had been twelve thousand employees present! Armed with driving directions, we decided to drive out and take a look at this unusual place.

It was PPG Heaven! That huge polo field looked even better from the ground. It was kept mowed like a lawn, perfectly level, with no holes or ruts. And there were grassy playing fields beyond the polo field that would make good emergency landing fields.

I was both elated and depressed. This place was so perfect that I knew we would never be able to get permission to fly here. This place was reserved for wealthy companies. NO WAY would the owner ever let us fly here. Nevertheless we decided to ask. Mike made some inquiries and finally made contact with the owner.

To my utter amazement, the owner welcomed us with open arms! Not only was he quite familiar with powered paragliders, he assured us that his polo field would be a perfect place for us to fly! We were invited to start flying from the polo field whenever we liked. We offered to pay for the use of the field, but the owner said that wouldn't be necessary. Just enjoy it!

After determining that I wasn't dreaming, I realized that the deal was too good to be true. I told Mike, "This guy wants something from us. I don't know what he wants, or who he wants killed, but there's going to be a price to pay."

It turned out that I was right. A few days later we found out what our Godfather expected from us. Actually it turned out to be quite reasonable. A large company was scheduled to have its annual company picnic at The Farm in only two weeks. And therein lay a problem.

A year earlier, at the same company picnic, another PPG pilot had been persuaded to fly over the area and drop a load of ping-pong balls for the kids to chase. Some of the balls were numbered, and the kids who found the numbered balls won prizes. The company CEO absolutely loved the idea.

Unfortunately the drop didn't exactly follow the planned script. The PPG pilot dropped the ping-pong balls from a very great altitude. The wind caught the balls and scattered them all over the surrounding fields, swamps, and forests. Naturally the kids didn't let a little thing like a barbed-wire fence, or impenetrable swamp, get in their way; not with prizes to be won! According to surviving eyewitnesses, the kids turned in a performance worthy of an elite squadron of Navy Seals fighting their way though a Southeast Asian jungle against hopeless odds.

Of course the company CEO didn't see it that way at all. (One of the perks of being the CEO of a rich company, is that reality conforms to you.) As far as he was concerned, a great time was had by all, and he wanted a repeat performance at this year's company picnic. And since he was paying the bill, nothing more needed to be said.

The owner of The Farm was in a real quandary. He couldn't say no to one of his best customers, but the company picnic was only a couple of weeks away, and he had no PPG pilot to make the drop. And then, as if in answer to his prayers, a couple of clowns suddenly show up on his doorstep, looking for a place to fly their PPG! Talk about a gift from Heaven!

"Duh, Mr. Property Owner, can we fly our PPG from your nice
field? We'd be happy to pay you for the privilege."

God certainly moves in mysterious ways. He also seems to have a great sense of humor.

So it was a pretty straightforward deal. If we flew over the picnic and dropped the ping-pong balls, we would get to use the polo field to fly our PPG. It seemed like a small price to pay for the keys to PPG Heaven.

As the more experienced pilot, the job of dropping the ping-pong balls fell on me. But I was only a beginner. I only had about a dozen PPG flights to my name. I'd never flown for a crowd, or dropped something in flight (at least not intentionally).

The owner of The Farm wanted me to drop the balls at precisely 5:35 p.m. At that hour, the winds were frequently light at The Farm, usually under five miles per hour. It would most likely require a forward launch.

I'd done numerous forward launches with an unpowered paraglider, so I wasn't entirely untrained, but I had yet to do a forward launch with a PPG. One of the first things I'd planned to do as soon as we found a suitable local field to fly from, was to perfect my forward launch technique. Now I had the field, but I also had to quickly learn to do a forward launch with the engine. I also had to figure out how to drop the ping-pong balls without sucking them into my prop. And I had to do all of this in front of three thousand people in only two weeks.

Welcome to PPG Hell.

I decided the first thing to do was to get familiar with the layout of The Farm. We drove out for a visit and walked all over the grounds. It truly was a beautiful place. It reminded me of the manicured lawns and grounds of a wealthy country estate. This place had to be worth millions, and it was going to be my private flying field. What a deal!

Provided I could drop those damned ping-pong balls.

The owner said he wanted the balls dropped in the amphitheater, at the far end of the polo field. I walked up to the end of the field to check out the amphitheater. It was just a big grassy depression, about ten feet lower than the rest of the field, and about two hundred feet in diameter. It was used to organize contests for the kids, and award prizes.

The amphitheater even had a zoo, consisting of three large pens. There were some miniature donkeys in one pen, a couple of double-hump camels in another, and two ostriches in the third. I walked over to take a closer look at the ostriches.

I'm a big man, and I look down on most people (literally). But the male ostrich sauntered up to the fence and looked me square in the eye. He was every bit as tall as me (but I am much prettier). I didn't like the way he was looking at me, so I hissed at him. He hissed back. I flapped my arms in a threatening manner. He flapped his wings in an even more threatening manner. He opened his huge mouth, and it looked big enough to swallow a bowling ball. He was walking around on the biggest drumsticks I'd ever seen. I remembered hearing that an ostrich could kick hard enough to kill a man. That's when I noticed that the fence between us was only about six feet tall. I started wondering how high an ostrich could jump.

A couple of days later I was out at The Farm, engine on my back, all warmed up, and the steering lines and risers in my hands. The wind was only a couple of miles per hour, and I was ready to attempt a forward launch. Mike was standing nearby with the video camera to record this Kodak Moment.

I ran forward and felt the wing start to come up behind me. As I ran down the field, the idling engine bouncing along on my back, I could see the wing as it came into view overhead. Instantly I hit the throttle. The engine screamed with power, and one hundred pounds of thrust suddenly shoved me forward

I looked up to see that the wing was a little off-center, to the left. I immediately changed course to the left and re-centered myself under the wing. Unfortunately this last-minute course correction also put me on a direct collision course with Mike, who was still trying get my first forward launch on video.

Mike finally realized that I was concentrating on the launch, and making absolutely no effort to avoid running over him. He lowered the camera and ducked out of the way. A few seconds later the camera swung up again, just in time to catch me lifting from the grass.

Hey! I'm flying! The forward launch worked! Heck, that was easy! Due to the lack of wind, I had to run a little farther than normal, but that was about all.

I found myself flying down the field, slowly gaining altitude. Suddenly I was passing directly over the amphitheater. The big male ostrich saw me, and flapped his wings to scare me away. I had no time to trade body language with him. I had to concentrate on clearing the big trees that were just ahead of me at the end of the field.

I cleared the first line of trees by about thirty feet. Unfortunately there was a scattering of Really Big Trees just a short distance beyond, and they still towered over me. In the hot, calm air, I wasn't climbing very fast. I had to make a few shallow turns to avoid hitting the taller trees before climbing safely above the forest.

I flew around The Farm for about half an hour. What a view! Open farmland on one side; mountains on the other. Scenic rivers and magnificent waterfalls. I made some practice approaches over the polo field. There was plenty of room for maneuvering and landing. Finally I cut the engine and prepared to land. Meanwhile the wind had completely died. This was going to be my first no-wind landing with the engine.

As I neared the ground, things got a little scary. With no wind, and with the extra weight of the engine, I was coming in hot and fast. I had to time my landing flare just right. Too high, and I'd end up falling to the ground after the wing quit flying. To low, and I'd find out what it was like to do a forward face plant at twenty miles per hour with sixty pounds of engine on my back.

At an altitude of about three feet, I pulled the brakes down to my shoulders. The wing leveled out in a fast glide. As my airspeed bled off, and I started to settle down to the ground, I pulled the brakes all the way down to my hips.

The wing virtually stopped, leaving me only a foot or so off the ground. I stepped lightly down onto the ground and ran a couple of steps to eat up the last of my forward velocity.

Touchdown!

Well, that had been easy. Now I knew that I could do forward launches and landings, with the engine, in no wind. Or was it just Beginner's Luck? Could I do it again? There was only one way to find out.

Two days later I was ready to try again. Not only was I going to try another forward launch with the engine, but I'd also made a small net bag to hold the ping-pong balls. The bag currently contained a half dozen orange ping-pong balls that I'd bought from the local department store. I was going to do a practice drop over the amphitheater, assuming I could get into the air again.

I tied the bag of ping-pong balls to the front of my harness. The net bag had a drawstring at the top to hold the bag shut, and I'd added an extra loop of line to the bottom of the bag. My plan was to put my left wrist through the bottom loop, then open the drawstring, hold the top of the open bag in my left fist, then fling the whole thing out sideways at the proper moment. The loop around my wrist should prevent the net bag from being dropped or sucked into the prop, and the force of my fling should send the ping-pong balls safely to one side, away from the cage and prop.

At least that was the theory. Now if only I could do all of this, still fly the PPG, and navigate, all at the same time. Man, if I could manage to pull this off it was gonna be great for my ego!

I warmed up the engine and made my takeoff run. Son-of-a-gun! Another perfect forward launch! Maybe I really could fly this turkey in no wind!

I circled over The Farm at about three hundred feet. One of the purposes of this test drop was to see how far the ping-pong balls drifted before reaching the ground. I wanted the ping-pong balls to end up in the amphitheater, and not in the swamp.

I crossed the south end of the polo field and headed for the amphitheater. I set the cruise control on my hand throttle to maintain altitude, and carefully untied the net bag from my harness. I put my left wrist through the bottom loop, and carefully opened the drawstring at the other end of the bag. If that bag got away from me, I knew I'd never get it back. And if it got into the prop, I knew that I might end up making an emergency landing with a shattered propeller. Must be very careful!

I clutched the open mouth of the bag in my left fist and hooked my left thumb back into the left steering line handle. Hmm. No problem steering with the bag in my hand. This just might work!

I steered the wing directly over the center of the amphitheater, planning to release the ping-pong balls just as I crossed the far side of the amphitheater. Whatever wind there was should carry the balls back toward the center of the amphitheater. I could see the ostriches below, in their pen. Both of them were looking up at me with great interest. Maybe they thought I was going to feed them.

Time to drop the payload. I released the throttle to reduce the engine power to idle. My left arm flung outwards. Exactly as I'd planned, the six orange ping-pong balls flew out of the net bag, cleared the prop cage, and were instantly swept away behind me. Perfect! I immediately made a right turn, to inspect the drop, but already the falling balls were lost to sight.

I stowed the net bag inside my vest and set up for my landing. I swooped down over the field and made another perfect, no-wind touchdown. I was getting good at this!

After landing, I walked up to the amphitheater to look for the ping-pong balls. I figured the bright orange color would be easy to spot against the green grass. But there was no sign of the balls anywhere in the amphitheater. Could they have drifted into the swamp?

Wait a minute! What was that damned ostrich looking at? I ran over to the ostrich pen. There were the ping-pong balls, lying just outside the fence of the ostrich pen. Each ball was only about five feet from its neighbor. They had barely scattered at all. If the wind was equally calm on drop day, I should have no trouble dropping the balls into the amphitheater, right into the arms of the waiting kids.

But wait! There were only five balls visible. Where was the sixth? Uh-oh.

It was inside the ostrich pen. Fortunately neither ostrich had spotted it. Yet. But I figured it was only a matter of time. I could just picture that ping-pong ball sliding down that long, stringy gullet, and getting stuck halfway down. And I could see the headlines in tomorrow's newspaper:

"PPG Pilot Murders Beloved Ostrich With Ping-Pong Ball."

"PPG Pilot Strung Up By Outraged Animal Lovers."

Unfortunately the ping-pong ball was too far inside the ostrich pen for me to reach it. And there was no way I could sneak inside the pen to get it. The big male ostrich was on constant guard, just waiting for a chance to get a piece of me.

The next day I called up the owner of The Farm and explained the problem. I pointed out the possibility of having the ping-pong balls fall into the ostrich

229

pen, and the danger of the ostriches eating the ping-pong balls. I discreetly avoided mentioning that one ping-pong ball was already in the ostrich pen. I just hoped it wasn't already inside the ostrich.

I tried to diplomatically suggest that perhaps the drop ought to be made out on the polo field, downwind from the ostrich pen. However the owner was not interested. He wanted the drop made in the amphitheater, where all the kids would be gathered, and where Mom and Dad, sitting on the sidelines, could proudly watch their offspring scramble for the ping-pong balls. And where the company CEO could see where his money was going.

The owner told me not to worry. He said that a ping-pong ball would most likely pass through an ostrich's digestive tract unharmed. Furthermore he said that these particular ostriches were scheduled to be slaughtered for their meat and feathers right after the company picnic. So their days were numbered anyway.

Two days later it was time for the real thing. The ping-pong ball drop was scheduled for 5:35 p.m. I planned to take off about twenty minutes earlier and make some passes over The Farm where the crowd could see me. The weather was overcast, but no rain. That meant no thermal activity to cope with. Good! No bumps in the air. It should be a nice, smooth flight.

I arrived at The Farm at 4:00 p.m. I was jittery, nervous, and anxious. I'd only made two forward launches with the engine, and even though both of them had been successful, the thought of making my third launch in front of three thousand people was unnerving. I wasn't really eager to have thousands of people watch me fall on my face. Also, I still had less than two dozen PPG flights so far. I was still a rank amateur, trying to pull off a stunt that really called for a highly-trained pilot. I had a sick feeling in the pit of my stomach, and I would be very glad when this day was over.

I was hoping for a west wind that would let me take off over the parking lot, avoiding the crowd of people at the north end of the field. Unfortunately the wind was directly out of the north. Damn! That meant I would have to fly down the length of the polo field, and right over the heads of the crowd in order to take off. That did not strike me as a good idea. I'd only be about fifty feet in the air as I passed over the crowd. If I had an engine-out at the wrong moment, I'd have to land right in the middle of the crowd. Not a good idea.

What to do? I could simply refuse to take off. I didn't think the owner would kick us off the field if we failed to drop the ping-pong balls, but I hated to take even the chance of losing our PPG paradise. Also, I didn't want to disappoint the kids.

Then I remembered a nearby hay field that I'd flown over on my last flight. The farmer had just cut and baled the hay, and most of the bales had been picked up. The field was plenty big enough for a takeoff. Best of all, it was deserted. No people to worry about. (And no one to see me fall down.) Why not take off from the hay field, then fly over to The Farm to make the drop?

Mike and I drove over to the hay field. The field was at least half a mile long, but not too wide. Unfortunately the wind was not blowing down the length of the field. It was blowing directly across the field. I would have to take off where the field was at its narrowest. And there was a line of trees that I'd have to get over, just after takeoff. Damn!

Nor was the hay field the smoothest field in the world. When I had flown over it earlier, it looked as flat as a billiard table. However on the ground I could see that it had many ruts and dips. I would have to watch my step as I ran, or I could end up taking a real fast tumble.

I laid out the wing and got the engine ready to fly. I had all the enthusiasm of a man on his way to the guillotine as I tied the bag of ping-pong balls to my vest. There were fifty balls in the bag, and ten of them had numbers written on them. The numbers ranged from one to five, and represented the amount of money a kid would win if he found the ball and turned it in.

It occurred to me that I could make this event much more interesting by writing a number on *all* of the balls, and make every ball a winner. Or I could add a zero to each number, and make it a *real* prize! That would certainly make things lively at the awards ceremony. Maybe I could even write FREE PONY on some of the balls? Nah, better not.

I glanced at my watch. It was twenty minutes after five. I knew that I'd better get in the air if I was going to make the drop on time. I picked up the risers and brake lines and started my takeoff run. I only managed to run about five feet when suddenly I felt something snag around my left foot. Instantly I stopped running and looked down. One of the wing suspension lines had snagged around my left foot. I'd forgotten to check the ground to make certain that all the lines were clear before I started to run. I'd never goofed up like that before. This was just the sort of jittery, stupid mistake that I was afraid I'd make. I was pushing my personal flight envelope, and I knew it.

Fortunately there was no damage, but the wing had been pulled out of position. I killed the engine, explained to Mike what had happened, and asked him to reposition the wing for me. As Mike worked to straighten out the wing, I backed up to the edge of the wing and got ready to run again.

Mike signaled that the wing was now ready for another launch attempt. I thumbed the starter button on my hand throttle. The engine instantly roared back into life. God bless electric start, and God bless that wonderful little DK engine! It started first time, every time.

I started my second takeoff run. I found that it wasn't as easy to run through the freshly-cut hay stubble, as it was to run on that beautifully manicured polo field. But I managed. I could feel the wing coming up behind me. I hit the throttle, and the engine roared.

I had to keep my eyes on the ground as I ran, to avoid the ruts and the holes. I glanced up at the wing. It was slightly off to one side, so I stepped sideways to re-center myself under the wing. A gust of wind suddenly caught the wing, blowing it to the other side, and again I moved sideways to re-center myself under the wing.

The field had a slight slope, and I found myself running uphill. This was quickly turning into my longest takeoff run yet. If I blew this launch I knew that I'd never have enough energy to make another one. Very well, I WILL NOT BLOW THIS LAUNCH!

I ran as hard as I could. I could feel the wing lifting, and trying to pick me up. Suddenly I ran into a slight dip in the field. Fortunately I had just enough lift to hold me up; like a cartoon character running off the edge of the cliff and running on air.

But I was airborne for only a moment. I reached the far side of the dip and I didn't have quite enough altitude to stay airborne. My right foot slammed into the ground. My whole body felt the jar, but I managed to keep running. I felt like Charles Lindbergh trying to get the Spirit of St. Louis off a runway that was filled with mud puddles and potholes.

Suddenly the bushes at the edge of the field were looming up in front of me. The bushes were only about ten feet tall, but if I didn't start climbing I'd never get over them. I pulled a bit of brake, and the wing suddenly lifted me completely off the ground. I held the brakes for a few seconds, then slowly started easing them off. I was climbing slowly but steadily.

I cleared the bushes with about six feet to spare, and continued to climb. I was determined to get this beast into the sky even if I had to get out and push!

And it was starting to look like I'd need a push. Behind the bushes was a line of short trees. I had enough altitude to clear the short trees, but behind the short trees was a line of tall trees, and I didn't have enough altitude to clear them. Fortunately there was a gap between two of the taller trees. There was just enough room to slip the wing between them, and that's exactly what I did.

The tall trees were quickly left behind as I flew out over open farmland. There were no more obstacles. It had probably been my most difficult takeoff ever, but I was airborne! I did it! Now on with the show.

I kept the throttle squeezed to the max as I continued to slowly climb. I dropped the footbar and kicked back into my seat. Okay, I was definitely a going concern. I was airborne, with plenty of altitude, and ready to head for The Farm. I glanced down to make certain the bag of ping-pong balls was still tied to my vest. For one horrible second I thought that I'd forgotten to bring the balls with me, but there they were. God, but I would be glad when this day was over!

I set the cruise control for level flight and flew over fields and forests on my way to The Farm. A few minutes later I passed over a golf course. Lots of people waved. Now I could see The Farm just beyond the trees. My God, look at all the people! Hundreds of heads were turning skyward as the sound of my engine reached them. Mothers were pointing at the sky and telling their kids to look up. Some people were looking up at me in open-mouthed disbelief. Obviously they'd never seen a powered paraglider before.

This was starting to get fun!

I made several passes over The Farm at about three hundred feet. The people seemed to be enjoying my presence. Truth is, there's just nothing prettier than a paraglider soaring through the sky.

I glanced at my watch. It was 5:32 p.m. Just three minutes to drop time. I made a gentle turn over the south end of the polo field and prepared to make my bomb run over the amphitheater. I spotted Mike in the car, burning up the highway and trying to get to the picnic in time to video the drop. I knew I could always go around for another pass, and give Mike more time to get into position.

I carefully untied the bag of ping-pong balls from my vest. For Heaven's sake, don't drop them now! I looped the bottom string around my left wrist, carefully opened the drawstring, and clutched the top of the open bag in my left fist. I hooked my left thumb back in the left brake handle and switched off the cruise control on my engine throttle.

I was now fully in control of the wing, ready for the drop, and approaching the edge of the amphitheater. Mike still wasn't in position to video the drop, so

I figured I'd go around and make another pass.

Except that I *couldn't* make another pass. My God, there must be five hundred kids down there, clustered in the center of the amphitheater, all looking up at me like I was Santa Claus. In the middle of the crowd of kids was one demented adult with a bullhorn, shouting and waving at me. I couldn't hear him, but it was obvious that he was telling the kids to get ready. I glanced at my watch. It was exactly 5:35 p.m. The kids were expecting me to make the drop on this pass. Video or no, I just couldn't disappoint them.

I released the throttle and the engine slowed to idle. The wing slowly started to descend. "IS EVERYBODY READY?" I shouted. The crowd roared something back, but I couldn't make it out through my ear plugs. A few minor steering corrections, and I was passing over the amphitheater. A few seconds later, and I was approaching the far edge of the amphitheater.

Time! My left arm flung the bag as hard as I could. The fifty ping-pong balls burst from the net bag like an exploding bomb. The wind instantly swept them behind me. Not a single ping-pong ball went through the prop. Perfect! I squeezed the throttle to halt my descent. I carefully stowed the net bag inside my vest, relaxed back into my seat, and permitted myself a very big grin.

I had done it! Mission accomplished!

Suddenly my thrill of accomplishment was replaced by a terrifying thought. Had the ping-pong balls missed the ostrich pen? I suddenly had this horrible mental picture of fifty ping-pong balls falling into the ostrich pen, and five hundred determined kids swarming over the fence, into the ostrich pen, with two giant ostriches who couldn't decide what to do first; eat the ping-pong balls or kill the kids.

"Buddy," I told myself, "if that's what happened, you'd better point this thing toward Canada and hope you have enough gas to make it across the border. Otherwise those parents are gonna have your hide for a rug!"

I made a sharp right turn and looked down, expecting the worst. But the ostriches were just standing quietly in their pen. A pen that was empty of children. The kids were racing around on the grass in the middle of the amphitheater, scrambling to get the ping-pong balls. No kids in the ostrich pen, no kids in the swamp, and no kids in the forest.

It had been a perfect drop. The ping-pong balls had completely missed the zoo. I breathed another big sigh of relief.

I flew around for a few more minutes, enjoying my post-drop glow. I made a few more passes near the picnic until most of the heads on the ground were no longer looking up at me. Obviously my fifteen seconds of fame were over. My job was done. I had given the people a good show.

I swung over the south end of the polo field, lined up for my approach, and cut the motor. Silently I drifted down to earth. I spotted Mike in the middle of the field, getting it all on video. I wondered how much of the actual drop he had managed to catch.

I flared for the landing, touched down lightly, and came to a stop. Instantly I spun around and collapsed the wing to the ground. I breathed another big sigh of relief. The flight was over. The Great Ostrich Ping-Pong Ball Drop was history.

I felt very good. Yes, I had pushed my personal envelope and had taken some risk, but my training and practice had paid off and had carried me through. I had been able to handle everything that had been thrown at me. My confidence level had just been ratcheted up a few hundred notches, and I now had this incredible sense of accomplishment and satisfaction that no amount of money could buy. It was moments like these that I lived for. It was a moment like this that let me know I was alive!

I slipped out of my trusty engine and lowered it to the ground. Mike came running up to congratulate me. A few of the picnickers were coming over to ask the inevitable questions.

I learned that Mike had reached The Farm just in time to record the actual ball drop. Then he had run up to the amphitheater to video the kids redeeming the ping-pong balls for the prize money. I watched the video later that night. The kids obviously loved the whole thing. It made me feel very good.

But now it was time to eat! The Farm was famous for its good food at these gatherings, and I figured that I'd earned the right to crash this party. Mike and I spent the next hour eating our way from one end of the picnic to the other. My appetite, which had been non-existent all day long, suddenly returned with a vengeance.

Before I left, I managed to talk with the owner of The Farm. He was absolutely delighted with my performance. He told me that it was perfect in every way, and that the company CEO had loved it. He was pleased, the boss was pleased, and I was pleased. Everybody was pleased.

The owner also told me that he wanted me to do it again, next year.

You bet! Wouldn't miss it for the world.

Before I left The Farm, I walked over to the ostrich pen. As I approached the fence, the big male ostrich sauntered over to stare back at me. I very carefully examined the ground inside the pen, looking for the orange ping-pong ball.

It was gone.

I looked back at the ostrich. I was pretty sure that I knew where I could find that missing ping-pong ball. But I'd need a long arm and a flashlight. And I might have trouble getting the ostrich to hold still.

"Bon Appetit," I muttered to the ostrich as I walked away.

Life was very good.

Chapter 19

Takeoffs Are Optional; Landings Are Not

I now had almost twenty flights on my powered paraglider and I was starting to feel pretty comfortable with it. I had recently acquired a small reserve parachute, and with my trusty reserve riding on my left hip, I had ceased to have a heart attack every time the wing rustled. All of my paragliding inventions were working nicely, and transporting and flying the engine was becoming pretty routine.

Except for the steering lines. I had lowered them ten inches to compensate for the raising of the wing attachment points on the PPG harness. No longer was it necessary to hold my arms high overhead like a soldier who has just surrendered to the enemy. Instead, I now held my hands level with my ears. This was a great improvement, but was still not totally comfortable. My hands needed to be in my lap. I decided to add some steering line extensions so that I could rest my hands in my lap, but still have control of the wing. The extensions were easy to fabricate and install, and we decided to go out to The Farm for a flight test.

The day was sunny, in the mid-70s, and the wind was blowing 4-5 mph on the ground. It would be a perfect day for flying except that the wind was now blowing almost directly from the east, right across the spine of the mountains. We were exposed to the turbulence and rotors being generated by the mountains.

There was no question where the wind was coming from. You had only to look up at the clouds streaming rapidly across the mountain peaks. Yet on the ground the wind was coming from the northwest at a gentle four or five miles per hour.

Now when the wind on the ground is blowing from the northwest, and the wind at four thousand feet is blowing from the east, it is possible to have a major wind shear going on. At such a junction there is likely to be plenty of turbulence and rough air. And this is where you definitely don't want to be flying.

For me, the choice was simple. The wind was blowing from the wrong direction, and it made our beloved field too dangerous to fly from. But Mike wanted to fly very badly. He pointed out that the turbulent air could be thousands of feet up, far higher than our normal cruising altitude of 500-1000 feet, and that as long as he stayed below this shear layer, he'd probably be okay.

I was skeptical. Even if we were below the shear layer, chances were good that the air would still be bumpy enough to take all the fun out of flying a PPG. Fortunately I knew how to test the air without having to fly in it. I got out my tank of helium, inflated a balloon, tied on a long string of brightly colored ribbon, and sent it aloft.

By watching the balloon's ascent I could tell that there were some bumps in the air, but nothing major. Interestingly, the balloon followed a steadily curving path to our left, rather than drifting away at a constant heading. I had never seen such a curved flight path before, so I decided to launch a second balloon about ten minutes later.

This time the balloon curved to the right! The wind had changed direction by about thirty degrees within the space of ten minutes. Obviously the conditions weren't so bad as to make flight impossible, but they were definitely more squirrelly than we had become accustomed to. However Mike said he was willing to give it a try.

At that point, I decided to fly. And I decided that I would fly first. If there were problems in the air, I had a much better chance of handling them successfully, owing to my greater experience. And I knew that if I judged it too dangerous for Mike to fly, he would stay on the ground.

While Mike laid out my wing, I started the engine and warmed it up for the usual three minutes. Then I stopped the engine, finished my preparations for takeoff, and got ready to fly. I got into position for a reverse launch, started the engine, and pulled the wing overhead. Something did not feel quite right, but I dismissed it as my usual pre-takeoff anxiety.

The wing kited overhead nicely. I turned 180 degrees, went to full power, and started to run. I hadn't even bothered to take my brake handles out of their velcro keepers on the risers. With a reverse launch, especially in low winds, I preferred to get airborne before grabbing the brake handles. It made for less clutter in my hands during takeoff. The only drawback was that it required me to give up control of the wing for several seconds during the launch. I wasn't entirely comfortable with this, but I was willing to experiment with different methods.

As soon as I squeezed the throttle to go to full power, something did not feel right. The engine did not sound right, and the thrust seemed to be much less than normal. In hindsight, I should have immediately cut the power and aborted the takeoff.

But I really wanted to launch, so I continued to run. It soon became apparent that I was not lifting off as quickly as I should have. I realized that I would need to add a little brake to lift off. That should have immediately told me that the engine was not developing full power. I frequently needed a little tug on the brakes to lift off in no-wind conditions, but never when there was enough wind to do a reverse launch.

But in spite of the warnings, I continued the takeoff. At this point I was running as fast as I could, but I still wasn't lifting off. If I ran any faster, I'd trip and stumble over my own feet. I grabbed the brake line handles, pulled them free of the velcro keepers, and gave a quick tug on the brakes to lift off. My feet left the ground, and I kept the throttle mashed as I started to climb.

But I wasn't climbing as steeply as I should. My angle of climb was more like that on a no-wind day. Something peculiar was definitely going on. But at least I was climbing. I knew I would clear the trees at the end of the field, and that was the important thing.

I stayed at full throttle for the next five minutes. The engine now sounded okay. Except for the long takeoff run, I could almost put the whole thing down to my overactive imagination.

But one thing that wasn't only in my imagination was the bumpy air. As soon as I cleared the trees, the bumps started, and they continued nonstop. Maybe the air would smooth out as I climbed higher. I turned toward a nearby golf course and continued to climb. My Cateye altimeter showed that I was gaining altitude at my usual rate of just over one hundred feet per minute.

Five minutes after launch I reached my cruising altitude of five hundred feet. I was now over the golf course and still getting bounced around like popcorn on a hot stove. The wing wasn't even close to any sort of collapse, but the flight was much too rough to take my hands off the steering lines. This meant that I would not be able to hook up my steering line extensions. The extensions were designed for easy steering in smooth air; not for keeping control of the wing in turbulent conditions.

After about a minute of this rough treatment, I decided that I'd had enough. I couldn't even enjoy the flight, much less test the steering line extensions. I glanced at the altimeter and got a surprise. Even though I was still at full power, the altimeter said I was descending. I realized that I must be in a sinking air mass. To hell with this nonsense. I decided to return to the field. I was glad that I hadn't let Mike go up in this turbulent soup. Even though the actual wind shear layer was thousands of feet above me, the wind near the ground was still too bumpy for fun flying. The lesson was clear: Don't fly near the mountains when the wind is coming from the other side, because you're basically flying in lee-side turbulence.

As I headed back for the field, I glanced at the altimeter again, and my eyes widened. I was still at full power but I was still descending. I was now barely above four hundred feet. I checked my tachometer, and I couldn't believe what it said. At full power the reading should have been approximately 6800 rpm. Instead it was reading only 6000 rpm! And as I watched, the tach started to fall below 6000.

Instantly I realized that something was wrong with my engine. It wasn't developing full power. Even as that thought raced though my head, I could hear the engine starting to rapidly fall off while the tachometer plummeted toward zero. *My engine was dying!*

I immediately released the throttle. The engine dropped back to idle and continued to run. I was now descending rather rapidly, so I cautiously squeezed the throttle to try to get enough power to maintain altitude. I knew that I would need about 5800 rpm to stop my descent.

I didn't even get to 4000 rpm. As soon as I squeezed the throttle, the engine coughed and died.

MY ENGINE WAS DEAD!

My God! I've just had my first in-flight engine failure! Even though I was always mentally prepared for it, I never really thought it would actually happen.

Fortunately I had always made certain to keep an emergency landing field within gliding range, so I wasn't worried about making a safe landing. In fact, I could easily make it back to my launch point at The Farm. However I would much prefer to finish the flight under power, so I thumbed the starting button on my throttle. My engine instantly roared back to life, and resumed idling. I decided not to take the chance of killing the engine again, so I just let it idle. I would try to save the engine in case I really needed it during the landing (and then hope that it didn't die again).

As I made my final approach, Mike was already out on the field. He'd heard the engine fail, and he knew that something was very wrong.

At fifty feet I deliberately killed the engine and slid forward in the harness in preparation for landing. I was over the end of the field, and getting bounced around a bit, but it was nothing I couldn't handle. In a few seconds I'd be safely on the ground.

But the Practical Joke department wasn't quite finished with me. Suddenly my rate of descent seemed to stop, and I floated down the field without losing any altitude. I realized that I must be in a weak thermal lift. It started to look like I might overshoot the field, and I was too low to make any turns to regain the field. Not that it was a real problem. If I overshot the field, I'd simply land in one of the soccer fields just beyond the amphitheater.

The thermal suddenly ended, and I resumed my normal descent. I finally made a feather-soft landing about halfway down the field. I stepped lightly down onto the ground, turned, and collapsed my wing. Mike was heading toward me with the utility cart.

I unhooked from the wing and attempted to restart the engine. It started instantly, and seemed to be running fine. I did a full-power runup, expecting the engine to die. The engine screamed with power, and the tachometer showed a healthy 6900 rpm. I eased off the throttle, allowing the engine to return to idle, then returned to full power. No problem. Obviously the engine hadn't been destroyed, or even severely damaged. What in world could be wrong with it?

I turned off the engine, unstrapped the harness, and lowered the engine to the ground. A careful inspection of the engine revealed nothing. Mike joined me, and we discussed what had just happened. Mike congratulated me on success-fully handling my first in-flight engine failure. I did feel good about it. It had been a bona-fide emergency, but I'd done everything that I was supposed to do, and everything had worked out okay.

The moral of the story is that if you're prepared for emergencies, and have taken the proper precautions, then when one finally happens, it's typically not a big deal. More inconvenient than actually dangerous. Of course if I'd been fly-ing low over water, or thick forest, when the engine quit, the story might have had a very different ending.

But what had killed the engine? Mike and I replayed all the pretakeoff prepa-rations. Had we forgotten something critical? Suddenly I realized that I'd forgot-ten to do a full-power runup after putting on the engine and restarting it. Normally I always did a full-power runup to make certain that the engine was developing full power before taking off. How could I have forgotten to do my runup? Simple human error. I had made nearly twenty motor flights, and the pretakeoff routine was starting to get....well, *routine.*

But the lack of a full-power engine runup had simply failed to alert me that there was a problem with the engine. It didn't explain what had caused the engine to fail.

We packed up everything but the engine, and prepared to leave. Before we left, I started the engine and did two more full-power runups. No problem at all. Whatever had killed the engine earlier was showing no effects now. But something had killed the engine in flight, and I would have to discover the cause of the failure.

That night I consulted my fellow PPG pilots on the Internet. I explained that I'd forgotten to do a full-power runup before taking off. Keith Pickersgill, who was very knowledgeable about engines, said that it was probably a heat-seizure, caused by failure to warm up the engine adequately. A heat-seizure took place when the piston had heated up and expanded more quickly than the cylinder. Going to full throttle before the engine was warmed up sufficiently would make this more likely to happen. Such a seizure could severely damage an engine. Although failure to do a full-power runup before takeoff will not cause an engine to seize, failure to warm up the engine adequately before going to full power could cause a seizure.

Keith told me how to open up the engine and check it for any signs of damage. Cautiously I removed the muffler and peered into the cylinders. Following Keith's instructions, I checked the pistons, rings, and cylinders. No sign of any damage. I put the engine back together and ran it up to full power. It seemed to be just fine. Yay!

Before I flew again, I made certain to add "Full-Power Runup" to my pretakeoff checklist. I wouldn't make that mistake again. The second thing I did was to increase my engine warm-up period from three minutes to five minutes, followed by a full-power runup. From now on I was going to make certain that my engine was adequately warmed-up before flying, and that my engine was developing full power before flying.

Nine days later, good weather allowed us to return to The Farm to fly again. The wind was still blowing out of the east, while the ground wind was still out of the northwest. I launched another pilot balloon. It was a little bumpy up there, but not too bad. However I had made it my personal policy not to fly when the winds aloft were so radically different from the ground winds. I remembered my last bumpy ride, and I didn't want a repeat.

However Mike was willing to give it a try. He simply wanted to take off and circle the field before landing. He wanted to practice his landings, and he wasn't planning to fly much higher than the trees. That seemed safe enough. I could have made a similar flight, but didn't care to go to the bother.

I helped Mike get set up for his launch. I warmed up the engine for him and then did a full-power runup. The engine seemed to work fine. I shut off the engine, Mike put it on, started it up again, and revved it a bit. No problem.

Mike took off without incident, and climbed out like a rocket. Obviously the engine was developing full power. I could see Mike's wing rock a bit as he climbed out and started to circle the field. There was some turbulence, but he seemed to be handling it okay. He circled the field, set up for his approach, and made a fine landing. After getting out of his flight gear, he reported that the engine worked perfectly. Our new warmup routine seemed to have solved the problem. However Mike decided that it was too bumpy to fly again, so we packed up and went home.

The following week, the wind was still out of the east, so we decided to try our luck at the County Fairground parking area. The parking field was not as nice as The Farm. The grass was a bit longer, and the ground a little rougher, but it did have the advantage of no trees at the end of the field. In fact, there was nothing but miles of open pasture all around. Since we'd never flown from this field before, I elected to fly first.

With the engine still strapped to the bumper carrier on the car, I started it up and let it idle for a full five minutes. Then I did a full-power runup and held the engine at full power for ten seconds. I let the engine return to idle before shutting it off.

I hauled the engine over to where Mike had laid out my wing. I hooked the engine up to the wing, got into my flight gear, and put on the engine. I started the engine again, let it idle for half a minute, and then just for good measure, I did another full-power runup. No problem.

Finally I was ready to launch. Since the wind was only about two miles per hour, I elected to do a forward launch. As the wing rose up overhead, I hit the throttle for full power, just as I always did.

The engine sounded good, and my takeoff run seemed normal. A tug on the brakes, and I was in the air. Damn but it felt good to be airborne again!

Once in the air, I simply held course and let the machine climb. A minute later I was at an altitude of just over one hundred feet, flying over pastures and cattle. I was looking forward to a nice long flight across the farmlands.

Suddenly I stopped climbing. I was at 125 feet, and leveling out, even though I was at full power. Oh no! Not again!

The tachometer read only 6,000 rpm. Damn! It was happening again! My engine was dying! I quickly released the throttle and returned the engine to idle. The engine continued to run. I immediately turned around and headed back to the field. But unless I could get some altitude or power, I knew I wasn't going to make it back to the field.

Not that it would be a disaster to fail to return to the field. I was flying over pasture land, and I could safely land almost anywhere. But most of these pastures were full of cattle, and piles of cattle doo-doo. Not the most pleasant place to land. Not to mention that it might be a long hike to the nearest road. Not to mention that some of the cattle might be bad-tempered, and fail to appreciate my Sky God status.

Unless I could get some power, I knew I was going to be on the ground in less than a minute. I squeezed the throttle, trying to coax some more thrust from the engine. The engine responded by sputtering and dying. Oh great! I had just had my second in-flight engine failure!

This time I didn't even try to restart the engine. I had just spotted a big grassy backyard behind a farmhouse that sat on a country road. No cows. No cow dung. Perfect! I had enough altitude to clear the last fence into the backyard, but not enough to turn around and land into the wind. Oh well, who cared? With the wind only blowing two or three miles per hour, it probably wouldn't make any difference which way I landed. (That turned out to be almost true.)

I swooped over the last fence and started my landing flare about three feet above the grassy yard. As planned, I leveled out in a fast glide above the earth. Uh-oh, this was a faster glide than I had anticipated. Better get ready to run!

As my airspeed bled off, and I started to settle to the earth, I went to full flare. Normally this would have slowed me almost to a complete stop. But not this time. Not while going downwind.

I ran as fast as I could, and I almost made it. I almost managed to remain on my feet. But not quite. My feet went out from under me, and I fell to the ground. Actually, it wasn't really a fall. The wing was still flying overhead, and was still generating lift, especially under full brake. I fell down, but it was a very slow, controlled fall. About like falling down on the Moon. I went down on one leg and forearm, and slid a few feet on the grass. I quickly came to a stop, totally unhurt. The wing collapsed on the grass in front of me.

I got to my feet, unstrapped the engine, and lowered it to the ground. The road was just thirty feet away, with only a low fence between me and the road. Nobody seemed to be home at the farmhouse. Perfect! Two dogs were barking at me from the farmhouse, but they seemed to be fenced in, and couldn't get at me. Nevertheless I quickly dug into the equipment pocket on the front of my harness and pulled out my little canister of pepper spray. Good for repelling unfriendly dogs, bad-tempered cattle, or any other beastie that the downed PPG pilot might encounter. I dug a little deeper into the equipment pocket and pulled out my cell phone. I didn't know if Mike had witnessed my engine failure, or had seen me land. Or if he did, he might not know exactly where I was.

As I was dialing Mike's cell phone, he suddenly came driving up. He had seen and heard the whole thing. We compared notes. Obviously the engine still had a problem. However I didn't see how it could possibly have been a heat seizure this time. I'd warmed the engine up for a full five minutes, and had done two full-power runups. Obviously the problem was elsewhere. We packed up the gear and went home.

After returning home, I decided to take the engine to a nearby ultralight engine repair center. It was time to seek professional help.

The engine repair center kept the engine for a full week. Unfortunately they couldn't make it fail. The engine ran like a Swiss watch. Finally they told me to come and get it. At least I knew there was nothing seriously wrong with my engine (no broken parts). But *something* was causing my engine to fail in flight. Repeatedly.

What to do? Take the engine up and try again? Hope that the problem has fixed itself?

I decided that I could just as easily simulate a flight on the ground, rather than actually going aloft. The engine wouldn't know the difference, and it would be much less risky. I strapped the engine to the bumper carrier on the car, started it, let it idle for five minutes, then did a full-power runup for ten seconds. I shut the engine off and let it sit for five minutes, just as if I were attaching it to the wing and getting ready to fly.

After the five minute rest, I restarted the engine, let it idle for about thirty seconds, then squeezed the throttle to full power, just as I would for a real takeoff.

The engine roared, and sent my cats scurrying to hide. I held the engine at full power for five minutes, simulating my usual climb to 500 feet, and then reduced power to 5800 rpm to simulate level flight.

The minutes passed slowly, and the engine appeared to be working perfectly. Maybe it really was okay.

Wait a minute! What was that in the fuel line? It was *bubbles!* A steady stream of tiny air bubbles was racing up the transparent fuel line, and into the engine. Already the engine was being starved for fuel, and the power was starting to fall off. It was just like the other in-flight engine failures!

Suddenly the engine quit. The fuel line was almost completely filled with air. Obviously there was a leak in the fuel line that allowed the fuel pump to suck air in from the outside, instead of drawing fuel from the tank. I had found the problem! Yay!

I repeated the test. This time the engine ran for fifteen minutes before the air bubbles started to appear in the fuel line, followed by the engine quitting. No doubt about it; I had uncovered the problem. It was an intermittent problem. Apparently it hadn't happened while the repair shop was running the engine. Actually I was very lucky that I happened to spot it. Otherwise I probably would have had a third in-flight engine failure to report.

Repairing the problem would be easy. The engine had one of the world's simplest fuel systems. The fuel line was just clear plastic tubing, about the diameter of a ballpoint pen. I went down to the local motorcycle store and bought six feet of new fuel line. Off with the old, and on with the new. I fired up the engine again, and let it run. Twenty-five minutes later there was still no sign of any air bubbles in the fuel line. Yay! The next day, I fired up the engine and let it run for another twenty minutes. Still no sign of air bubbles. Problem solved.

In Hindsight, What Would I have Done Differently?

The next time I have an engine failure, I'll have a much better idea of what to look for. Two-cycle engines are very simple devices. There is very little to go wrong with them. Given fuel, spark, and compression, they run. And when they fail to run, it's frequently due to insufficient fuel. This is why it's a good idea to replace the fuel lines at least once a year. My fuel lines had been long overdue for a replacement. They looked fine, but when I finally removed them they were stiff and brittle rather than soft and flexible. No wonder they had cracked and leaked air.

Before I took my engine in for repairs, I should have replaced the fuel lines. That would have solved my problem. And had I replaced the lines after they were a year old, I would never have had a problem in the first place. Preventive maintenance is a wonderful thing. It lets you fix problems on the ground, rather than try to cope with them in the air. Highly recommended.

Chapter 20

Upgrades, Hipbelts, and Farewell

After my two engine failures, I took a long hard look at my engine. Winter was setting in, and the flying season was pretty much over for the next six months.

My engine was rated for just over one hundred pounds of thrust, and I had found this to be somewhat underpowered for my weight (220 lbs.). The best rate of climb I could manage was only one hundred and twenty-five feet per minute. Also, my no-wind takeoffs required some extra running. Sometimes I would bounce once or twice during the takeoff before I finally stayed in the air. No big deal, but I knew that some extra thrust would make one helluva difference. Also the 1.7 gallon fuel tank permitted barely one hour of powered flight, and I wanted at least two hours.

So I upgraded my machine. This included a bigger prop (carbon-fiber composite, and *very* expensive at $800) and a correspondingly larger prop cage. I also added an external fuel pod that strapped to the bottom of my machine and permitted me to carry an additional three gallons of fuel. The fuel pod made the whole machine about a foot taller.

So now I've got a bigger prop that's supposed to give me around 140 lbs. of thrust, which should give me a much better rate of climb, and I have almost triple the fuel capacity I had before. Yeah!

Of course the new prop cage came with the usual lousy prop netting that would permit a wing line to be sucked through the netting and into the prop. The first thing I did was to remove the old netting and replace it with fishnetting. It took an entire evening of painstaking work, but the end result was a prop cage that would keep the wing lines out of my propeller.

The addition of the external pod gave me a fuel capacity of nearly five gallons. Of course since the fuel was in two separate tanks, it meant that I would have to install a fuel selector switch on the engine, so that I could switch tanks when the first tank went empty. But then I realized that just the new tank alone would give me at least two hours in the air, and that was plenty for me. So I simply connected my fuel line to the external fuel pod, bypassing the 1.7 gallon internal tank.

The additional three gallon fuel tank simply hung by a strap from its plastic handle inside a protective framework of aluminum tubing. This allowed the tank to swing and sway and bump into the aluminum frame. To prevent this, I cut a piece of plywood to fit into the bottom of the fuel pod frame, and strapped the fuel tank down onto the plywood floor. I also bought a quick-disconnect coupler for the fuel line. This allowed me to unhook the fuel line, unstrap the fuel tank, and completely remove the fuel tank from the engine. This not only permitted easy fueling, away from the engine, but after flying, the fuel tank could be removed from the engine and the remaining fuel emptied out for safe transport.

Some experts say that you should not fly with an old fuel mixture. They say that the fuel deteriorates quickly after being mixed with the oil, and should be dumped out after flying. Some recommend just pouring the leftover fuel into the gas tank of your car. This is much easier to do if you have a removable fuel tank.

The new propeller, prop cage, and external fuel tank looked pretty snazzy on my machine. Unfortunately the new infrastructure also added about fifteen pounds of weight to the machine, and the extra gas that I would be carrying would add another nine pounds. Add the weight of the reserve parachute, and I was going to be carrying a machine that had increased in weight from only sixty pounds originally, to nearly ninety pounds! *Ouch!* But I told myself that I would only be carrying the machine for a minute or two, so the extra weight wouldn't matter. (What a delusion!)

But what did matter was that winter was setting in. So for the next six months, as the wind howled and the rain fell, I could only stare at my beautiful upgraded engine, wondering what it would be like to finally fly it.

Just after Christmas, my financial picture improved somewhat, and I was able to buy a nice, big, used Ford Econoline van. Plenty of room for hauling the assembled engine in the back. No longer would it be necessary for my engine to ride on the bumper carrier, exposed to vandals and the elements.

Since my PPG engine had been upgraded, I decided that I needed to upgrade the utility cart as well. With the external fuel pod, I no longer needed the folding table flap. Instead, the engine could now sit on the ground, and I only needed to sit on a small camp stool to put on the engine. At the time, it seemed like an improvement.

I realized that loading my equipment would be a different process with the van, so I found a new utility cart that would make the process easier. The new cart had an extra set of wheels at the top, near the handle. I made a new plywood floor for the cart, large enough for my new engine, and cut two large slots in the floor to fit my hands. Now I could wheel the engine to the van, tilt the cart so that the top wheels rested on the floor of the van, put my hands in the slots in the bottom, and lift and roll the whole thing into the van. It was much like loading an accident victim into an ambulance. Unloading was even easier. Now all I needed was some good weather for flying.

In late March we had a few days of unusually warm weather. Since spring was just around the corner, I took the wing over to a nearby playing field to make sure my ground handling skills were still up to snuff.

The field was on the top of a high ridge, on the lee side of the prevailing wind. It was sunny, but an earlier rain had left the grass wet. Winds were variable, blowing from zero to eight miles per hour, with occasional higher gusts. In addition, the wind was blowing around lots of trees and homes and other obstacles, creating a great deal of turbulence. I thought that ground handling in the turbulence would give me some good practice in case I ran into the real thing while airborne.

With the gusting wind and the turbulence, this was definitely not good flying weather. But I wasn't worried, because I wasn't going flying. I was just going to practice ground handling my wing. Can't get hurt doing that, right?

I put on my boots and gloves, laid out the wing, and slipped into my training harness. I clipped into the wing, took the brake lines in one hand and the front risers in the other, and started ground handling the wing. I needn't have worried about losing my ground handling skills. It was just like riding a bicycle. I tugged on the front risers and built a very nice wall in just a few seconds. The wind was blowing about five miles per hour, so I decided it was time to pull the wing up into the air.

I pulled sharply on the front risers and the wing promptly shot up into the sky. It stopped directly overhead, and flew there like a big kite. I steered with the brake lines while I constantly stepped from one side to the other to stay centered under the wing.

It wasn't easy. With the gusty wind and turbulence, the wing bucked and shook like a wild horse. I had to steer constantly to keep the wing facing into the wind. I was getting one wing collapse after the other (and just as quickly pumping them back out). I didn't care. I was getting some good practice in active piloting, and it just felt good to be standing under a flying wing again!

The air was so turbulent that I couldn't keep the wing in the air for more than a few seconds at a time. The wind would die abruptly, and the wing would collapse to the ground. So I would wait a few seconds for the wind to start blowing again, and then pull the wing back up into the sky. Lots of good practice!

This happy state of affairs went on for about fifteen minutes until I suddenly realized that I wasn't wearing my helmet! Idiot! I kept the wing on the ground while Mike fetched my helmet from the car. As Mike handed me my helmet, he asked, "Do you really need a helmet on the ground, surrounded by all this grass?" His words proved to be prophetic.

About a minute later, with my helmet in place and my wing once again flying overhead, the wind suddenly failed and the wing started to drop. As the wing fell toward the ground, I let go of the brakes and started to relax. I knew that it could be as much as a minute before the wind started to blow again.

And I was wrong. The wing had not quite reached the ground when a really HUGE gust of wind suddenly kicked up. It caught the wing and instantly turned it into a drag chute. A very large drag chute.

Suddenly I was being pulled across the grass as fast as I could run. I was taken completely by surprise. I was running so fast that I couldn't even look down at the risers to start the collapse process. Suddenly I tripped over a big rut in the grass, flew forward through the air, and slammed into the ground like a ton of bricks. I hit the turf on my left side, mostly on my shoulder. I was momentarily stunned while the wing continued to drag me across the grass. When I had been dragged about a hundred feet from my starting point, I managed to pull in a brake line, finally bringing the wing to a stop. Thank God I was wearing my helmet! My left side was covered with mud where I had plowed a trench through the wet grass.

About an hour later, my left side was really hurting. I had to use pain pills to get some sleep that night. I was afraid that I might have broken another rib, so the next day I went to the doctor. He took an x-ray, but found no sign of any broken bones. He said it was most likely just soft-tissue damage, and should heal in a week or two.

So I learned a couple of valuable lessons from the School of Hard Knocks. Even if you're just kiting your wing, ALWAYS WEAR A HELMET! And even if you're just kiting your wing, DON'T DO IT IN WILD, GUSTY AIR! The wing can suddenly grab you, and take you for a very wild ride. That sudden gust of wind caught me completely off guard, in the most vulnerable position possible. I was just lucky that I was only dragged over grass. If there had been any rocks or trees, I could have been injured much worse.

A few weeks later, I moved into a new house. After six months of being grounded by engine problems, winter storms, and an injured shoulder, I now had a whole new set of responsibilities that kept me out of the air. More delays! Would I ever get to fly again?

Finally the weather, my shoulder, and my schedule all coordinated so I could try out my new engine. The weather was perfect; sunny, no clouds, and a smooth wind blowing about five miles per hour. I also had a new flying field. It was a huge grassy field, located in the middle of a little-used airport, with no obstacles for thousands of feet. It just didn't get any better! So Mike and I loaded up the van and took off.

At the new field, I poured three gallons of newly-mixed fuel into the new tank. I pressed the starter button, and after sitting for six months, the motor started up with no problems. Yay!

I let the engine warm up for several minutes, and then tried a full power run up. With the bigger prop, I expected a much stronger push, but I can't say that I noticed any significant increase in thrust. Then I glanced down at the fuel line and saw a couple of tiny air bubbles racing up the fuel line. Oh no! Not another air leak!

The only possible place for air to enter the fuel line was at the quick-disconnect coupling. Every few seconds, another tiny bubble would suddenly race up the fuel line. The quick-disconnect was definitely leaking air. However the very slow air leak did not seem to be having any noticeable effect on the engine.

I reached down to the quick disconnect, jiggled it a bit, and twisted it back and forth. The bubbles stopped. I stopped the engine and made sure that the two pieces of the coupler were firmly snapped together. I started up the engine again, and revved it up to full power. This time there was no sign of any air bubbles. I jiggled the quick-disconnect some more. Still no bubbles. I figured that the quick-disconnect must have been seated improperly. I watched the fuel line for several more minutes, and when no more bubbles appeared, I decided that it was safe to fly. Even if I took off, and suffered a major air leak, and an engine failure, I had gobs of open field to land in. Besides, I WANTED TO FLY!

But then I noticed something else that was very disturbing. My engine was not reaching the speed it used to reach. With my original thirty-six inch propeller, the tachometer always read about seven thousand rpm at full power (the factory spec). Now, with the bigger propeller (forty-seven inches), my tach read only 6300 rpm at full power.

Hmm. Could something be wrong? I hadn't changed any of the carburetor settings. In fact, I'd never even touched them. They were still on factory setting. My takeoff altitude was unchanged. Could the bigger propeller account for the lowered rpm setting at full power? Was 6300 rpm with the bigger propeller, the equivalent of 7000 rpm with the smaller propeller? I didn't know. The engine upgrade had not come with any instructions for changing the carb settings, or made any mention of a different rpm setting at full power. I decided the only way to find out was to see how it flew. Either I'd get airborne, or I wouldn't.

I slipped into my flight jacket and helmet, and pulled on my gloves. I removed the engine from the utility cart and set it on the ground. It rested solidly on the external fuel pod. Then I unfolded my camp stool and slipped it under the harness seat. I sat down on the stool, slipped my arms through the shoulder straps, and fastened all of the harness straps.

I tried to rock forward and stand up. I could not! Sitting down, with my legs out in front of me, and with nearly ninety pounds on my back, I could not get enough leverage with my legs to stand up! Mike came to my rescue, and pulled me up onto my feet. Obviously this part of the process was going to need some additional work. With a ninety pound PPG engine, it's more important than ever to be able to put on the engine while standing up!

Once on my feet, I noticed the extra weight right away. Also, the balance was not nearly as good as before. I attributed this to the fact that the new fuel tank hung about a foot below the original fuel tank. This meant that the engine no longer ended at hip level. Instead, the new fuel tank extended about one foot below my hips. Wearing the machine, I looked sort of like a fat dinosaur with a stubby tail.

Another problem was that when I bent forward, the gas tank was no longer resting on the small of my back. Now it was hanging out in space, below my butt. This created a pretty good lever arm effect, like the end of a seesaw, and put extra force on my shoulder straps.

Okay, so the new machine seemed a lot heavier, and didn't balance as well, but what the hell? I only needed to carry it for a minute or two. Let's go flying!

The engine was warmed up, I was hooked into the wing, and the wind was blowing about four miles per hour. It was 6:30 p.m., and I had nearly two hours of daylight left. I was looking forward to a wonderful flight with plenty of fuel (for a change).

The wind was barely strong enough for a reverse inflation, so I decided to give it a try. I gave the front risers a good pull. The wing came up overhead, but was a little crooked and started to drift to the right. I tried to run sideways, to re-center myself under the wing, but I found that I couldn't run fast enough with my heavy engine. With the extra weight, and altered balance, I couldn't maneuver as nimbly as I used to. When I realized that I couldn't keep up with the wing, I was forced to let it collapse to the ground.

I quickly repositioned myself for a second launch attempt. The wind had picked up a little, and this time when I pulled the wing into the air, it shot straight up and flew overhead beautifully. I spun around and squeezed the throttle, and started to run forward for my takeoff. That's when I realized that my risers were still crossed over my head! Once again I was forced to abort the takeoff.

What had happened? Apparently, after my wing crashed to the ground on my first takeoff attempt, it somehow got turned over, and reversed the cross in my risers. So when I attempted to take off the second time, my turning around to fly did not uncross the risers, but simply wound them tighter.

Damn! If only I'd noticed the difference in the cross, earlier. I could have either corrected it before starting the launch, or else simply turned around in the opposite direction for takeoff. I had blown a perfectly good launch because I'd failed to notice that the risers were crossed in the wrong direction. Part of the problem was the increased weight of my engine. It was so heavy that any extended ground maneuvering quickly drained the energy right out of me. So by the time I made my second attempt to take off, I was so fatigued that I failed to notice that the risers were now crossed the wrong way.

I was too exhausted for another launch attempt, so I stopped the engine and slipped out of the harness to rest for a few minutes. Fifteen minutes later, the wind speed had fallen to about three miles per hour. I would need to do a forward launch. I got the wing laid out and properly positioned. Mike helped me put the engine on, and helped me get to my feet. I backed up to the edge of the wing, and started running forward. I was giving this launch attempt all I had left (which wasn't much). I noticed right away that my forward run, while carrying the heavier engine, was slower than normal.

But the wing popped up overhead in a fine forward inflation. I squeezed the throttle and felt the push from the propeller. As I raced across the field, I realized that I was getting a little bit to the right of the wing, so I moved slightly to the left. I pulled a little brake for some extra lift, and felt my feet leave the ground.

I was flying! I made it! Yay!

Well, not quite. Something was wrong. Instead of climbing into the sky, I just skimmed the ground. Not good! I felt myself starting to sink, and I was worried about hitting the ground with the bottom of the external fuel pod, so I touched down on my feet and started to run again. A few seconds later, I was picked up into the air again.

But the machine still wouldn't climb. I was simply skimming along over the grass, no more than a foot in the air, barely maintaining level flight. I was at full throttle, but the machine just wouldn't climb. I realized there was no point in continuing, so I killed the engine and ran to a stop. I was totally exhausted, and was panting and wheezing like an old steam engine. I unstrapped the machine and lowered it to the ground. That had to have been the shortest (and lowest) flight in the history of powered paragliding.

Mike came running up, and we discussed what had gone wrong. Could an air leak in the fuel line have robbed me of my power? I promptly fired up the engine again, and revved it up to full power. No sign of an air leak, but the tachometer still wouldn't go higher than 6300 rpm. Nor did the machine feel like it was developing 140 pounds of thrust. It felt more like 100 pounds. Could it be that I was only developing enough power for level flight, with nothing left over for climbing? The empirical evidence surely pointed to that. There was no point in trying to fly again; at least not until I could get an informed opinion on that low tachometer reading. So we packed up to leave. I was quite disappointed. After waiting six months to fly my new, upgraded machine, it didn't work!

The sun was setting as we finished loading the van. Rather than driving out the way we came in, we took a short cut across the field. Big mistake. About one hundred feet from the road, we suddenly hit a wet spot that was concealed by the grass. The van promptly sank about one foot into the thickest, stickiest, gooiest patch of gumbo mud I had ever seen. I tried putting some throw rugs under the rear wheels, for traction, but the mud was like grease, and the wheels just spun. I pushed on the rear of the van while Mike gave it the gas. The wheels spun, and the van didn't move, but something in my shoulder did. I felt something give, followed by a sharp, stabbing pain. Obviously I'd aggravated my old shoulder injury. Damn! I wondered how long it would take to heal this time? This just wasn't my day!

Except that the day wasn't over yet. We still had to get the van out of this damned mud hole. Two hours later, a huge tow truck with a hundred feet of steel cable pulled the van out of the mud, and onto the road.

"That will be $70 please, and thank you for calling Triple-A."

Back home, I had plenty of time to think while I waited for my shoulder to heal. I decided that I just *had* to do something about the weight of the engine on my back. Having ninety pounds, hanging on two shoulder straps, was just too much!

As any backpacker will tell you, the way to carry a heavy load is with your hips, rather than your shoulders. Backpackers had switched to hip belts years earlier. The hip belt was simply a thick, padded belt that strapped around the hips. The bottom of the pack attached to the sides of the hip belt, and *voila!* No more load on the shoulders! All of the pack's weight now rode on the hips, where it belonged.

I decided that if it worked for backpackers, it should work for me. I went to the local camping supply store and bought the biggest hip belt I could find. I sewed a couple of attachment straps to each side of the belt, and tied the ends of the straps to the base of the PPG engine. I slid my arms through the shoulder straps, put on the hip belt, cinched it tight, and snugged up the attachment straps. Then I stood up straight.

What a difference! The weight of the engine was now completely off my shoulders! My hips now carried the entire load. Since the load was no longer on my shoulders, my balance was vastly improved, and my arms were free to maneuver and manipulate the wing instead of being pinned down by the shoulder straps.

With the weight of the engine on my hips, I walked around my backyard for at least fifteen minutes, carrying my heavy engine. Normally I would be desperate to take the engine off after only a minute or two. Normally my shoulders would be screaming for mercy. Not this time. With no weight on my shoulders, I was not panting and sweating after only a few minutes of carrying the engine. *Yes!!!*

This was definitely the way to carry a PPG engine. The hip belt made it easy! I wondered why no one had ever tried this before?

I even hung the engine from the rafters, just as it would hang under the wing, just to make certain that the hip belt did not interfere with any aspect of flight. As I suspected, it had no effect. The hip belt was simply a way to make it easy to carry the engine on the ground, but in flight it changed nothing. I was looking forward to trying the hip belt in an actual flight.

While I fiddled and tweaked with the design of my hip belt, I also investigated the lack of thrust with my upgraded engine. I learned that the prop for my engine had actually been designed for a later model engine, and might need some plastic shims to change the pitch of the prop in order to give me full thrust.

I was preparing to order the shims when I received an unexpected offer to buy my PPG engine. I considered the offer very carefully. At the moment, I did not have a flyable unit. I would have to experiment with the shims for the propeller to see what pitch would give me the maximum thrust. Unfortunately I had no good way to measure the thrust from the engine, other than running it up to full power and feeling how hard it pushed on me. Not very scientific. It was also possible that this newer propeller just wouldn't work properly with my older engine. In that case, I would have to revert to the original propeller, which could only provide a little more than one hundred pounds of thrust. And that wasn't really enough for a pilot of my weight.

I thought about some of the other aspects of my current engine. Even with the hip belt, the balance wasn't as good as I would have liked. I didn't like the fuel pod hanging low as it did, with the increased danger of striking the ground during takeoff and landing. I preferred a design that kept everything above hip level, like a backpack. Also, there was the fact that my harness was too small for me. It really hadn't been designed for a pilot of my size. Even with my tweaking and fiddling, it never really fit me very well.

So perhaps this was a good time to sell the old girl and buy something better suited to my needs. I knew there were PPG engines out there that came standard with 2.7 gallon fuel tanks, and thrust levels of at least 130 pounds. In addition, most other machines came with ordinary wooden propellers that cost less than $200 to replace, compared to the whopping $800 for my present carbon-fiber composite propeller. If I sold my engine, I could afford to buy a new engine that came with everything that I wanted and needed (including a bigger harness), rather than buying various add-ons and upgrades that weren't always the optimum solution. And I knew that everything I had learned about powered paragliding, including my newest hip belt invention, would easily transfer to a new PPG engine.

And so, after much soul-searching, I sold my beloved DK Whisper Plus engine. And while researching the various new engine options, I decided to take the time to write this book. I wanted to tell you everything, good and bad, that happened to me during my first year's experience with powered paragliding.

I know one thing for certain. I'm going to take my time in selecting my next PPG engine. This time I know exactly what I'm looking for (see Appendix G for details). I just hope I can find it. I may have to wait a couple of years for the technology to catch up to my wishes. But it's coming!

In this book, I've tried to give you an honest, accurate look into the sport of powered paragliding. I haven't left out anything, and I haven't tried to gloss over anything. I hope that I've given you the information you need, in order to decide if you want to participate in this sport (hopefully without scaring the hell out of you in the process). Because flying a powered paraglider isn't for everyone. But then, no sport is. The trick is to determine if the sport is for *you*, before you spend a lot of time and money and sweat.

Was it worth it for me? Yes! Thanks to my participation in this sport, I now have memories that are priceless. I will never forget that moment when I ran madly across the sand, the engine roaring at my back, and my feet first lifted from the ground. You couldn't pay me enough money to buy that memory away from me. Nor will I ever forget that moment when my feet touched lightly down on the sand, ending my first powered flight. I will never forget watching those kids scramble for the ping-pong balls I had just dropped for them. And I will never forget that angry eagle, chasing me away from her nest!

For me, it was worth it.

In the meantime, I hope you've enjoyed reading this book. I know I've certainly enjoyed writing it. I hope you've had a laugh or two, and maybe even learned something useful. Powered paragliding is the most fantastic form of flying in the world, but it's a new sport, and there's a lot of room for development and improvement. So have fun being one of the pioneers, but try not to take too many of the arrows!

Until next time—Happy Flying!

Appendix A

Powered Paragliding – The Bottom Line

So what's the bottom line on the sport of flying a powered paraglider? Is it practical? Does it make sense for you? Is it safe? Just because other people are doing it doesn't mean that *you* should be doing it. After all, there are people who wrestle alligators and who run races with refrigerators strapped to their backs — all in the name of fun.

Why should you fly a PPG? For starters, it's the most fantastic form of powered flying in existence. Over the course of thirty years I've flown everything from ram-air parachutes to fixed wing aircraft. There is simply nothing like a PPG. You are flying with the absolute minimum of equipment. You can literally pack your flying machine in the trunk of your car. And there is something incredibly exciting and romantic about clipping on a wing and running off into the sky, just like a bird. In the air, the view is unmatched by any other form of powered flying. There is literally nothing between you and the rest of the world.

Once in the air, piloting the PPG could not be simpler. Most of the time you don't do anything, and the PPG flies itself just fine. You don't have to worry about maintaining your airspeed, keeping your wing level, or flying straight; the wing does that automatically. You steer, and you work the throttle to go up or down. Powered flying just doesn't get any simpler. When it's time to land, you shut off the engine and swoop down to a gentle, stand-up landing on your feet. You watch your wing collapse into a little pile of string and cloth on the ground, and you have an indescribable feeling of accomplishment.

That's the magic of powered paragliding, and it's very real. It's what the dealers and sales brochures talk about endlessly. But along with the magic comes the hard reality that the brochures typically don't mention. But that's been the purpose of this book; to give you the pluses and the minuses. We've seen the magic, so let's take a moment and talk about the problems and shortcomings of powered paragliding.

The mechanics of the sport are still being developed. The sport of powered paragliding is still in its infancy, and it's extremely undeveloped. A powered paraglider is a conglomeration of parts, mostly borrowed from other sports. The wing and harness are borrowed from the sport of unpowered paragliding. Many of the engines were originally designed to be used in motorcycles and motor scooters. One of the more common engines used today was designed over thirty years ago as an agricultural water pump. Only recently has a wing (Reflex) been specifically developed for powered paragliding. And I know of no engine developed specifically for powered paragliding. This isn't to say that a lot of developmental work hasn't been done in the sport. It has. But the sport is still finding its way. We're still trying to figure out the best way to hang an engine on a man and let him fly.

After-sale support and information can be limited. The sport of powered paragliding worldwide is only a few years old, and the initial growth was quite slow. The U.S., in particular, lags greatly behind most of the rest of the world in the sport. No PPG engine is manufactured in the United States. Some engines may have only a single dealer or importer in the entire U.S.! Getting replacement parts can be expensive, frustrating, and time-consuming. Qualified PPG trainers are few and far between, so one may be forced to travel great distances, at considerable expense, just to get trained. Some PPG dealers are total flakes. There are very few PPG pilots in the U.S. compared to other forms of sport aviation. The comprehensive book on powered paragliding has yet to be written (but some of us are trying). Unlike other branches of sport aviation, an American PPG pilot will not find much of a support structure in place if he runs into problems. He will have to scratch for answers to his questions, and to get help.

What about getting help via the Internet? There are few areas of modern life that haven't been touched by the Internet, and powered paragliding is no exception. However like everything else on the Internet, the quality of PPG information tends to vary tremendously. You can find Web sites and mailing lists that deal with every branch of aviation, including powered paragliding. These web sites and mailing lists can prove very helpful in locating other fliers who will be happy to share their knowledge and experience with you.

However I must sound a cautionary note about the mailing lists. Unlike the newsgroups, which are usually unmoderated, the mailing lists are frequently run by individuals (called Moderators) who have very little knowledge of what it takes to operate a successful mailing list. Most Moderators have never heard of free speech. They regard the list as their private property, and if you say something they don't like, they will kick you off their list. (I've been kicked off of several.) As a result, the really knowledgeable pilots tend to avoid such lists. They will not spend their time and energy contributing to a mailing list, only to be told by the Moderator that they are forbidden to speak on a particular topic. Such mailing lists tend to end up populated by the "me too" gang who think it's more important to get along with each other, and present a sweet image to the rest of the world, rather than getting at the truth. In other words, you end up with a mailing list populated by mediocrities who are happy to censor themselves in order to keep the peace. Caveat Emptor!

There are various powered paragliding organizations that regularly come and go. They can be useful sources of information while they exist, but they also tend to be heavily censored. Caveat Emptor!

The engines are too heavy. Unfortunately there's not much that can be done about the weight of the engines used in powered paragliding. The technology for a lightweight engine strong enough to propel a PPG with a two hundred pound pilot, simply isn't available yet. Some PPG engines can weigh 100 pounds with a full load of fuel, and this is a tremendous amount of weight to place on the pilot's shoulders and spine. And the pilot must be able to run with this weight on his shoulders, and must be ready to quickly maneuver from side to side to keep himself centered under the wing. This can be difficult to do when you're so top-heavy. Without proper technique, which few students acquire immediately, the student may very well find that the tasks are so physically challenging that he soon gives up on the sport. There are lots of eighty pound PPG engines for sale at large discounts by discouraged, would-be PPG pilots who discovered that it's just too damned difficult to maneuver with that much weight on your back.

Ideally, a fully-fueled PPG engine, good for two hours of flight and putting out at least 130 pounds of thrust, would weigh no more than thirty pounds (including the harness). Such an engine would open the sport of powered paragliding to almost everyone. Alas, such an engine is still very much in the dream stage. Currently such a proven engine, fully fueled, weighs at least 70 pounds, which automatically excludes many people from the sport. Clearly there is much room for improvement. There are always reports of wonderful new lightweight PPG engines about to be released (and some actually do get released). My advice is to give any such engines at least a year of trials in the field to see if they really hold up. It's easy to get extra power from a lightweight engine by running it too fast and too hot. This makes the engine look very impressive on paper, with a high power-to-weight ratio, but the problem with this approach is that it tends to burn up the engine fairly quickly.

Engine technology has not quite caught up to the idea of powered paragliding. The present-day technology barely gets the job done for some people (and not at all for most people). That's why many people who are initially interested in the sport of powered paragliding lose interest when they find out how much the typical PPG engine weighs (and costs).

However there are plenty of skilled, dedicated people who are trying to reach PPG engine Nirvana, so let us hope that one of them succeeds.

Disclaimer: The following statements are part fact, part conjecture based on fact, and part consensus among PPG pilots. The sport of powered paragliding is still so new that reliable accident statistics are hard to come by. Powered paragliding is regulated by the FAA only to the extent of FAR 103 which governs the rules for operation of ultralight aircraft. There is no law that requires the reporting of injuries or deaths that take place while flying a powered paraglider. The novice PPG pilot can find it difficult to accurately determine just how dangerous the sport really is.

Please understand that I am not here to tell you whether or not it is safe to fly a powered paraglider. Safety is a relative thing. Some people accept more risk than others, and safety levels among pilots will vary greatly because of differences in training, experience, attitude, and innate skill. Only *you* can determine if the sport is for you. I want you to be armed with information that will help you to accurately estimate the risks. As in every branch of aviation, the risks are there, and they are very real. You can get killed if you get careless.

So with that disclaimer in mind, let's look at the real risks of flying a powered paraglider:

PPGs are more dangerous when flown at low altitudes. Any PPG flying done at less than 300-500 feet is inherently risky. Some PPG instructors even recommend doing the bulk of your flying at an altitude of at least 1,000 feet. Even if the pilot is careful not to hit anything on the ground, the PPG wing can collapse unexpectedly in bad turbulence. Recovery from a collapse is normally automatic, but can eat up more than 100 feet of altitude. If the pilot runs out of altitude before the wing recovers, there is nothing to cushion his collision with the ground. So except for landings and takeoffs, when you can't help being close to the ground, keep some altitude under your wing!

If you want to fly really low to the ground, consider flying a powered para-chute (PPC) where the wing is more resistant to collapse, and where you have some armor and wheels to protect you from an impact with the ground.

PPGs are more dangerous to fly during the middle of the day. For me, this was the most serious limitation on PPG flying. Turbulence in general, and thermal activity in particular, is highest during the middle of the day, typically from late morning to late afternoon. During this time the PPG wing is especially vulner-able to collapse from powerful thermals and other forms of turbulence. This is definitely not the time for a novice PPG pilot to be flying. As a rule, it is much better to fly only in early morning or late afternoon/early evening when winds are usually calmer and thermal activity is reduced.

When I first got into powered paragliding, this was one limitation that I sim-ply could not understand. The no-fly rule for powered paragliding is in appar-ent contradiction to the rules for flying an unpowered paraglider. Unpowered paragliding uses the same wings as powered paragliding, and a great deal of unpowered paragliding is done during the middle of the day when thermal ac-tivity is at its peak. If paragliding wings can be flown unpowered during the turbulent part of the day, why can't they be flown under power during the middle of the day?

There are several reasons. First, without an engine, an unpowered paraglider pilot is in much closer "contact" with his wing. Through the brake lines and suspension lines, the PG pilot feels every twitch of his wing. This allows "active flying," which means that the pilot flies with a constant slight tension on his brake lines. This allows him to feel what the wing is doing, and to take any cor-rective action that might be needed. Frequently the pilot gets warning signs that the wing may be about to collapse (a brake line suddenly starts to feel "mushy" as one side of the wing starts to lose pressurization). If the wing takes a collapse, the pilot is forewarned and is ready to pump out the collapse, using the brakes. If the wing starts to surge forward, the pilot applies more brake to stop the surge. If the wing falls back, the pilot releases the brakes slowly. It also helps that the PG pilot is generally flying in a laid-back, semi-reclining positioning, so it's very easy for him to keep the wing in constant view.

The situation is very different for a PPG pilot. Engine noise and vibration make it more difficult for the pilot to be aware of what his wing is doing. His first hint of a wing collapse is usually the realization that his craft has just gone into a steep turn without his input. Also the PPG pilot must typically fly while sitting upright (because the engine must remain upright for balanced thrust), so it's much harder for a PPG pilot to keep his wing in constant view. At one point I flew with a convex mirror strapped to one leg, just to make it easier for me to see what my wing was doing without having to bend my head back sharply.

PPG pilots also typically fly with no brake pressure, because wings under power fly best with no brakes. But without tension on the brake lines, the PPG pilot is unable to "fly actively." The PPG pilot can easily miss all of the warning signals that are available to an unpowered paraglider pilot.

The whole thing is a complicated interplay of variables, but the bottom line is that powered PPG flight is not the same as unpowered PG flight.

This is not to say that PPGs can't be flown in the middle of the day, but additional training must be obtained, and extra precautions must be taken before doing so. The pilot should be experienced in flying a paraglider. He should be wearing a reserve parachute, and he should have received training in advanced canopy control maneuvers so that he is familiar with wing collapses and knows how to deal with them. It's also recommended that the bulk of the mid-day flying be done at higher altitudes, typically several thousand feet, where the thermals lose much of their strength. And this leads us to the next safety point about the sport of powered paragliding:

You can't see the dangerous air when flying a PPG. Somebody once said that if you could see the turbulence in the sky, you'd never go flying. There's probably some truth in this. Unfortunately, just because you can't see the turbulence doesn't mean it's not there. A column of thermic air, rising swiftly at fifteen hundred feet per minute, looks exactly the same as still air.

For rigid-wing pilots, thermals and turbulence are merely annoying bumps and jolts. Flying on a bumpy day might scare the hell out of a first-time passenger, but the Cessna pilot knows that his wings aren't going to fall off, even in very bumpy air. The PPG pilot has no such assurance. For him, every bump is a potential wing collapse.

Rigid-wing pilots can largely avoid life-threatening turbulence such as thunderstorms, tornadoes, and hurricanes, merely by looking at the sky. They can *see* the dangerous air. PPG pilots cannot. A warm, clear, sunny day, without a cloud in the sky, can easily be too dangerous for a beginning PPG pilot to fly in. Especially if it's during the heat of the day when the thermal activity is at maximum strength.

This was the thing that constantly bothered me when I was flying my PPG. I never knew for certain when the air was sufficiently safe to fly. On my way to the flying field, in the afternoon, I would constantly glance at my watch and then at the sky, wondering when the thermals would die down enough for safe flying. But there was simply no way to know for certain. A good rule of thumb is to confine your flying to three hours before sunset, or after sunrise, and this is what I always did. Sometimes the air was smooth, but usually there were some bumps. I tried to ignore the bumps, but I couldn't. In the end, the only way I could get sufficient peace of mind while flying in bumpy air, was to wear a reserve parachute.

Sometimes the air was very bumpy. I remember one particular flight when I took off in late afternoon. No sooner had I cleared the tree line than the wing began to rock and shake almost non-stop. Every few minutes there would be an especially big bump that would set my heart pounding and glue my eyes to the wing, looking for any signs of collapse (it never did). I flew around the countryside for nearly twenty minutes, looking for calmer air, but I never found any. It was like the entire atmosphere was being stirred by a gigantic Cuisinart. And this was late afternoon, on a warm summer day, without a cloud in the sky. It wasn't even gusty, and the ground wind was blowing at a steady six miles per hour. It should have been ideal weather for a PPG flight, but it wasn't. The atmosphere was simply very turbulent on that particular day.

This is a real problem with PPG flying. Even the "good" weather can turn out to be too rough. Unfortunately the only real way to find out, is to go aloft and see firsthand. Nobody has yet invented a detector, or special set of glasses, that will permit the PPG pilot to see that the air is too rough for safe flying before he takes off, except in very obvious circumstances.

The PPG pilot has no protection from impact. The freedom of flight in a powered paraglider is unmatched by any other powered aircraft. There is nothing to block your view in any direction. There is nothing between you and the sky and the ground. However this also means that there is nothing to protect you from impact in any direction. Every freedom has its price.

When you fly a PPG, you are flying totally unprotected. Your landing gear is your feet, and your shock-absorbing system is your legs. After that, the next thing to strike the ground is the base of your spine. Some PPG instructors claim that your engine and propeller cage can be expected to provide some crash protection for your back. Others disagree. Take your pick. Personally, I always thought an air bag on the bottom of the engine would be a good idea.

By contrast, in a powered parachute (PPC), or rigid-wing aircraft, you have wheels, a metal frame, a shock-absorbing system, and a padded seat between you and the ground. PPCs can hit the ground hard enough to break the wheels and bend the frame, and yet the PPC pilot frequently walks away unharmed.

Because of the inherent risks in flying a PPG, there are constant efforts to lessen the risks. If you're worried about your wing collapsing in flight, you can carry a reserve parachute. If you're worried about smashing your spine into the ground, you can tie an air bag to the bottom of your engine. Unfortunately all of these things add both weight and bulk to the PPG (which is why most PPG pilots don't use them).

The truth is, there's probably no way to eliminate the inherent risks in flying a PPG, any more than we can eliminate the inherent risks in riding a motorcycle, or engaging in any other sport. Any attempt to remove the risks also eliminates the reasons for operating such a craft in the first place; the freedom, the simplicity, and the openness. This is why we don't see protective steel cages, air bags, or seat belts on motorcycles, and why we're not likely to ever see the equivalent on PPGs.

PPGs require smooth air for relaxed flying. The air is not always a smooth highway. Most of the time it's a bit bumpy. The sun heats the ground unevenly, causing columns of warm air to rise. As these columns rise, they displace cooler air which then falls. This results in rising air and sinking air in close proximity to each other. When you fly through such air, you experience the different motions as bumps and jerks. The occasional bump is not a problem, but when they become more frequent it can quickly take all of the fun out of flying.

It's hard to know when you've been properly trained to fly a PPG. Ram-air wings are a remarkable invention. With only some cloth and string, it's possible to fly. This permits wings to be made very inexpensively (compared to other aircraft), and has opened the sport of foot-launched aviation to almost everyone. Because of the "pendulum stability" afforded by the weight of the pilot hanging below the wing, the wing is self-stabilizing and self-flying. This means that a ram-air pilot can learn to fly a wing with just a few days of training. No license is required. Ram-air wings provide an inexpensive, easy-to-learn entry into the sport of aviation, and have made sport flying available to almost everyone.

Alas, there is just one little flaw in this rosy picture. Because they require constant pressurization to maintain their aerodynamic shape, ram-air wings are vulnerable to ordinary everyday turbulence. The turbulence can cause the wing to lose its pressurization and to collapse. And if the collapse takes place close to the ground, the pilot may strike the earth before the wing has time to recover. Every year a few unpowered paraglider pilots are killed in this manner. It even happens to expert paraglider pilots. Fortunately motorized pilots do not have to seek out unstable air with rising thermals. That makes powered flying much safer, but the risk is still there.

Someone once said that a paraglider is the world's easiest craft to fly when conditions are good, and the world's most difficult craft to fly when conditions are bad. There is much truth in this statement. Learning to fly a PPG is basically learning to fly a paraglider. The engine simply lets you take off from level ground and permits you stay in the air without having to find a rising thermal. When conditions are good, the paraglider is very easy to fly, but when conditions are bad, the paraglider can quickly become an uncontrolled nightmare, even for an expert pilot. In a severe collapse, the shape of the wing is constantly changing, and if the pilot does the wrong thing at the wrong time, he can actually make the situation worse. A collapse can be so severe, and so unpredictable, that even a trained expert cannot make a successful recovery in time. In such a case, the only other option is to throw the reserve parachute (assuming you have one).

When I flew a PPG, the question that always haunted me was, *"How much training do I need in order to fly safely?"* I never got a satisfactory answer to that question. Even worse, I'm not sure that anyone really knows the answer. When I learned to fly a PPG, I had two weeks of excellent training in the basics, but no training at all in how to handle an emergency situation in case I ran into some bad turbulence and suffered a severe wing collapse. And I *did* run into some bad turbulence during my basic training. See the chapter, "The Demon Behind The Rock."

You can learn the mechanics of getting a PPG into the air in just a few days. In a week you can go home and fly without an instructor. But eventually you may start to wonder just how safe you are while flying. And you ask the question, "Can I be safer?" If you ask such a question, here is what you will find.

If you study the books and videos for unpowered paragliding, you may start to wonder just how risky it is to fly a paraglider. You read about asymmetric collapses, frontal tucks, negative spins, and stalls. You see all of the violent collapses that a paragliding wing can undergo, and how even the experts can't always recover from a collapse. You read really horrible stories of PG pilots who stalled their wings, and then ended up falling into them when the wing surged forward violently. Not good!

This sort of thing can start to worry you. You realize that your basic PPG training didn't really prepare you to cope with such things, so you look around to see if there is any sort of advanced training you can take to handle such in-flight emergencies. And there is. There are Maneuvers Clinics that are devoted solely to the subject of advanced canopy control. In these clinics, while flying over water and wearing a life jacket and reserve parachute, you deliberately induce all sorts of collapses in your wing and learn how to recover from the collapse. Many PG pilots attend such clinics every year, just to keep their safety skills current. It's supposed to be a great confidence builder.

So you attend such a clinic and you are gratified to learn just how badly the typical paraglider wing really wants to fly. You learn just how quickly it will normally recover from collapses, and how easy it is to recover from most collapses.

Are you safe now? Well there's no question that you're safer than before. You're much less likely to do the wrong thing, and perhaps make the situation worse. Are you now safe from the danger of wing collapse?

Well, no. The truth is, a genuine wing collapse, in turbulent air, can be *much* more violent and complicated than a deliberately-induced collapse in calm air. That's why virtually all unpowered paraglider pilots now wear reserve parachutes. Skydivers have used them for years to save their lives when their parachutes failed to open, and many paraglider pilots already owe their lives to their reserve parachutes. There are documented cases of paraglider pilots who suffered a collapse below one hundred feet of altitude, tossed their reserve parachute, and walked away unhurt.

So you buy a reserve parachute and learn how to use it. Are you now safe from wing collapses?

Well, there's no question that you're safer than before. With a reserve parachute you always have a second chance. But that's all it is; just a second chance. Even a reserve parachute is no guarantee of survival. If you're too low when the wing collapse hits, the reserve may fail to open in time. Or the reserve may get tangled up in your collapsed paraglider wing and fail to open. Unlike skydiving pilots, paraglider pilots don't cut away from their collapsed wing before deploying their reserve parachutes. (Not enough altitude.)

The truth is, you can get into an emergency situation while flying a paraglider wing that can defeat your best efforts to recover from it. Even if you're highly trained in handling collapses, and are carrying a reserve parachute, you can still suffer a wing collapse and end up crashing through no fault of your own. Even the best recovery techniques are not guaranteed to be successful, and you may need every foot of altitude to get your reserve open in time.

In this regard, paragliding is different from most other forms of aviation. In most forms of flying, death or injury is almost always to due to pilot error or bad judgment. In almost every case the pilot can look back and say, "I should have known better. I could have prevented that accident." But his accident will not be due to the fact that his aircraft fell apart in the air!

Unfortunately this is not always the case in paragliding. You can do everything right, have the best training, be carrying the best safety equipment, carry a reserve parachute, and still get injured or killed through no fault of your own. It's like being hit by a drunk driver on the road. It's simply a risk that must be accepted.

This was the thing that bothered me most about being a PPG pilot. I could read about the various sorts of wing collapses that might happen, and the recommended way of dealing with them. But I knew that without actual training, without actually going up in the air and experiencing such collapses and practicing recovering from them, I was just kidding myself that I was trained to handle such emergencies. I knew that if I actually experienced such a collapse, about all I could do was hang on, wait for the wing to recover, and try not to do anything to make the situation even worse. (In other words, about the same thing I had done when I encountered the turbulence behind Moro Rock.) Every time I went up in my PPG, I knew that I was taking risks that I wasn't really trained to cope with.

The truth is, the PPG industry largely fails to acknowledge this risk to newcomers entering the sport. Certainly when I was researching the sport of flying a PPG, none of the dealers (who were eager to sell me a PPG) ever told me about the very real hazards of flying a paraglider; powered or unpowered. I simply assumed that once I got into the air, the paraglider could be counted on to remain flyable, just like any other winged aircraft. It wasn't until after I had bought my PPG, and started my flight training, that I started to learn about all the bad things that can happen to a paraglider wing in flight.

The industry tends to gloss over this risk by pointing out that PPG pilots fly beginner-rated wings that are more stable and resistant to collapse than the higher-performance wings used by many unpowered PG pilots. They point out that PPG pilots normally fly only in the early morning and late afternoon/evening hours, when turbulence is much less active

But while this is all true, it's still true that wing collapses can occur at any time of the day. I personally know of a PPG pilot who took two severe collapses while flying during the supposedly "safe" time of the day. He survived both, without injury. Nevertheless, the PPG industry, as a whole, provides almost no training for handling wing collapses.

How much training in emergency procedures does a PPG pilot really need to fly safely? Probably nobody knows yet. The sport is still too young and undeveloped. So we give the new pilot a week of training, send him out to fly, and see what happens. In another ten years we should have some definitive answers. But in the meantime, the truth is that we're sending PPG pilots out to fly with little or no training in handling emergency situations. We're sending them out to fly in craft that can suddenly collapse into a very out-of-control situation.

This is the critical point that I want to make clear to you. The sport of powered paragliding is very new and undeveloped. Even the experts are still feeling their way. Both equipment and training are still evolving. One only has to look at the early days of hang-gliding, with its grisly toll of dead and injured pilots, to see that the pioneers truly do take the arrows.

On the other hand, the sport of powered paragliding seems to have demonstrated a pretty good overall safety record so far, with very few fatalities or serious injuries, so maybe we're mostly doing things right. One seldom hears reports of injuries to PPG pilots due to wing collapses. Falling down while taking off, or landing, seems to be the main source of injury. So perhaps I am overstating the risk. I certainly hope so.

If you want to fly a PPG, here are your basic choices when it comes to safety:

Play the odds. Learn the basics of launching, flying, and landing the PPG. This can be done in about one week of good training, although two weeks would be much better. Then limit your flying to early morning or late afternoon, and just accept the risk, knowing that a severe wing collapse is not very likely under such circumstances. And even if you do suffer a collapse, chances are it will promptly fix itself. This is what most PPG pilots do.

Get advanced training in dealing with wing collapses. Become a knowledgeable, experienced, powered paraglider pilot. Take advantage of the training that has been developed for unpowered paraglider pilots. Attend a Maneuvers Clinic and practice dealing with collapses while in the air. Then if you ever get hit with a major wing collapse, you'll have the best possible chance of successfully dealing with it.

With either choice, you can greatly improve your odds of survival by carrying a reserve parachute. Reserves are proven lifesavers. Unfortunately they also add weight and bulk to an already-heavy PPG rig. This is why many (if not most) PPG pilots don't carry them.

I'm frequently asked if I would get a P2 paraglider rating before learning to fly a PPG, in order to fly more safely. My answer is "no," even though that's exactly what I did. The problem is that a P2 rating simply teaches you the basics of flying a paraglider, but normally does not teach you to handle wing collapses or other in-flight emergencies. (I do not consider watching videos, to constitute training in handling wing collapses.)

It's true that the development of the ram-air canopy has permitted people to become airborne at a very low cost, and with very little training. But it's also true that the ram-air canopy makes it possible to put large numbers of pilots into the air who have very little training in dealing with emergency situations, and who have very little understanding of the principles of flight.

It's not my intention to frighten anyone away from the sport of powered paragliding, because the danger is actually pretty slight. I simply want you to understand exactly what you're getting into before you spend a lot of money and time learning to fly a PPG. Because the sad fact is, a lot of would-be PPG pilots get into this sport, learn the hard realities of the sport only after they've spent a ton of money, and then leave the sport, disappointed and discouraged. I don't want that to happen to you. I want you to walk into this wonderful sport with both eyes open.

I don't want to give the impression that flying a powered paraglider is some sort of uniquely dangerous sport. It isn't. Statistically it seems pretty safe, especially when compared to other forms of recreational aviation. One simply does not hear of regular deaths or serious injuries in the sport of powered paragliding, the way one does with rigid-wing ultralights, or general aviation, or even unpowered paragliding. Of course this may have something to do with the relatively few pilots who are flying PPGs. But falling down on the ground while wearing your engine, and breaking the prop, is probably the most typical PPG accident.

The truth, of course, is that every sport has its unavoidable risks that can be minimized, but never eliminated. If you swim in the ocean, you risk getting attacked by a shark. If you hike or camp in the mountains, you risk getting attacked by a bear. If you ski, you risk getting hit by other skiers, or running into a tree. So the risk itself is never a reason for not participating in a sport. It's what sort of risk *you* are comfortable taking, and what sort of goal *you* are trying to accomplish.

Appendix B

PPG vs. PPC – Which is Safer?

This is a debate that used to rage all the time. So we're probably getting close to another round of debate. When I first got into the sport of powered paragliding, I had no idea there was any sort of safety difference between a powered parachute (PPC), and a powered paraglider (PPG). My first clue came from the powered parachute dealer who gave me a demo ride. When I mentioned that I'd also been looking into buying a powered paraglider, he said "There's no way I'd fly one of those things. The wing can collapse."

I wasn't exactly sure what he was talking about, and since I wasn't convinced that he'd be completely objective on the subject, I decided to look into it myself. I found an Internet database of accident reports for unpowered paragliding, and was surprised to learn that paraglider wings frequently took collapses in flight. Sometimes these collapses were so severe that the wing was unable to recover. Then the pilot would be forced to open his reserve parachute (if he had one) in order to save his life. Sometimes the collapse took place at such a low altitude that the pilot had insufficient time to react, and he struck the ground hard enough to be badly injured, or even killed. Every year, about one paraglider pilot in a thousand seems to meet death in this fashion.

This worried me. When I had flown a ram-air skydiving parachute, twenty years earlier, collapses had never been a problem. I investigated further, and learned some interesting things.

All ram-air wings maintain their shape from internal air pressure. The weight of the pilot forces the wing to move downward through the air. It forces air into the openings at the front of the wing, pressurizing it and causing the wing to inflate like a giant air mattress. This pressure is quite low, but it's enough to keep the canopy inflated into a wing shape that can fly.

If the wing encounters a band of air moving the wrong way (as can be found in thermals or turbulence), the wing can be momentarily robbed of its pressurization. This can cause the wing to collapse and stop flying. Usually only a small portion of the wing collapses, while the rest of the wing continues to fly. The collapsed portion normally quickly re-inflates, and no harm is done (except perhaps to the pilot's nerves). However an extensive collapse can cause the wing to lose altitude before the wing manages to re-inflate. If this collapse occurs too close to the ground, the pilot may strike the earth before the wing resumes normal flight.

Powered parachutes (PPCs) use ram-air canopies directly descended from skydiving ram-air canopies. The PPC wings are simple, reliable, and highly resistant to collapse. Powered paragliders (PPGs) use wings that are much more sophisticated in design, and have much higher performance and maneuverability, but are more vulnerable to collapse. In aviation, it's always a tradeoff. PPG wings have roughly twice the glide ratio of PPC wings. This means that in case of engine failure, the PPG wing would be able to glide almost twice as far as a PPC wing, and would also descend much more slowly. This means that the PPG pilot would have four times as much area to land in, as would a PPC pilot. That gives the PPG pilot a much greater chance of reaching an emergency landing field.

But the higher performance of the PPG wing comes with a price tag. Because of its lower internal air pressure, the PPG wing is more susceptible to collapse than the PPC wing. It became apparent to me that any ram-air wing had the potential to collapse if the turbulence became sufficiently severe. PPG wings were obviously more likely to collapse than PPC wings, given the same amount of turbulence.

This is as far as many pilots seem to take the argument. PPG wings are more likely to suffer collapses than PPC wings, therefore it's safer to fly a PPC. But as I continued to study the evidence, it soon became obvious that it wasn't this simple. (In aviation, it almost never is.)

As I read the accident statistics, several important facts emerged. First, not all PPG wings are created equal. Most powered paraglider wings are simply unpowered paraglider wings that have been selected for their ease of launch and stability in the air. Frequently they are the same wings used to teach unpowered paragliding students. Such wings are certified to self-recover from any sort of collapse or difficulty, even if the pilot does nothing.

Such wings are ideal for powered paragliding. A PPG pilot has an engine to give him power and lift. Unlike an unpowered PG pilot, he does not need a higher-performance wing to get the maximum amount of speed or air time, or to wring the maximum amount of lift from the thermals. In fact, a PPG pilot has no need of thermals, and typically goes out of his way to avoid such turbulent air.

PPG flying is done from flat fields, typically far away from mountains. A PPG pilot has an engine, which gives him the ability to launch from a flat field and to keep him in the air even if no thermals are present. If a PPG pilot runs into turbulent air, his wing may rock and shake, or even momentarily collapse, but there is no mountain for him to run into. The accident statistics seemed pretty clear on this point. Stay away from mountains and turbulent air, and PPG wings appear to be as reliable, and as free of dangerous collapses, as PPC wings. But if a collapse does happen, there seems little doubt that a PPC wing is more likely to self-recover, and to recover more quickly. Undoubtedly the accident statistics would reflect this.

Well no, that wasn't quite true either. If anything, the PPCs seemed to have a higher rate of accidents, injuries, and fatalities. How could that be? The PPC was supposed to be inherently safer. Could it simply be a reflection of the fact that PPCs were more numerous than PPGs (at least in the United States)? No, that didn't make sense. Even in Europe, where PPGs were far more numerous than PPCs, injuries and fatalities were still very low.

It didn't make sense. PPCs had more stable wings, they had wheels, and they had sturdy metal frames that gave the pilot greater protection in the event of a crash. I examined the accident rate of the PPC more closely. It appeared that the greatest cause of injuries and fatalities was due to running into power lines. Such accidents were virtually unheard of in the PPG world. What was the explanation?

Suddenly the truth hit me. *PPCs fly lower!* Because they have wheels, and frames, PPCs can safely fly much lower to the ground. They can even fly low while flying downwind. On the other hand, because they lack wheels, and because their wings are somewhat less resistant to collapse, PPG pilots normally refrain from low-level flight. If a PPG pilot hits the ground while flying low, at full speed, he will not be able to run fast enough to remain on his feet. He will fall down, and is quite likely to break his propeller, propeller cage, or damage his engine (or himself). Or a sudden wing collapse could cause the PPG pilot to hit the ground, again damaging the pilot or his equipment. So PPG pilots normally fly at least three hundred feet off the ground. This normally gives their wings enough time to reinflate in the event of a collapse. And if you're flying at three hundred feet, you don't have to worry about hitting powerlines.

I finally concluded that PPCs appear to have a higher accident rate than PPGs, not because they are more dangerous, but because PPC pilots frequently like to fly at altitudes where they are more likely to hit something.

So which is safer? PPCs or PPGs?

I think the accident statistics show that both types of craft are roughly equal in safety. A PPC wing is less likely to collapse in flight, but a PPG wing will carry a pilot twice as far in search of an emergency landing field in case of engine failure. Both craft, if flown in non-turbulent conditions, have little to worry about in terms of wing collapses. Both craft, if flown at sufficient altitudes, can always be assured of reaching an emergency landing field in the event of engine failure. And if a power pilot likes to fly in turbulent air, then he probably shouldn't be flying any type of ram-air wing, but instead should be flying a fixed-wing craft.

If a PPG pilot flies a safe, beginner wing, is he guaranteed to be safe from wing collapse? No. Any ram-air wing can collapse, given sufficient turbulence. And if the collapse takes place near the ground, the pilot may impact the ground before the wing can re-inflate. The same risk is also present in a PPC, though the risk is smaller, and the PPC pilot has wheels and a metal frame to give him an added measure of protection. The possibility of such crashes is simply one of the risks of flying a ram-air wing.

Since the PPG pilot has a higher risk of wing collapse, is there anything he can do to mitigate this risk? Yes. He can normally fly at least three hundred feet above the ground. This will normally give his wing sufficient time and altitude to recover from most collapses. He can attend safety clinics that will teach him how to avoid collapses, or how to deal with them if they happen. He can also carry a reserve parachute. Reserves are proven lifesavers. They have been successfully deployed as low as one hundred feet, and still saved the pilot's life. Nothing is guaranteed, of course, but it's nice to know that if your PPG wing suffers a catastrophic collapse, you have a backup chute that can safely lower you to the ground.

Can PPCs use reserve parachutes? Yes. A ballistic reserve parachute has been developed for the PPC, but it's quite expensive. The general consensus in the PPC world seems to be that a reserve parachute is so expensive, and so seldom needed, that the cost of the system is not justified by the risk. Each to his own.

Bottom line: The PPC pilot simply takes his chances with wing collapse, knowing that the actual risk is very small. The PPG pilot lives with a larger risk of wing collapse, but can carry a reserve parachute to mitigate the risk. Again, it probably comes out about the same. In fact, many PPG pilots don't even bother to carry reserves, since they consider the risk of fatal wing collapse, in good weather, to be too small to worry about.

Some people claim that PPG wings are easier to stall than PPC wings. This is not true. Both types of wings have what is called "pendulum stability." In non-turbulent air, the pilot's suspended weight serves to maintain a proper angle of attack, keeps the wing flying at a constant speed, and keeps the wing from stalling. This is one of the nicer features of flying ram-air canopies. Even if you do nothing, the wing will fly just fine, all by itself, without stalling or requiring pilot input.

Nevertheless, it's a fact that one frequently hears about PG wings being stalled, while one seldom hears about PPC wings being stalled. What accounts for this discrepancy? Actually both types of wings will stall if the brake lines are pulled down too far. It's easier to pull the brake lines down too far, in a PPG, than in a PPC. With a paraglider wing, the pilot has complete control over the brake lines. The ends of the lines hang next to his head, and he can pull them as far down as he wishes. If he pulls the lines all the way down to his waist, and holds them there, he will very likely cause the wing to stall, although it takes considerable effort to do so.

A PPC has the brake lines arranged differently. Instead of pulling directly on the brake lines, the pilot pushes his foot against a hinged steering bar, to which the brake line is tied. Thus, by regulating the length of the brake line, and the length of the steering bar, an automatic safety feature is introduced. Even if the pilot pushes both steering bars as far as he can, it will not normally be enough to cause the wing to stall. Of course if the length of the steering line has not been properly adjusted, the PPC pilot can get a very unpleasant surprise!

This is another reason why PPCs require less time to learn to fly safely. They have been "idiot-proofed" to a greater degree than PPGs. One of the things that is taught in PPG training, is how to avoid pulling the steering lines down too far, and causing a stall. By contrast, the unpowered paraglider pilot spends most of his time trying to remain within a narrow thermal. Thus he frequently flies with the brakes already pulled far down, to slow the wing as much as possible, and may not be far from a stall. Suddenly he realizes that he's just flown out of the thermal, and so he quickly turns in order to get back into the thermal (since that's where the lift is). However if he forgets to first ease up off the brakes, and simply jams one brake line down even farther, to make the turn, he may stall one side of the wing.

This is the origin of the mistaken notion that paraglider wings are easy to stall. It's not that the wings are easy to stall, but that it's easy to forget that you are already deliberately flying close to a stall, while flying as slowly as possible to stay within the thermal, and to suddenly slip over the edge into a stall.

PPG flying does not normally suffer this problem. Having an engine makes thermal hunting unnecessary. Unlike an unpowered paraglider, a powered paraglider normally flies with little or no brake pressure. Even when making turns, the PPG pilot seldom pulls the brake lines below his shoulders, and therefore does not normally come close to a stall.

In the end, it depends on what sort of risks a pilot feels most comfortable with. If avoiding a wing collapse is your highest priority, then fly a PPC. If reaching an emergency landing field in the event of engine failure is your highest priority, then fly a PPG. If flying thirty feet off the ground is something you like to do, then definitely fly a PPC. If turning off the motor, and soaring in thermals is something you like to do, then fly a PPG. And if flying like a bird is your most important criteria, then definitely fly a PPG!

The critical point is to know how to fly your craft safely. PPCs and PPGs are probably the world's safest form of aircraft, but if you are careless, and take unnecessary risks, you can get killed in either one.

Appendix C
Flying Tips

Here is a collection of basic flying tips that I've discovered over the course of my first year of flying. I hope you find them as useful as I have.

Pre-Flight Checklist: No matter what you fly, every PPG pilot should have a pre-flight checklist. If you stick with this sport, sooner or later you'll get complacent and forget something before takeoff. I'll never forget the time that I made a perfect takeoff, and then looked down to see that I was still wearing my tennis shoes. I'd forgotten to put on my paraboots! On another occasion I forgot to fasten my chest strap. I've even been told of a case where a PPG pilot forgot to fasten his leg straps, gunned his engine, and ran down the field. His machine took off just fine, however the pilot never left the ground.

Everyone will have his own ideas as to what is needed on a pre-flight checklist. Here's a copy of mine to get you started:

Boots

Helmet

Gloves

Ear Plugs

Altimeter

ELT (Emergency Locator Transmitter)

Hook Knife

Cell Phone

Pepper Spray (for unfriendly animals)

Leg Straps

Vest

Chest Strap
Harness Locking Pins
Risers - attached
Hand Mirror
Footbar - hooked
Reserve straps - removed
Reserve pins - secured
Master Switch - on
Overview
Engine Run Up

The Overview item is performed by my flying buddy, Mike. He simply stands back and looks me over, in general, to see if anything looks out of place.

I added the Engine Run Up item after I started the engine, warmed it up, and then took off without first running up the engine to full power. I didn't think I could possibly forget to run up the engine before takeoff, but I did. Never trust your memory! If an item is important, then put it on the checklist.

Hook Knife: No PPG pilot should ever go up without a hook knife. If you are forced to make a water landing, you can easily find yourself underwater and entangled in the wing lines. If you find it necessary to use your reserve, you can find yourself getting dragged across the ground by your reserve after landing. In such circumstances the hook knife can save your life.

Any sharp knife will do, as long as you have a way of carrying it safely. However a hook knife is ideally suited for the job. A hook knife is just a little plastic handle with a curved end, with a razor blade embedded in a slot inside the curved end. The slot leading to the blade is too small for your fingers to enter, but a suspension line, or even a piece of nylon webbing, will readily slip inside. And as soon as the line or strap hits the razor blade, it's cut. With a hook knife, you can instantly sever a two inch wide nylon strap. Highly recommended. Cost: $10-20.

Tachometer: There are only three instruments that you Really Do Need for flying a PPG. One is the Wind Speed Indicator (see below). Another is the Wind Direction Indicator (see below). The other is the Tachometer. Most PPGs come with tachometers, but if yours doesn't, it's very easy to add.

The tachometer gives you a constant readout on the speed of your engine, in revolutions per minute (rpm). Not the speed of your propeller, but the speed of your engine. This information is very important, because anything seriously wrong with your engine will very likely affect its speed. So if you see an unexplained change in your engine speed, that's a pretty good sign that something's wrong with your engine, and that you should land immediately. For example, if your engine is running too fast, it can burn up. If it's running too slow, it may be starved for fuel. Neither condition is desirable when airborne.

The tachometer can also keep you from taking off with a defective engine. If you start up your engine on the ground, and see that it's not idling at its normal speed, that's an excellent indication that something is wrong. If you do a full-power runup on the ground, and your engine does not reach its normal rpm setting, that's also an excellent indication that something is wrong. Obviously you don't want to take off if your engine is not developing full power.

The tachometer is about the size of a pack of chewing gum, and weighs about as much. You can easily attach it almost anywhere on your harness. Typically there are two wires on the tachometer. One wire grounds to the body of the engine, and the other wire simply wraps around your spark plug wire. The tachometer works by sensing and counting the electrical pulses that run to your spark plug, and translating this into engine rpm.

Cost: About $40.

There are other engine instruments that you can add to your PPG engine. The CHT (Cylinder Head Temperature) gauge will do just that, while the EGT (Exhaust Gas Temperature) gauge will tell you the temperature of the gas coming out of your muffler. If your engine starts to overheat, or do other types of shenanigans, these gauges can be helpful in preventing damage, but most PPG pilots fly only with the tachometer.

Wind Speed Indicator: If you're experienced in judging wind speed, then you don't need a wind speed indicator. However if you're like me, your ability to judge wind speed pretty much ended with "There's not enough wind to fly my kite!" In such a case, the wind speed indicator is a fabulously useful instrument. You simply hold the indicator up to the wind for a few seconds, and it tells you how fast the wind is blowing. This will tell you if the wind is blowing fast enough for a reverse launch, or slow enough that you need to do a forward launch. It will also tell you if the wind is blowing too fast to launch, period. Even more important, if you take several wind speed readings over a period of several minutes, you'll know how much the wind is gusting. Too much gusting is an excellent indicator that conditions are too turbulent for safe flying.

The wind speed indicator is basically just a little propeller on a plastic handle, with some electronic circuitry and a battery inside the handle. You hold it up to the wind, the wind spins the propeller, and the electronics measure the rpm of the propeller and translate it into wind speed. The speed is then displayed on a little digital readout. The whole assembly is smaller than a pack of cigarettes, and weighs next to nothing. You can put it on a string and hang it around your neck.

If you're like me, you'll be amazed at just how lousy a judge of wind speed you really are. But after a few months of actually measuring the wind, you'll get yourself calibrated and start to become a pretty good judge of wind speed.

There are several good brands of wind speed indicators. I bought the "Skywatch" brand.

Cost: $70. And worth every penny.

The only thing I didn't like about my Skywatch wind speed indicator is that it refused to work when the air temperature fell below 40 degrees Fahrenheit. The bearings on the little propeller contracted in the cold, and eventually stopped the propeller. So if you're flying in cold weather you might want to see if the company has solved this particular problem.

Wind Direction Indicator: This is even more important than the wind speed indicator. You *must* take off directly into the wind, or you won't get airborne. And no matter how fast or slow the wind may be blowing, you always want to land *into* the wind. If you land in any other direction, you will very likely fall down and may injure yourself or your equipment.

You can spend good money buying a fancy wind sock like they use at the airport, but a hunk of brightly colored ribbon, tied to a stick and stuck in the ground, works almost as well. Ribbon is very cheap, and sticks are readily available. Fluorescent Orange ribbon is the easiest to see.

My personal preference is to use an empty plastic bleach jug. Jugs of bleach can often be found in the laundry room. Pour the bleach down the sink and rinse out the jug. Just don't tell your wife. When she can't find the bleach, blame it on those damned kids that she insisted on having.

Pour some gravel or lead shot into the empty bleach jug to make it bottom-heavy. Then go to the hardware store and buy a dowel rod exactly one and one-eighth inches in diameter, and three or four feet long. Stick the dowel rod into the mouth of the jug (it will be a perfect fit) and tie a three or four foot length of brightly colored ribbon to the other end of the dowel rod. The gravel or lead shot will keep the whole thing from tipping over in a high wind. You now have a superb wind direction indicator. When you're done flying, pull the dowel rod out of the bleach jug and put the cap back on. This will prevent the gravel or lead shot from spilling out. Now the whole thing will store easily in your trunk. I suggest drilling a hole in the plastic cap, and tying it to the jug handle with a short length of string. Then you can't lose the cap.

I am forever indebted to Tyson Russell, of Seattle, Washington, for suggesting the use of the plastic bleach jug. If you want to tell Tyson's wife what happened to her bleach jug, it's okay. I don't need him anymore.

Altimeter: You can safely fly a PPG without an altimeter, but it's a lot more fun if you have one. Not only will know just how high you are, but you'll also know if you're climbing or descending, which is not always easy to tell by eye alone.

As an ex-skydiver, I had a really excellent skydiving altimeter that I tried to use for powered paragliding, but it didn't work very well. The problem was that the dial on my skydiving altimeter went from zero to twelve thousand feet. But powered paragliding is frequently done at altitudes of less than one thousand feet, and that barely caused the needle on my skydiving altimeter to move. I realized that I would need a much more sensitive digital altimeter that was fairly accurate (say to the nearest five or ten feet).

Excellent digital altimeters are available for unpowered paragliding. These typically strap around your leg, and almost always include a built-in variometer so you know exactly how fast you're going up or down. But these altimeters are fairly expensive (around $400). I was lucky enough to discover a smaller, less-expensive altimeter called the Cateye. I had to import mine from South Africa, but I believe they are now available in the United States from various shops that sell bicycle equipment. The Cateye is the size of a large wristwatch, and weighs very little. You can strap it around your wrist or around your leg. It doesn't have much of a variometer, but you really don't need a variometer for powered paragliding. The Cateye only costs about $100. Highly recommended.

There are various "altimeter watches" available, but I've found that these don't work very well for powered paragliding. They're fine for hiking or skiing, but they don't update the altitude reading fast enough for any kind of sky sport. One model only updates the altitude reading every thirty seconds! You can gain or lose a lot of altitude in only thirty seconds. The nice thing about the Cateye altimeter is that it was designed for sky sports, and it updates the altitude reading almost constantly.

Global Positioning System (GPS): You can safely fly a PPG without a GPS indicator, but it's a lot more fun if you have one. The GPS will always tell you exactly where you are, and will always show you exactly which way to fly to get home. Believe it or not, it *is* possible to get lost while flying a PPG. Of course you can always land and ask directions. (Unless you're a man, in which case forget it!)

Another nice feature of the GPS is that it will always tell you your ground speed. Not your air speed (which is constant), but your ground speed (which is constantly changing). It doesn't take much of a head wind to bring a PPG to a halt in the sky. So if you know that your PPG has an airspeed of twenty miles per hour, and you glance at your GPS and see that you're flying downwind at thirty-five miles per hour, you'll know that you're going to be bucking a fifteen mile per hour headwind on the leg home, and that your ground speed will only be about five miles per hour. Information like this can help you judge how far to fly downwind or upwind, so that you can be certain you have enough fuel to make it home. A very nice instrument to have.

Most GPS units come with some sort of plastic carrying pouch. Cut a hole in the pouch so you can see the GPS display screen, and tie the whole thing to your leg strap or chest strap. Then you can simply glance down, in flight, and read the display.

Cost: The sky is the limit. All of the really useful features can be had in a unit costing less than one hundred dollars. Moving map displays are nice if you have the extra bucks to spend, but they aren't really necessary. Do you really care to know the name of the lake, river, or town below you?

Emergency Locator Transmitter (ELT): If you can afford it, this is a very, very nice instrument to have when you fly. It can save your life. The ELT is simply an electronic beeper that puts out a steady signal on the Emergency Channel of 121.5, which is monitored by lots of people. If you crash, and survive, and you have your ELT, all you have to do is stay conscious long enough to extend the antenna and flick the activation switch. For the next twenty hours or so, your ELT will be screaming its head off on the Emergency Channel. Anyone who hears it, such as a passing plane or satellite, will know that you're in trouble and will alert the authorities to send help. Best of all, the authorities can use the ELT's signal to help determine your location, even if you're hanging in a tall tree in the middle of a vast forest. Or if you were smart enough to tell someone that you were going flying, that person can notify the authorities that you're overdue, and the rescuers can start listening for your signal. Highly recommended.

The ELT is a metal box about the size of a pack of cigarettes, and about eight times as heavy. Mine has a carrying loop that I attach to my harness so that I can always reach it, even if I'm hanging in a tree with a broken arm.

Cost: $300-$500. Available at pilot supply stores and from various catalogs. Expensive? Yes, but what is your life worth? If you have an ELT, the rescuers can find you, no matter how well-concealed you are. Otherwise you are just a very small speck in a very large world.

Cell Phone: I always keep my cell phone attached to my harness, typically right next to my ELT (see above). If you run out of gas, or have engine failure and have to land out in the middle of nowhere, you can probably call for help on your cell phone. Even though your ELT will ultimately bring the rescuers, it might take awhile. With a cell phone you can call for help immediately (assuming you have coverage). If you're seriously injured, having a cell phone just might save your life.

Cost: I paid $800 for my first cell phone. Now they're giving them away for free. Warning! Don't use your cell phone while in the air unless it's a genuine emergency. Don't use it to call up your wife or girlfriend to tell her that you're flying over her house. The FCC doesn't like that at all. I know one guy who got fined $10,000 for using his cell phone while flying.

Radio: If you want to talk to someone on the ground while you're in the air, then you need a radio. You can fly low, and shout to someone on the ground, and be heard, but I guarantee that you will never hear the answer. Personally I've never flown with a radio while flying a PPG. The good radios cost money, they add weight and complexity, and I fly to get away from the rest of humanity; not to stay in touch with it.

Instead of using a radio, I worked out a simple system of hand signals to communicate with my flying buddy, Mike, on the ground. We have signals for Land Immediately, Don't Land, Wind Direction, Wind Speed, etc. If something interesting happens on my flight, I'd rather talk about it over a cup of coffee after the flight. Still, radios can be nice. Especially if you can afford one. And there's no question that they increase your safety.

Of course, carrying a radio while being trained is a completely different story, and is highly advisable.

Cost: Many good handheld radios are available from dealers like Aircraft Spruce or Sporty's Pilot Shop. Expect to spend a couple of hundred dollars for a good one. You can buy cheaper radios intended for everyday consumer use. Quality and reliability varies.

Pilot Balloon: Many a pilot has taken off in perfectly calm conditions, only to discover that it's very bumpy and turbulent one hundred feet above the ground. How to avoid this? Send up a Pilot Balloon! A Pilot Balloon is simply a kid's balloon, filled with helium, with about ten feet of colored ribbon tied to the balloon to make it highly visible. You can follow the balloon's ascension with binoculars. After a couple of minutes you'll know exactly what the wind is doing. If it's bumpy, you'll see the balloon suddenly jerk in a different direction. If the balloon is constantly jerking back and forth, then it's *very* bumpy, and probably best not to fly. If the winds aloft are blowing in a different direction, you'll see the balloon gradually change direction. If the balloon suddenly changes direction, you may be seeing a wind shear, and you definitely don't want to fly into that! I never fly without first sending up a pilot balloon. If it looks questionable, I sometimes send up a second balloon.

To launch Pilot Balloons, you need helium. Go to the K-Mart, or Wal-Mart, and go to the party supply section. For about twenty dollars you'll get a tank of helium about twice the size of a bowling ball, a package of colorful latex balloons, and some colored ribbon. You'll get enough helium to inflate several dozen balloons. When the tank is empty, you simply throw it away.

Always use latex balloons for your pilot balloon. They are biodegradable. Mylar balloons last forever, and clutter up the countryside. Also the mylar balloons cost more, and since you're never going to get the balloon back, why pay more?

If you want to be Environmentally Pure, you can always try to recover the ballon. Just walk up and down the countryside, after each flight, asking everyone you meet, "Have you seen my balloon?"

A tethered pilot balloon also makes an excellent wind direction indicator. Fill one of your pilot balloons with helium and tie about twenty feet of brightly colored ribbon to it. Then tie the other end of the ribbon to something on the ground (like your car bumper). It makes a superb wind direction indicator, and you can easily see it when you're getting ready to land.

If the weather is too bad to fly, you can always pass the time by sucking up a lung full of helium and talking like Donald Duck. It scares the hell out of the cat. Warning! Never suck helium directly out of a pressurized tank. You may overpressure your lungs and damage them. Suck it out of a balloon, instead.

Safety Helmet:
Never fly without a safety helmet!
Never fly without a safety helmet!
Never fly without a safety helmet!
A broken arm or leg will heal. A broken brain will not. My safety helmet has saved me from serious head injury on at least three separate occasions.

Just abut any kind of helmet will do, provided it has a rigid shell and some thick padding (like styrofoam) that will absorb and spread the impact. I have a regular motorcycle helmet that I use when the weather is cold, and a vented bicycle helmet for when the weather is hot. Some pilots think that bicycle helmets or motorcycle helmets don't afford enough protection, and that only a full facial helmet is appropriate. They're probably right, but a full facial helmet can make you sweat like a pig on a hot day. It can be dangerous to launch with your eyes full of sweat. Caveat Emptor.

Boots: Whenever you fly, always wear a good pair of study, high-topped boots. Paraboots, or Paragliding boots, are particularly nice as they are specifically made for the foot-launching pilot, and provide maximum ankle support. However hiking boots, or sturdy work boots, are cheaper and will usually get the job done. They just don't look nearly as sexy.

Don't fly in tennis shoes or low-cut boots. Your feet are your landing gear. Normally they are the first and last things to touch the ground. If all goes well, your landings will be feather-soft, and you could probably make them barefoot. But if you flare a little too high, or land a little too fast, especially while you're still learning to fly, good boots can make the difference between no injury, and a broken or sprained ankle.

Ear Plugs: Never fly without some sort of ear protection. PPG engines are incredibly noisy, and prolonged exposure to the noise can damage your hearing. I use the foam ear plugs that many aircraft pilots use. Just roll them between your thumb and finger to make them real small, then stick them in your ears. The foam expands, filling your ear and conforming exactly to the shape of your ear canal. It's a perfect custom fit. You'll be amazed how much noise the ear plugs eliminate. After landing, just pull them out and reuse them. Throw them away when they start looking really gross.

Cost: A couple of bucks.

Don't forget to wear your ear plugs whenever you start your engine, even if you're not flying. Noise is noise.

Ratio-Right: All PPG engines require a mixture of oil and gasoline in the fuel tank. Depending on the engine, the mixture ratio can be anything from 25:1, 50:1, or even 100:1. How do you know how much oil to add to the gasoline to get the right mixture? Well, you can figure out how many fluid ounces of gasoline you have, and then measure out the proper number of ounces of oil. Or you can use a Ratio-Right.

A Ratio-Right is basically a measuring cup for measuring out the proper amount of oil to mix with your gasoline. Basically it's just a plastic measuring cup, but instead of being marked in ounces, it's marked in gallons of gas, and oil ratios. The Ratio-Right cup typically has several sets of markings on the side, depending on what ratio you want (25:1, 40:1, 50:1, etc.). Whatever fuel/oil ratio your engine requires, chances are the Ratio-Right is already calibrated for it. Within each ratio, the cup is marked in gallons of gasoline. Simply determine the number of gallons of gasoline you have, and then fill the cup with oil until you reach that gasoline mark. Dump the oil in your gasoline and shake it up to thoroughly mix it. *Viola!* A perfectly mixed batch of gasoline and oil, at exactly the right ratio.

The Ratio-Right cup takes all the guesswork and effort out of determining how much oil to add to your gasoline. A marvelous little tool. Highly recommended.

Cost: Under $10 at most motorcycle shops.

Tip: Here's an even easier way to mix your fuel. You can usually buy your oil in eight ounce, or sixteen ounce plastic bottles. Multiply the ounces of oil by the ratio you need, then divide the result by 128 to determine the gallons of gas required. Take your empty gas can to the filling station, pump exactly the gallonage you just calculated, then open up a bottle of oil and dump the whole thing into the gas tank. Result? A perfectly mixed batch of fuel, and you didn't even have to get out your Ratio-Right to measure the oil. What could be simpler?

Example: My DK Whisper called for a 25:1 ratio of gas to oil. An eight ounce bottle of oil, multiplied by 25, would require 200 ounces of gas to get the right ratio. 200 divided by 128 (the number of ounces in a gallon) gave 1.56 gallons of gas needed to get the proper mixture when mixed with eight ounces of oil. I went to the filling station, pumped 1.56 gallons of gasoline into the gas can (easy to do with the meter on the pump), dumped in an 8 ounce bottle of oil, and had 1.6 gallons of perfectly mixed fuel to pour into my Whisper's fuel tank. By coincidence, this just happened to be the amount of fuel needed to fill the Whisper's fuel tank. You may not be quite this lucky, but you can see how easy it is.

If I had a bigger fuel tank, I would simply pump 3.12 gallons of gasoline, then dump in a 16 ounce bottle of oil. A perfect 25:1 ratio. No muss, no fuss.

If you have any leftover mixed fuel after flying, dump it into your car's gas tank. Don't store mixed fuel. It deteriorates too quickly, and you risk having it gum up your carburetor and causing engine trouble in flight. It's not worth the risk. Always mix up a fresh batch of fuel just before flying.

It's also a good idea to mix your fuel in a separate tank, and then dump it into your PPG's fuel tank. That way if you make a mistake while mixing, you can easily dump the whole thing out and start over. Not so easy to do if the mistake is already in the PPG's fuel tank.

Training Harness: The secret to successful launches of a PPG is ground handling. You must be able to control your wing at all times while on the ground. It's not a difficult skill to acquire, but it does require practice. And if you don't fly regularly, your ground handling skills can start to get rusty.

So practice your ground handling on a regular basis. Go out to a park or playing field, spread your wing, clip it to your harness, and practice pulling it up into the air. Great way to keep in practice. Also a great way to meet chicks.

But there's just one little problem. Your harness is attached to your motor. You certainly don't want to practice ground handling for any length of time with your heavy motor on your back. You can detach your motor from your harness, of course, but that's probably a lot of bother.

So what's the answer? Buy a training harness. Schools that teach unpowered paragliding will usually be happy to sell you a used training harness for very little money. Or you can buy a brand new training harness for about $150. Personally I use my old skydiving harness, and just clip the wing risers to the reserve attachment rings on my chest.

With a training harness you can easily stay proficient in your ground handing skills without ever touching your motor or flying harness.

Mushroom Bag: When the flying is done, it's time to fold up the wing and pack it away. And your wing probably came with a backpacking-type bag to pack it in. No doubt your instructor showed you how to lay out your wing on the ground, carefully fold it up in sections, squeeze the air out of the cells, and finally stuff the folded wing into a tiny little packing bag. And after about the tenth time of packing your wing, you looked at that tiny little packing bag and said, "There's gotta be a better way!"

Well, there is! If you're wondering why the packing bag included with your wing is so small, there's a couple of reasons. First, your wing was probably designed for unpowered paragliding. The poor bastards who fly without engines frequently have to hike up hills and mountains to find suitable launch sites. So they want compact bags that are easy to carry up the mountain. Second, have you ever seen a van or station wagon loaded with half a dozen unpowered paragliding enthusiasts? They need a shoehorn to get everybody, and all the wings, into the van. Unless the wings are packed up into bundles that are as small as possible, they'd never get everything inside.

But those of us who have been selected by God to be powered paragliding pilots don't have any of these problem. Space in the vehicle is not nearly so critical. This means we can use mushroom bags to pack our wings.

What is a mushroom bag? Basically it's just a flat piece of circular plastic with a drawstring around the edge. You lay the bag out flat on the ground, pick up the wing, and dump it onto the plastic. Then you steadily cinch up the drawstring as you tuck the wing inside the drawstring. In just a minute or two, the drawstring has been pulled up snug, and the whole wing is completely enclosed inside a plastic bag that looks exactly like the top of a giant mushroom about three feet in diameter. The bag has a carrying handle in the middle, and even has a couple of shoulder straps if you want to carry it like a pack. Best of all, there's no folding or packing of the wing. You just pick the wing up, set it down on the bag, then snug up the drawstring. It takes about two minutes to pack up a wing, and it's the very best way to transport and store your wing. Because the wing is not tightly folded, you don't have to worry about putting any permanent creases in the fabric.

Mushroom bags are sold by several paragliding equipment distributors. I bought mine from Larry Pindar at Over-The-Hill Paragliding, and have been absolutely delighted with it. The bag is both waterproof and sunproof, so you can quickly pack up your wing and get it out of the weather. Highly recommended.

Cost: About $65.

Riser Bag: No matter how you pack up your wing, you'll find that when you unpack it, your suspension lines are frequently in a tangled mess. After you've untangled the mess for the tenth time, you'll find yourself saying, "There's gotta be a better way!"

Well, there is! It's a very simple solution. Before you pack away the suspension lines, clip the ends of the risers together. A carabiner is ideal for this. With the ends of the risers fastened together, it's almost impossible for them to twist or tangle. Then take the risers and shove them inside a little bag, and tie the neck of the bag shut around the suspension lines above the risers. A little nylon camping gear bag, with a built-in drawstring, is perfect for the job. Stuff the suspension lines inside your wing transport bag, and finally stuff the riser bag in with the lines. When you're ready to unpack the wing, pull out the riser bag, followed by the suspension lines, followed by the wing. I guarantee that you will not have a tangle or twist anywhere.

If you were smart enough to buy a mushroom bag from Larry Pindar at Over-The-Hill Paragliding, you'll find that there's a built-in riser bag already attached to the mushroom, with a velcro neck closure. Perfect!

Cleaning Out The Wing Cells: No matter how careful you are, your wing is bound to scoop up sand, dirt, and other detritus. This junk will end up rattling around in your wing cells. If you fly at the beach, you're virtually guaranteed to pick up a load of sand in each cell. You might think that all you have to do is hang the wing upside down, and all of the detritus will fall out. Hah! You have a lot to learn, Grasshopper. Each cell of your wing has a curved nosepiece. This nosepiece will catch everything that falls out of your cells, and automatically return it to the cells as soon as the wing is no longer upside down. It's a fiendishly clever system. Banks are studying it as a way to protect currency from theft.

So how do you get the crud out? Two ways. Lay the wing face down, tail end facing into the wind, grab the tail, then violently flap the whole wing up and down. This will not only move the crud to the front of the wing, but the violent flapping will cause it to be dislodged from the nosepiece and fall to the ground. Your arms are only long enough to flap a few cells at a time, so you'll have to repeat the process all the way down the length of the wing. After you've flapped about a dozen cells, you'll vow to never again let any crud get inside the wing cells. Good luck. It's a worthy goal.

The other way is to hang the wing upside down, so all the crud falls down into the nosepiece, then walk along the nosepiece with a vacuum cleaner and suck out the crud. Or you can lay the wing down on the ground, on its back, then grab the tail and shake all the crud down into the nosepiece. Then with the wing still lying on its back, walk along with your vacuum cleaner and suck out the crud.

Videotape Landings and Takeoffs: This is absolutely the best way, bar none, to identify your landing and takeoff errors. Get a friend with a video camera to videotape your landings and takeoffs, then play them back later to catch your errors. This technique works so well that I'm always amazed to learn that so many instructors don't use it. As a bonus, you can play the tape at parties, and really impress your non-flying friends. They will have absolutely no idea that they're actually watching you screw up.

Filter Your Fuel: This is absolutely the most important thing you can do to keep your engine running. Fuel from the gas station can be contaminated with all sorts of crud, water, and sediment. And it takes very little sediment to clog the carburetor jets of your engine and kill it. So buy a good filter funnel and use it to filter every drop of gasoline that goes into your engine. I recommend the "Mr. Funnel" brand of fuel filter. Mr. Funnel will even filter out any water in the gasoline. Amazing! I bought mine from the "SkySports" catalog. Call 1-800-AIR-STUF.

Cost: About $10.

Appendix D

Useful Inventions

During my first year in powered paragliding, I came up with several inventions that seemed to make the sport easier and more enjoyable. Here is a list of them. I'll start with the simplest things, and work my way up.

Hand Mirror: Every PPG pilot needs to be able to check his fuel level, in-flight, to avoid running out of gas. But the fuel tank is behind you, where you can't see it. Solution: A hand mirror.

The only problem with a hand mirror is that it's easy to drop. And you'll find that your wife or girlfriend does not appreciate having her mirror stolen out of her purse, and then lost forever. Also, where do you store the mirror, while flying, when you're not using it?

I went to the auto supply store and bought one of those little, round, convex mirrors; the ones that Cause Objects To Appear Further Away Than They Actually Are. Then I cut a piece of velcro and glued it to the back of the mirror. Then I cut two corresponding pieces of velcro and sewed them to my left glove (the one that doesn't hold the throttle) One piece of velcro went on the palm, the other piece of velcro went over the back of my hand.

Before takeoff, I simply velcro the mirror onto the backside of my glove where it's out of the way and doesn't interfere with my ability to grip the lines. After launching, when I'm safely in the air, I transfer the mirror from the back of my hand to my palm. With the mirror on my palm, it's very easy to reach behind me and check my fuel level. Having the mirror on my palm means that I can easily aim the mirror in order to see the fuel tank. It's much easier than if the mirror is mounted on your wrist (which I also tried).

Just before landing, I transfer the mirror to the velcro holder on the back of my glove. It would probably be a good idea to tie a short length of string between the mirror and the glove, to make it impossible to drop the mirror.

I find that a convex mirror works better than a flat mirror. A flat mirror is more difficult to aim properly. The convex mirror works over a much wider range of angles.

I've also tried mounting a mirror on the prop cage so that I can simply glance over my shoulder and see the fuel level, but at some engine speeds the vibration can render the mirror useless.

Lowered Brake Handles: As soon as you start to fly your PPG for more than a few minutes at a time, you'll start to notice how tired your arms get while holding them high over your head, gripping the brake handles. It's sort of like being crucified. Unlike unpowered paragliders, PPGs fly best with no brake pressure. But you still need to have the brakes in your hands in order to make turns. You also want the brakes in your hands if you suddenly hit some turbulence and need to keep the wing under your active control or, God forbid, have to pump out a wing collapse.

The first time I noticed this problem was on my extended beach flight. I wondered why the brake handles had to be so high over my head. When I was flying my wing, unpowered, the brake handles were just about level with my ears, and were much easier to reach.

Then I realized what was causing the problem. My paragliding wing was designed for unpowered flight. It was designed to clip onto a harness just above my hips. This placed the brake handles down around my ears, where they were easy to reach. However on a powered paraglider, the wing clips onto the harness much higher. On my DK Whisper, the wing attachment points were almost one foot higher than they were on my unpowered paragliding harness. Unfortunately this also put the brake handles one foot higher, putting them high above my head where they were much more difficult to reach. On PPGs with over-the-shoulder suspension bars, the problem would be even worse.

Once the problem was identified, the solution was obvious. If the wing has been raised, then lower the brakes! All I had to do was lower the brake handles about one foot, and they would be back at ear level where they belonged. There was plenty of extra brake line below each brake handle, so I simply untied the brake handles, moved them down about one foot, and retied the lines. Of course the brake handles were now much too low to be held in place on the risers by the original metal snaps, so I made new keepers out of velcro. I sewed one piece of velcro to the brake handle, and the other piece of velcro to the lower end of the riser strap. (Velcro brake holders are also much easier to use than metal snaps.)

What a difference! The next time I flew, I simply reached up and pulled the brake handles out of their velcro holders and spent the flight with my hands at ear level, rather than held high overhead.

Did the lowered brake handles affect my landing? Not at all. Putting the brake handles back to ear level simply returned them to the level where they had always been before I started flying the motor. So the performance of the wing was quite unchanged.

In my opinion, this is the way a PPG wing ought to be made. But until they start coming this way from the factory, it's easy enough to modify them yourself.

Highly recommended.

Riser Handles: If you have a little bit of wind, reverse inflations are the best way to launch a PPG. You just face the wing, grab the front risers, pull the wing up into the air, spin around, hit the throttle, and go. But doing a reverse inflation can be a handful. Literally. With both brakes in your left hand, and your throttle in your right hand, you still have to make room for both front risers in your right hand. Finding a place for those front risers when your hand is already full of throttle, can be difficult. When I first started flying, I squeezed the front risers between my thumb and the plastic housing of the throttle. While this made it possible to pull on the risers, and get the wing in the air, it was difficult and clumsy at best.

Then it occurred to me that I only needed my index finger to work the throttle. This left the three remaining fingers on my hand with nothing to do. I tried grasping the front risers with my three lower fingers, but found that I still couldn't get a very good grip.

Then I realized that if there was some sort of handle on each riser, I could use my three lower fingers as hooks to grab the handles and get a good strong pull on the risers. So I bought an extra pair of brake handles and clipped a handle to the metal ring at the top of each riser where the risers connect to the suspension lines. Then when it was time to fly I simply strapped the throttle to my right hand, as usual, then hooked the two riser handles over my bottom three fingers, immediately in front of the throttle.

What a difference! Since I didn't have to squeeze my three fingers to hold onto the risers, there was no temptation to squeeze my throttle finger. And with my bottom three fingers hooked into the riser handles, I was easily able to exert a good strong pull on the risers to pull the wing into the air. It turned a very awkward task into a piece of cake.

Highly recommended.

Very Important! In flight, the riser handles simply hang from the tops of the risers. Be sure to always distinguish the riser handles from your regular brake handles. Pulling the riser handles down, in flight, will simply cause the leading edge of your wing to collapse (and give you an unwanted thrill ride).

Tachometer On The Throttle: You can mount your tachometer just about anywhere, as long as you can see it in flight. However my very favorite location is to mount it on the side of my throttle housing, just above my hand. This puts all the wiring together (throttle cable and tachometer cable), plus it's very easy to simply glance to your right (assuming you're right handed) and see the tachometer on the side of the throttle housing. Since your right hand is normally holding the throttle, just a few inches from your face, it's a particularly good location.

I fly a DK Whisper, and its large plastic housing is particularly well-suited for mounting the tachometer on the throttle. I drilled a small hole in the throttle housing for the tachometer wire, threaded the wire down through the housing, and ran it out the bottom with the throttle cable. Both cables fit very nicely in the cable sheath that runs from the throttle to the engine.

If your hand throttle isn't big enough to mount the tachometer on it, you can always mount the tachometer on the throttle cable, just below the throttle unit.

Footbar Hook: I've only flown a DK Whisper, and I'm familiar with its footbar, so I don't know how useful this tip will be for other PPGs.

The footbar on the DK Whisper is held in place, under the seat, by a pair of elastic loops. Some people release the footbar and simply let it dangle from the seat before takeoff. Personally I never liked this. I don't like having the footbar banging against the back of my ankles while I run, and I'm always afraid that I may catch the tip of my boot on the footbar, while running, and trip and fall.

I always launched with the footbar stowed in the elastic loops under the seat. However the seat is always tucked up behind my butt while I launch, and once in the air, the footbar can be hard to locate and release. And until the footbar is released, I can't use it to pull the seat down and forward, and slide back into it.

Finally I realized that if I was going to take off with the footbar undeployed,

I needed to find a better way to deploy it in flight, rather than just groping blindly beneath the seat for it. Obviously the easiest way to deploy the footbar would be if it were hanging from my harness, in front, rather than tucked away behind me under the seat. So I added a small S-hook to one end of my footbar, pulled the whole thing around my left hip and up in front of my harness, and hooked the S-hook to the nearest D ring near the bottom of my vest.

This works extremely well. After takeoff, I simply reach down to the bottom of my vest, unhook the S-hook from the D ring, and let the footbar drop. Then it's a simple matter to catch the footbar with my foot, and slide back into my seat. Perfect! No more fumbling for the footbar beneath my seat. Now it hangs from the bottom of my vest, within easy reach, where I can instantly and easily release it.

Pulse Battery Charger:

Question: In a six thousand dollar PPG engine, with electric start, why do they only include a two dollar battery charger?

Answer: Ran out of fifty cent ones.

Electric starters are nice, but the battery chargers that are typically included with the starter battery are an abomination. Most starter batteries are nicads, and if you leave the battery on charge for too long, it overcharges and gets damaged. Also, if you charge a battery that still has some juice in it, the infamous "memory" effect of nicads can cause the battery to end up with greatly reduced capacity. And if you decide to run the battery down, before recharging, to avoid the memory effect, I guarantee that you will one day be surprised with a dead battery just as you're trying to start your engine for takeoff.

I decided that there just had to be a better battery charger out there, somewhere, so I went looking for it.

A couple of years earlier I had faced exactly the same battery problems with my cellular phone. Either the battery was always getting fried through overcharging, or else it was dead when I tried to use it. Then I heard of a company in Seattle called Pulse Power. They made a charger called a "pulse charger." I didn't know how the charger worked, but the beauty of it was that you could recharge a nicad phone battery, at any stage of discharge, without getting a memory effect. Furthermore, you could leave the battery on charge, constantly, without damaging it. I decided to contact the company and see if they could sell me a similar charger for my PPG starter battery.

It turned out that the company had a charger that could be modified to charge my nicad starter battery. It wasn't cheap (about $200), but it let me go flying, come home, throw the battery on the charger, and forget about it until I was ready to fly again. Whereupon my battery would be fully charged and ready to go. Nice!

It's a pity these chargers aren't in mass production for PPG starter batteries. They're expensive, but they sure are convenient. And you will get the maximum life from your expensive battery. You can contact the company at:

Sage Electronics, Inc.

14691 N.E. 95th Street

Redmond, WA 98052

Phone: 1-800-225-3404

Give them your battery voltage, capacity, and type of battery, and they'll tell you if they can make a pulse charger for it. Good luck!

Reserve Straps: If you fly with a reserve, you probably keep it permanently attached to your harness, just for convenience. I know I do. However when you're not flying, you want to be careful not to accidentally deploy your reserve. It's easy to do; just snag the handle on something while you're lugging the engine around. When I carried my engine outside the car, on a bumper carrier, I had visions of the reserve accidentally deploying while I was driving seventy miles per hour down the freeway. There were several possible endings to this scenario, and none of them were particularly appealing.

To keep this from happening, I went to a camping supply store and bought a couple of nylon tie-down straps. The straps were about an inch wide and about six feet long, with an adjustable friction buckle to let you cinch up the strap as tightly as you wished. My reserve is square shaped, so I put two straps on it at right angles to each other, and cinched them tight. Now, even if the reserve handle is pulled, nothing moves and nothing deploys.

Very Important! Just don't forget to remove the straps before flying, or nothing will happen when you pull the reserve handle in an emergency. Make the strap removal an item on your pre-flight checklist!

Fishnet Prop Cage Cover: Early in my PPG career, I tried to fly with my motor before I'd been taught how to ground handle my wing. During one of my takeoff attempts I managed to get the wing into the air, but before I could get airborne I managed to collapse the wing and drop it down onto my engine. One of the wing suspension lines was sucked through the prop cage netting and shattered my $400 propeller. *Ouch!*

The problem was that my prop cage netting wasn't really "netting" at all. It was just some heavy cord that zigzagged across the face of the prop cage. This formed a series of long, narrow wedges, like slices of pie. If a wing line happened to fall across the wedge, no problem. However if the line fell lengthwise, parallel to the sides of the wedge, then it was easily sucked into the propeller.

No doubt this "zigzag" netting was cheaper, and required less labor to install than ordinary fish netting, but in my opinion it simply didn't do an adequate job of keeping the wing suspension lines out of the propeller. So I decided to remove the zigzag netting and replace it with ordinary nylon fish netting. The best netting for the job is also sold to cover batting cages in Little League baseball parks, and so should not be too difficult to find.

I purchased a few square yards of netting, with mesh openings about one inch square. Any smaller, and I was afraid that I might start restricting the airflow to the propeller. Any larger, and I was afraid that a suspension line might get sucked into the propeller. Total cost of the netting was only about twelve dollars. I simply laid the netting over the prop cage, squared off the individual mesh cells, then started to tie the netting to the propeller cage. In some places I used little nylon tie wraps, but most of the time I simply wound a piece of strong nylon string through the mesh netting and around the edge of the propeller cage. By using nylon string, I guaranteed that the wing suspension lines would still be able to slip up and around the edge of the propeller cage, during wing inflation, without snagging on any bumps or protrusions.

Installing the netting took most of an evening. It was boring, painstaking work, but the end result looked pretty snazzy. Now I don't have to worry about sucking a suspension line through the propeller cage, and into the propeller.

Bumper Carrier: A PPG engine can be disassembled for easy transport. The propeller can be removed, and the propeller cage usually will break down into several smaller pieces. The whole thing can easily be packed into the trunk of an average-sized car. Indeed, this is frequently touted as a major advantage of the PPG; it's the only aircraft in the world that you can carry around in the trunk of your car!

Unfortunately, you'll quickly find that having to assemble your motor every time you go out to fly, followed by disassembling the motor when you're finished flying, gets old real quick.

If you're lucky enough to have a van or truck, you can haul your motor in one piece. This is the very best way to transport your machine; especially if you have a van. Your machine is inside, safe from the weather and curious hands.

However if you only have a car, you can still transport your motor in one piece using a bumper carrier. The PPG carrier is largely the same as the carriers used by cyclists to haul their bicycles around on the bumpers of their cars.

I had originally thought that I would simply buy a bicycle carrier and modify it to suit the needs of my PPG engine. However none of the commercially available bicycle carriers was shaped exactly right, and they were all very expensive. So I decided to make one.

First I had a standard, Class II trailer hitch installed on the back of my car. This cost about $150, but the hitch can also be used to haul trailers, bicycle carriers, cargo platforms, and many other things. The hitch is simply a square piece of steel tubing, about two inches on a side, that mounts on the frame of your car, under the bumper. This tubing is called the "receiver."

The PPG carrier is another piece of square steel tubing, about two feet long (called the "shank"), that slides inside the hitch receiver. A removable steel pin locks the two pieces of metal together. I welded a couple of pieces of one-inch square steel tubing at right angles to the shank, to give me a solid base. We'll call these the cross braces. Then I cut a piece of plywood about 14 inches square, and one inch thick, and bolted it to the cross braces. I cut a couple of slots in the plywood so that I could run a nylon strap over the footbars of my PPG engine, and then down through the slots in the plywood to anchor the engine securely to the base.

With the bottom of the motor firmly tied down, I added a vertical mast to the carrier so that I would have a solid anchor point for the top of the motor as well. I used inch and a half square steel tubing for the mast, with the top end of the mast cut and welded into a hook. After the engine was strapped to the plywood platform, I inserted the bottom end of the mast into the base of the carrier, and then dropped the hook on the top end of the mast down over the engine crossbar, locking the engine in place.

That's just how I happened to fabricate my bumper carrier for my PPG engine. There's nothing special about the design. The idea is to have a strong, stable platform on which you can strap down your engine and transport it, in one piece, to and from the flying field. Using a trailer hitch means that you can easily remove the carrier from your car after you've finished flying. If you're at all handy with tools, a bumper carrier is easy to make. If you're not handy with tools, a machine shop, or a good welder, can easily cut and weld the steel tubing for you.

If you want to buy something ready-made, you can buy a cargo platform that's designed to slide into your hitch receiver. The platform is made of steel, and is typically sixty inches wide and twenty inches deep. The platform will carry about five hundred pounds of cargo. Cost is about one hundred dollars. There's no mast on the platform to anchor the top of the engine, but a mast could be easily added. Or, alternatively, you could brace the top of the engine with a couple of ropes running down to the bumper. The only reason I didn't buy and use one of these ready-made cargo platforms was because the thing was much wider than I actually needed. My custom-made platform was only fourteen inches square. This made the carrier much lighter and easier to handle.

If you want to protect your PPG engine from rain while you're driving down the road, you can easily buy or make a waterproof cover for it. I used a Sears barbecue grill cover. Just make certain that your propeller cage, when covered, can take the strain of acting like a giant sail as you go whizzing down the freeway at seventy miles per hour. Alternatively, you could probably make a smaller cover that would cover just the engine, and leave the propeller and propeller cage uncovered. This would eliminate any problem with wind resistance while driving down the road. Rain, or other bad weather, won't hurt most propellers or propeller cages.

Utility Cart: Of all the things I've invented to make my PPG career easier and more fun, this would probably have to rank as the Number Two Most Useful Invention. PPG engines are heavy, and you'll quickly get tired of lugging your engine around on the ground. The problem is that PPG engines aren't designed to be carried. They're designed to fly.

Carrying the engine is not much of a problem when you can simply unload the engine from your vehicle, set up, and fly. Unfortunately not all flying fields are so conveniently located. There may be a fence with only a small gate that is too small for your car to pass through. Or cars may be forbidden on the field. The fact is, it's frequently necessary to haul the engine some distance from the car to get to the flying field. What finally broke my back was carrying my engine to the launch site on the beach, over soft, loose, beach sand. For an out of shape couch potato like me, this was pure hell. There had to be a better way.

My solution was a wheeled utility cart. I bought a two-wheeled hand cart from the hardware store for about sixty dollars. It's the sort of cart people use to move refrigerators, or dressers, or other heavy objects. The cart has a flat piece of steel, or nosepiece, just in front of the wheels so that you can slip the nosepiece under the refrigerator, then tip the refrigerator backwards onto the cart's wheels and roll it away. I figured that if it was good enough for a refrigerator, it was good enough for my engine.

The cart's nosepiece was plenty wide enough for the base of my PPG engine, but not deep enough. Too much of the engine's weight was hanging, unsupported, out over the front edge of the nosepiece. So I cut a larger nosepiece out of three-quarter inch plywood and bolted it to the metal nosepiece. Then I picked up the engine and set it on the nosepiece with the harness side of the engine next to the cart, and the propeller cage facing forward. I secured the top of the engine to the top of the cart with an elastic bungee cord. I grabbed the twin handles of the utility cart, tipped the whole assembly back onto the two wheels, and *viola!* Now it was easy to wheel the engine wherever it needed to go. Since I had bought a cart with big, balloon tires, it rolled quite nicely even over loose beach sand.

My engine transportation problem was solved. But the motor still presented me with one annoying problem. The normal way to put on a PPG engine is to sit down on the ground, in front of the machine, and strap yourself in. But then you face the daunting task of getting up off the ground with a sixty or seventy pound (or more) load on your back. Anyone who has ever tried to get up off the ground while wearing a heavily loaded backpack will know exactly what I'm talking about. And if the ground is wet, or dirty, or sandy, it gets all over you and the harness.

It didn't take a rocket scientist to figure out that it would be much easier to put on the engine while standing up. So I added a hinged table flap near the top of the cart to support the engine while I put it on. I used u-bolts to attach a piece of plywood to the vertical frame of the cart, and then used hinges to attach the table flap to the first piece of plywood.

I ended up with a folding table flap. When using the cart to transport the engine, the hinged table flap simply folded down against the frame of the cart, out of the way. After I removed the engine from the cart, I simply raised the table flap and inserted a large dowel rod under the table flap to hold it up. Then I could pick up the engine and set it down on the table flap.

Putting on the engine was now a piece of cake. I simply set the engine on top of the table flap, then backed up to the engine and slipped my arms through the shoulder straps. Then I walked away with the engine on my shoulders. No more sitting on the cold, wet ground; no struggling to get to my feet with seventy pounds of engine on my back. Heaven! Roll the cart out of the way, and I was ready to fly. Best of all, I wasn't exhausted from struggling to get to my feet with the heavy engine on my back.

Warning! Don't walk away and leave your engine perched on top of your utility cart. It doesn't take much wind to topple the whole assembly.

Hip Belt: Of all the things I've invented to make my PPG career easier and more fun, this would probably have to rank as the Number One Most Useful Invention.

PPG engines are normally carried on the ground with two shoulder straps. This is absolutely the worst way to carry a heavy load. It destroys the pilot's balance and makes it difficult for him to maneuver on the ground. All of the weight of the engine is on the pilot's shoulders, and ends up on his spine instead of his hips (where it belongs).

It's true that the PPG pilot only has to carry his engine for a minute or two, during launching, but it's also true that a minute or two is quite sufficient to leave the pilot totally exhausted.

If the weight of the heavy engine on the pilot's shoulders was simply uncomfortable and exhausting, that would be one thing. But it's also a safety issue. After carrying a heavy engine for a minute or two, the pilot is desperate to get airborne and to get the weight off his back. His mind becomes fuzzy and fatigued, and he is desperate to fly. He becomes willing to cut corners. Safety is largely forgotten. If the wing is not fully-inflated during his takeoff run, or if a few suspension lines are tangled, who cares? I'll take care of that once I'm in the air and no longer carrying this damned heavy engine!

And it's all so unnecessary! There is a much better way.

Backpackers, who frequently carry heavy loads for hours at a time, learned many years ago that the best way to carry a heavy load on your back is to let the weight ride on your hips rather than your shoulders. So they invented the hip belt. The hip belt is simply a large, padded belt that straps tightly around your hips. The bottom of the backpack is connected to the belt by some sort of

303

suspension system (usually a pair of straps). The result is that the weight of the backpack rides on the hips, rather than on the shoulders.

After struggling to launch with a heavy engine, I decided that what was good enough for backpackers was good enough for me. I went to a camping supply store and bought the thickest, most luxuriously padded hip belt I could find. The cost was less than thirty dollars. Then I sewed a couple of strong nylon straps to either side of the belt, and attached the straps to the bottom of my engine.

What a difference! With the weight of the engine on my hips, I felt like I had just shrugged the weight of the world off my shoulders. With the weight of the engine on my hips, my arms were once again free to move, rather than being pinned down by the shoulder straps. My balance was restored, and I could once again run and maneuver. The difference was literally night and day. With the hip belt I was easily able to carry my engine for fifteen minutes without becoming exhausted. Without the hip belt, a minute of two of carrying the engine quickly drained me of all energy.

With a hip belt, you can take your time to do the launching right. You're in no particular hurry to get into the air. And that makes all the difference in the world.

The hip belt seems to have no effect on the actual flight. It's simply a way to carry the engine on the ground. Once airborne, you can even unfasten the hip belt, if you wish.

Highly recommended!

Appendix E

No-Wind Launches

Launching a PPG when the wind is blowing at least five miles per hour is easy. You simply execute a reverse launch by facing the wing and pulling it up into the wind. As soon as the wing is flying overhead, turn around and hit the throttle and go. Piece of cake.

A no-wind takeoff in a PPG requires more skill, but once you get the technique down, it's easy. Here's how I do it:

I'm a big man. 6'4" tall, and 220 lbs. I fly a DK Whisper Plus that puts out about 115 lbs. of thrust (or so the factory claims). I also fly a big wing; a Pro Compact Design 37. The wing can handle a payload of 300 lbs. If the wing were any bigger, it would be a tandem wing.

Are forward launches, in no wind, difficult? I used to think so, but not anymore. Now I consistently nail my forward launches. In fact I prefer forward launches, rather than reverse launches in higher winds. In no wind I can fly in any direction and not have to worry about fighting a head wind when it's time to return home. Here is what works for me and my flying friends. I spent the last year working out the details.

My forward launch technique has three important points:
1. Proper Layout.
2. Hit The Wing Hard!
3. Apply power early.

1. Proper layout:
You can't build a good house without a good foundation. It's the same with forward launches. You MUST start with a good layout. If you skimp on the

layout, you'll pay for it later with a blown launch. Remember, if there's not enough time do it right the first time, there's always enough time to do it over later!

The absolute most important thing for a proper layout is to lay the wing out FACING INTO THE WIND! And I mean facing DIRECTLY into the wind; not a few degrees to one side or the other. If the wing is not facing directly into the wind, it will come up crooked, or not at all. Then you will have to do some fancy running to get yourself centered under the wing, or be forced to abort the takeoff and start the whole thing over.

How do you ensure that your wing is facing directly into the wind? You need a wind direction indicator, and the back of your neck.

A wind direction indicator is just a long stick with a ribbon tied to it. No PPG pilot should be without one. The ribbon tells you which way the wind is blowing. I use an empty plastic bleach jug weighted with some lead shot. Then I stick a 1 1/8" wooden dowel rod in the jug (perfect fit) and tie some orange ribbon to the end of the stick. You can buy fancy windsocks, but the ribbon works just as well. The whole thing comes apart easily for transporting. (Save the jug cap so you don't spill the lead shot. In fact, drill a small hole in the jug cap and tie it to the jug handle so you don't lose it.)

The best place for your wind streamer jug is downwind from your wing. Lay the wing out, facing into the wind. Then set the wind streamer jug on the other side of your wing, downwind, about thirty feet away, and lined up with the center of your wing. Then when you stand upwind, on the other side of your wing you can look across the center of your wing, at the jug, and easily see if your wing is exactly perpendicular to the blowing ribbon. If the wing isn't perpendicular, make it so! It will pay off later.

Do a final wind check with the back of your neck. If you haven't already noticed, the back of your neck is a remarkably sensitive instrument for determining wind direction!

After your wing is perpendicular to the wind, make certain it is lying flat on the ground with no folds or tucks. Remember, you are trying to inflate the wing, and the easier it is for the air to get inside and fill the cells, the better. While keeping the wing flat, bend it into the shape of a gentle horseshoe. This helps to ensure that the center section inflates first, followed by the tips. If the tips inflate first, the center section will frequently fail to inflate, the wing will fold in two, and collapse. I get my wing into the horseshoe shape by first pulling back on the center cell, then I walk along the leading edge, out to each wingtip, giving a

306

progressively lesser tug on each of the cells as I approach the wingtip. The end result is a nice, gentle horseshoe shape.

Now run the suspension lines. Run each riser strap separately. Make certain there are no knots or tangles in the suspension lines. You want to make it easy for your wing to inflate. It can't do this if the suspension lines aren't free to separate.

With your engine on your back, and warmed up and ready to go, and the brakes and front risers in your hands, walk forward until the front riser suspension lines have a little tension on them. Don't pull too hard, or you'll pull the leading edge of your wing out of alignment and have to start over. Just make certain that the front riser suspension lines are equally tense. This tells you that you're properly centered on your wing. Look back on either side to be certain of your centering. This is very important. If you're not centered on your wing, it will not leap straight up into the air when you start pulling, and will probably fall off to one side. You will then be in a condition known as "screwed."

Now you're ready to launch.

2. Hit The Wing Hard!

In no wind, the only thing that can inflate your wing and pull it into the air, is you. Until the engine can take over, you are the engine. If you fail to impart enough kinetic energy to your wing, it will not be able to fly. But you are woefully underpowered compared to a gasoline engine. So how do you get the job done? You run! Your body and engine add up to a lot of weight. Get that weight moving! Get that weight moving as fast as possible before you start pulling on the wing.

So back up for your takeoff run. Back up all the way to the edge of the wing. Forget what it says in the paragliding manual about taking "one or two steps backward." You're not launching from a hill, with the assistance of gravity. You're launching from level ground. You need all the help you can get! So back up all the way to the edge of the wing. (Just don't walk on the wing or the suspension lines.) You want to be moving as fast as possible before you start pulling on the wing. You want to hit that wing as hard and as fast as you can.

I'm always amazed to see PPG pilots failing to back up all way to the edge of the wing before starting their takeoff run. It's like watching a thirsty man pour his precious water into the sand.

Now lean forward and run, run, run! You want to be just like a plow horse pulling a heavy wagon. Don't pull with your arms; pull with your chest. Your arms should simply be used as "feeler gauges" to tell you where the wing is at any given moment.

You'll feel the suspension lines go taut, and the wing will start to rise off the ground. Keep running! With all that momentum you built up with your long takeoff run, the wing will snap right up into the air. About two seconds after it leaves the ground, the wing will enter what I call "Drag Chute Mode." Drag Chute Mode simply means that the wing is presenting its full flat surface to the air, and thus generating the maximum amount of drag. It hasn't started to fly yet.

This maximum drag seems to happen when the wing has risen to about a forty-five degree angle. There is so much drag that it can easily bring you to a complete stop. You'll feel like you're tied to a tree. Now is the time to run even harder! Even if you can't actually move forward, lean forward and dig in with your feet as hard as you can. Even if you've stopped moving, remember that the wing is still climbing into the air. Press forward on the front risers to help "tease" the wing into the air. But don't press too hard on the front risers or you may cause the leading edge of the wing to collapse. Pushing forward on the front risers is like giving the wing a few extra miles per hour of airspeed. It can make the difference between success and failure. If you stop running (or straining forward) at this point, the wing will stop climbing and will fall to the ground.

Never stop running! Never stop running! Never stop running!

3. Apply Power Early:

As the wing continues to climb overhead, it will pass out of Drag Chute Mode and into normal flight. You'll suddenly find that you can run forward again. You'll also find yourself straightening up. The wing is now more than halfway up, but it's still not flying overhead. Now is the time to go to full power! Don't wait until the wing is completely overhead, and you're running down the field. At that point the wing will probably be starting to collapse due to insufficient airspeed, and if you go to full power you may end up sucking a line through the prop. That's what I did on my first launch attempt. So hit the power early, as soon as you're out of Drag Chute Mode. It makes all the difference in the world. Remember:

Air speed cures all problems!

Air speed cures all problems!

Air speed cures all problems!

If you hit the throttle just as the wing comes out of Drag Chute Mode, it's like kicking in the afterburner on a jet. Suddenly the whole system is flooded with power. The wing climbs smoothly into flying position, and both you and the wing will go hurtling down the field for a perfect takeoff.

As you're running down the field, engine at full power and rapidly gaining speed, look up at the wing! Unless the ground is so rough that you must keep watching it to avoid falling down, keep your eyes on the wing. You MUST stay centered under the wing to achieve takeoff. If you keep your eyes on the wing during your run, it's easy to stay centered.

If you're a heavy pilot (like me), flying an engine with less power than you would like, you may get to the point where you're running as fast as you can, but you're still on the ground. Your feet seem to be holding you back and are threatening to slow you down every time they hit the ground. If so, give a gentle tug on the brakes to lift off.

Using this launch system I have achieved 100% success on forward launches in no wind. So have my flying friends. I now prefer forward launches in no wind, rather than reverse inflations in higher winds. Not only are the forward launches very easy to do, but the lack of wind lets me fly in any direction I wish, without worrying about bucking a head wind on my way home.

May you be as fortunate.

P.S. Before you ever try to fly with a motor, you should become an expert ground handler with your wing. Buy a cheap training harness, or else take the harness off your engine. Practice doing launches without the engine. When you can successfully launch the wing consistently, then practice launching with the engine on your back, but with the engine turned off. If you're worried about damaging the prop or the cage, take them off. You'll know when it's time for the real thing.

Happy flying!

Appendix F

PPG Hype vs. PPG Reality

Hype: *PPG is the world's smallest aircraft. You can store it in the trunk of your car.*

Reality: It's true that a powered paraglider is the world's smallest aircraft. It's also true that almost any PPG can be stored in the trunk of the average-sized car. The problem is that you have to take it apart before you can store it in the trunk. You must remove the propeller and the propeller cage. Now this is not difficult to do, nor does it take very long. The propeller cage is typically held together with velcro straps and will quickly break down into several pieces that are easy to store and carry. Even a three-bladed propeller is typically held on by no more than six nuts and bolts, and so is fairly easy to remove.

But taking your engine apart, and putting it back together, every time you want to fly, gets old real quick. The best way to transport your PPG is in a van or pickup truck. Then you can transport it in one piece. Very nice! Or if you only have a car, you can build or buy an external bumper carrier which will let you carry your engine in much the same way that bicycles are carried on the bumper. This lets you can carry the engine in one piece. Very nice! The only drawback is that your engine is out in the open, exposed to weather and strangers, and must be constantly watched. When I carried my PPG engine on a bumper carrier, I kept an old bedsheet handy to throw over it whenever I stopped for any length of time. Otherwise the sight of that engine attracted people like moths to a flame.

Hype: *PPGs are easy to learn to fly. You can learn to fly in only one weekend! No license is required!*

Reality: It's true that PPGs are one of the easiest aircraft to learn to fly. Probably only a PPC (powered parachute) is even easier to learn to fly. And it's true that you don't need a license to fly a PPG. But you can't learn to fly a PPG in only a weekend. You can learn to *solo* a PPG in only a weekend, and there are plenty of unscrupulous dealers who will sell you a PPG, give you enough training to make a solo flight, and then send you home. Whereupon you will try to fly again, fall down, and shatter your propeller. Your PPG will end up sitting in your garage, collecting dust, and eventually be sold for ten cents on the dollar.

Plan on spending 5-10 days to learn to safely fly a PPG. At that point you're ready to go out and fly on your own *in ideal conditions* (i.e. early morning or late evening when the air is smooth and conditions are calm). You are *not* ready to go out in the middle of a summer day, when the thermals are booming, and play tag with those big, beautiful cumulous clouds that are filling the sky.

In one respect, flying a PPG is like flying any other aircraft. It doesn't take too long to learn to take off, fly around the airport, and land. But once you've mastered that, you'll want to do more. That's when you'll discover that extra skills and training are necessary in order to do it safely.

When I first learned of PPGs, I had visions of learning to fly it in a few days and then being able to fly anywhere, any time I liked. I pictured myself soaring high over mountain ranges, circling snow-capped volcanoes, and dropping down into remote mountain valleys that would normally require days of hiking to reach. Well the truth is, you can't go out and do that sort of flying in a Cessna, or a Learjet, *or* a PPG. You first need to become an experienced, skilled pilot, and learn to how to safely fly under such conditions.

Hype: *PPG is the world's safest aircraft. If your engine quits, your parachute is already deployed!*

Reality: It's true that a PPG, properly flown, is a very safe aircraft. Unlike other aircraft, the PPG literally flies itself. All the pilot does is steer, and work the engine throttle to go up or down.

But a PPG wing is not a parachute. It is a *wing*, and it must be flown like a wing. If you stall it, it will stop flying and you will fall like a rock. Unless it is actually flying, and generating lift, a PPG wing is too small to make an effective parachute. This is why some PPG pilots carry reserve parachutes. In case the PPG wing ceases to fly, for any reason, they can toss out an ordinary round parachute and float safely to the ground.

Most PPG pilots don't carry reserve parachutes since they only fly in calm conditions, when any kind of a wing collapse is very unlikely. However it's never a bad idea to carry a reserve parachute whenever you're flying. If nothing else, it can bring considerable peace of mind when your PPG wing hits a bit of stray turbulence, and shakes for a few seconds.

Hype: *PPG is the world's smallest aircraft. You can store it in a corner of your garage.*

Reality: Here's a case where the reality equals the hype. It's true! The engine only takes a few square feet of floor space, and the wing packs up into a bag the size of an ordinary backpack.

Appendix G

What To Look For When Buying A PPG

What are the primary things you should look for when buying a PPG? What features are really necessary, versus merely nice to have?

Let's take them one at a time.

The *Wing* is the most critical item in a PPG. Be sure you are flying a paraglider wing that is rated for a beginner pilot. You want a good, stable wing that is unlikely to collapse in turbulent air and send you plummeting toward the ground. Stay away from the higher-performance wings that are sometimes used in unpowered paragliding. Pilots who fly unpowered paragliders must rely on rising air for lift, so they are always looking for increased performance from their wings. But since you have an engine, you have no need for a high-performance wing.

The *Engine* is the second most critical item in a PPG. The three important factors to look for in a PPG engine are *thrust, weight*, and *fuel*. Let's take them in the order of importance.

Engine Thrust is the most important factor. If you don't have sufficient thrust, you won't get off the ground. Extra thrust also gives you extra safety in the air if you suddenly find it necessary to climb over an obstacle in your path, or find yourself in a sinking air mass.

Generally speaking you need at least one hundred pounds of thrust. If you're a heavier pilot (over 200 lbs.), you'll need more. I weigh 220 lbs. and flew a PPG engine that put out just over one hundred pounds of thrust. It wasn't enough. I could fly, but my takeoff runs tended to be long, and my rate of climb in the air was seldom more than one hundred feet per minute. Even in level flight I had to constantly run the engine at 80% of full power. Not only did I have to find larger fields in order to safely launch, but once in the sky I tended not to want to lose altitude since it took so long to regain it. Thus I usually resisted the temptation to drop down and look at something on the ground more closely (which took a lot of the fun out of the flying).

Most of the PPG engines are currently based on the Solo 210 design. It's generally agreed that this engine can be tweaked to put out about 130 pounds of thrust. (One manufacturer claims 155 lbs. of thrust.) Pilots who don't weigh much more than 200 pounds seem to report good results with this engine.

If you're a heavier pilot, say around 250 pounds, then you'll probably need one of the big, Zenoah-based paramonsters. These engines are intended for heavy pilots, and for tandem flying. They can typically handle as much as four hundred pounds of pilot payload, and they typically put out over 150 pounds of thrust. However they also weigh more than eighty pounds, without fuel. Fully-fueled, they can easily tip the scales at 100 pounds. Which brings us to the...

Engine Weight is the second most important factor. If you're young, in excellent condition, and have muscles like Charles Atlas, then you probably won't be too concerned about the weight of the engine. But if you're like most of us couch potatoes who are Weekend Fliers, you'll find that the weight of the engine is critical. It can make the difference between fun flying and acute suffering.

Keep the weight of the engine as low as possible. You'll be glad you did. Remember, every pound must be carried on your back during launching. And the difference between a seventy pound engine, and a one hundred pound engine, is night and day.

I consider a seventy pound paramotor to be about the maximum practical weight to carry on your shoulders. Anything more, and it starts getting heavy, real fast. If you blow your first launch attempt with such a heavy engine, you may very well find it necessary to stop and take the engine off, and rest, before making a second attempt.

Unfortunately most PPG pilots will find it very difficult to keep the weight of their engine under seventy pounds. Without fuel, most engines weigh at least sixty pounds. Add 2.7 gallons of fuel (16 pounds), and you have a total weight of 76 pounds. So if seventy pounds isn't doable, try to keep it under eighty pounds.

Fuel is something that the engine can't fly without. Most PPG engines have 2.7 gallon fuel tanks (ten liters). This typically gives about two hours of flying time, and for most pilots this seems to be long enough. There are some PPG engines that will carry up to five gallons of fuel, but unless you are an endurance freak, you'll probably never need this much. Also, keep in mind that five gallons of fuel weighs thirty pounds, and that PPG engine weight is normally given without fuel.

Some PPG engines have only a 1.7 gallon fuel tank. This typically gives about one hour of flying time. This is the sort of PPG engine I flew, and I quickly discovered that one hour of flying simply wasn't enough for me. If I wanted to return to my takeoff field, I couldn't afford to fly more than twenty-five minutes away from the field before having to turn back. However one hour of flying time might suit you just fine, and if so, a fuel supply that only weighs ten pounds is very nice.

Now that we've discussed the critical engine items, let's look at some of the less-critical items:

Electric Start is a feature that I have very mixed feelings about. On the one hand it's a very nice, convenient feature to have. You can warm up your engine on the ground, stop the engine, put it on, and instantly restart the engine with just the touch of a button. Very, very nice. I had electric start on my first PPG engine, and I adored it. Pushing a button to start the engine is much easier than pulling on a starting rope, and is much sexier! An electric starter also allows you to restart the engine in the air.

On the other hand, the electric starter adds weight. You have both a starter and a battery (typically nicad). Together they add about eight pounds to the weight of the engine, and that's a lot. Also, the starter is something else to go wrong. The tiny little starters that they put on PPG engines aren't the most rugged things in the world, and they sometimes wear out rather quickly. They can be expensive to replace.

Another problem with electric starters is the danger of in-flight fire. If a nicad or lead-acid battery is short-circuited, it is quite capable of frying the wiring and setting your harness on fire. A fire is not a good thing in an airborne PPG! If you get a PPG with an electric start, examine every wire and connection before every flight!

If I typically flew a PPG alone, I would probably get an electric starter so that I would be able to restart the engine after warming it up, stopping the engine, putting it on, and getting ready to fly. I would not want to have to start the engine on the ground, and then sit down and put it on while it was running. It can be done, but it's somewhat hazardous.

However I always fly with a friend, and if your engine is properly warmed up, you can stop the engine, put it on, and then have your friend give the starting rope a yank. Almost as easy as an electric start, and without the extra weight. So

I think that my next PPG engine will not have electric start. The whole idea of PPG is to keep it as simple and lightweight as possible.

Some of the newer PPG engines claim to have their starting rope positioned so the pilot can simply reach overhead and give the rope a pull. Or they have a foot stirrup that you can slip over one foot and attach to the starting rope, enabling you to "kick start" the engine in the air. I have no experience with either of these, but they might be worth looking into.

The ability to *Jettison The Motor,* in flight, can be found on at least one brand of PPG engine. The pilot merely twists a couple of safety interlocks, and the entire motor, prop, cage, and fuel tank drops away from the wing and harness. The pilot can then fly just like any other unpowered paraglider.

The only circumstance I can think of, under which you would want to jettison your motor, is if it caught fire while in the air. Then you could instantly jettison the motor instead of going up in flames like a World War I fighter pilot. In-flight fires of PPG engines are pretty rare, but it has happened.

Cruise Control is a nice feature to have on your throttle. You can level out at your desired altitude, set the cruise control, and not have to keep the throttle squeezed with your finger. I had cruise control on my first PPG engine, and it was handy, but it's not essential. Keeping the throttle depressed is very easy, and if you change altitude a lot, the cruise control may be of little use. Cruise control on a PPG is very much like cruise control on a car. Nice when driving across the country, but not much good in heavy traffic.

There's not much to say about the *Engine Harness,* except to make sure that it fits. My first PPG had a harness that was too small for me. Not only did it make it difficult to get in and out of the harness, but I had to fly hunched over, to keep the shoulder straps from cutting into my shoulders. So before you buy any PPG engine, insist on trying it on. Walk around while carrying the engine, and insist on hanging the whole thing from a pair of ropes so that you can see exactly how it will feel in flight. Comfort is a very subjective thing. Don't simply take the dealer's word for it.

As far as harness safety goes, I would tend to avoid any harness that uses zippers. Zippers can jam, and trap you in the harness. Insist that all harness fastenings be done with quick-release buckles. If you end up landing in the water, you must be able to get out of your harness quickly. My first PPG engine had a zippered vest, and the zipper was always jamming. To solve this problem I simply added a couple of quick-release buckles to the vest, and left the zipper unzipped. End of problem, and much safer. Metal snap buttons might work just as well.

Some PPG engines hang the harness from a pair of over-the-shoulder bars that hang from the wing. It's claimed that this reduces the engine vibration that is otherwise transmitted to the pilot. Other PPG engines hang the wing directly from the harness. It's claimed that this permits easier turns via weight-shifting in the harness, as well as giving slightly easier ground handling and takeoffs, but also makes the harness more difficult to get into. My first PPG engine used the latter style, and I can vouch for the difficulty of getting into the harness. The shoulder straps were also used to support the seat, in flight, so when I pulled the seat up behind me, to get into the harness, this also put extra tension on the shoulder straps and made them more difficult to get into. On my next PPG I'll probably try the over-the-shoulder bars.

Unless you have deep pockets, the engine *Propeller* should be made of wood. Wood is heavier, and not quite as sexy-looking as carbon-fiber composite, but it's one hell of a lot cheaper. On my first PPG engine, I had a 3-blade carbon-fiber propeller. On one of my first launch attempts, I managed to suck a wing line through the prop cage netting and into the prop. The tips of all three blades were instantly shattered. The prop was only 36 inches in diameter, but it still cost me nearly four hundred dollars to replace it. Later on I flew with a 47 inch carbon-fiber prop that would have cost me eight hundred dollars to replace!

By contrast, a wooden propeller can usually be replaced for less than $200. Sometimes much less. Go with wood. Falling down and breaking your propeller is an occupational hazard for PPG pilots. So keep the propeller replacement cost as low as possible.

Propeller Cage Netting is an area where I can claim to be an expert. In my opinion, virtually every PPG manufacturer is grossly negligent in this area. The netting that they put over their prop cages simply can't be counted on to keep the wing lines out of the propeller. The openings in the netting are much too large. It makes me wonder why they bother to put any netting on at all.

When I was preparing to buy my first PPG engine, I noticed that the earlier models of the engine used ordinary fish netting to cover the propeller cage. The openings in the netting were only about one inch square, and this guaranteed that a wing line could not be sucked through the netting and into the propeller. On my engine, the factory had changed the design. Instead of fish netting, they simply used a piece of nylon cord strung across the face of the prop cage in a zigzag pattern. Instead of tiny little square openings, there were now long, wedge-shaped openings, like slices of pizza. I suppose the labor costs of installing the zigzag cord were much less, but I was very dubious when I saw the new design.

It looked to me like a wing line could easily slip between the adjacent cords and go right into the prop.

And that's exactly what happened. I managed to collapse the wing on top of myself before I could get airborne, and a wing line was sucked through the cage netting and into the propeller. The propeller was instantly destroyed, and it cost me nearly four hundred dollars to replace the prop. What the hell good is netting that won't keep the wing lines out of the propeller?

I promptly went out and bought some ordinary nylon fish netting, with openings about one inch square, and covered the entire prop cage with it. Result: No more destroyed propellers. Unless your prop cage already has good fish netting on it, I urge you to do the same.

A *Removable Fuel Tank* is a very nice thing to have. PPG engines require you to mix the oil with the gasoline in the fuel tank. But the oil/gas mixture starts to deteriorate almost instantly after mixing. So you want to mix your fuel just before you fly. After flying, you want to discard any leftover fuel. If the fuel tank is removable, you will find the whole process to be much easier. You can completely remove the fuel tank from the engine for easy, safe fueling, or for easy dumping of the leftover fuel.

My first PPG engine had a fuel tank that was bolted to the engine frame, and so removing it was not practical. Unfortunately the fuel tank opening was right next to the spot where I had attached my reserve parachute. I managed to overflow the fuel tank while filling it, and got fuel on my reserve container. Fortunately no harm was done. When I was done flying, the only way to get the remaining fuel out of the fuel tank, was to siphon it; a very messy, awkward job. With a removable fuel tank you can simply unhook the fuel line and dump the remaining fuel into your car's fuel tank (no need to waste the leftover fuel).

A very highly recommended feature.

A *Hip Belt* is something that is just starting to get noticed by the PPG world, but I would insist on it. And if the PPG engine had a hip belt, I could forgive almost every other shortcoming in the design.

Present-day PPG engines force the pilot to carry the weight of the entire engine on his shoulders. This is very stupid. It's the worst possible way to carry a heavy load. Not only does it ruin the pilot's balance, but the load on the shoulders ultimately ends up on the spine, which can cause all sorts of back problems.

The hips are the part of the human body designed to carry heavy loads. All backpackers know this, and this is why their packs all have hip belts. A hip belt is simply a large, padded belt, worn snugly around the hips, and attached to the base of the pack. This results in the weight of the pack being placed on the hips, rather than on the shoulders.

PPG engines are frequently even heavier than backpacks, so why PPG engines fail to use a proven method for carrying heavy loads is a mystery to me.

When you buy your PPG engine, ask the dealer and manufacturer why the engine lacks a hip belt. Maybe if enough of us ask for it, they'll get the message.

A *Reserve Parachute* is something that I also have very mixed feelings about, since it forces you to choose between weight and safety. If you're going to fly with a reserve parachute, make sure that your PPG engine has some form of attachment loops for the reserve bridle somewhere near your shoulders, preferably on the harness shoulder straps. If you have to land under a reserve parachute, you want to come down on your feet; not on your back, stomach, or side. On my first PPG, the shoulder straps had an additional pair of nylon loops sewn to the underside of each shoulder strap. These loops were intended for use with a reserve parachute. This meant that if I ever deployed the reserve, the load would be taken by my shoulder straps and I would descend feet first.

The problem with a reserve parachute is that it adds about eight pounds of weight to your engine load, and that's a lot of weight. It's also true that reserve parachutes are so seldom used by PPG pilots that most pilots don't bother carrying them. I personally know of only one reserve deployment by a PPG pilot in a genuine emergency situation. It was low-altitude wing collapse, and the pilot promptly threw his reserve and landed safely.

When I first started flying a PPG, I did not carry a reserve. Then I ran into some turbulence that shook me up pretty badly, even though it failed to collapse my wing. After that I bought a reserve and started wearing it. I really hated the extra weight, even though I loved the feeling of security it gave me in the air. And it made a great arm rest for my left elbow.

The other problem with reserve parachutes is that PPG engines aren't yet designed to accommodate reserve parachutes. While the engine may have attachment loops for the reserve bridle, usually no real provision is made for attaching the container of the reserve parachute to the engine. The reserve typically comes with a few attachment straps, and the pilot simply straps the reserve to his harness or engine (or both) as best he can. The end result is frequently a bulky, awkward arrangement.

PPG engines need to come with some sort of mounting pocket for a reserve parachute, as is commonly found on unpowered paragliding harnesses. Perhaps the reserve could be mounted under the base of the engine, in a recessed pocket to protect the reserve from contact with the ground.

Should you wear a reserve parachute? Well, it's simply a question of how much safety you want, and how much weight you are willing to carry.

For additional copies of this book, send a check for $27.95 ($24.95 + $3 shipping) to:

Jefferson Technology Press
4810 SW 325th Place
Federal Way, WA 98023-1920

Or visit our website at www.jeffcomp.com and order on-line!

Questions or comments? E-mail us at jtp@jeffcomp.com.